# Renewing Christianity

# Renewing Christianity

## A History of Church Reform
## from Day One to Vatican II

*Christopher M. Bellitto*

PAULIST PRESS
New York/Mahwah, N.J.

On the cover: *The Church at Auvers,* June 1890, by Vincent Van Gogh (1853–90) (Musée d'Orsay, Paris, France). Used courtesy of Scala/Art Resource, N.Y.

The Scripture quotations contained herein are from the New Revised Standard Version Bible, copyright 1989 by the Division of Christian Education of the National Council of the Churches of Christ in the U.S.A. and are used by permission. All rights reserved.

The Publisher gratefully acknowledges the use of excerpts reprinted from *Luther's Works,* volume 31, edited by Harold J. Grimm, copyright © 1957, Fortress Press. Used by permission of Augsburg Fortress.

*Book design by Theresa M. Sparacio*

*Cover design by Cheryl Finbow*

Library of Congress Cataloging-in-Publication Data

Bellitto, Christopher M.
   Renewing Christianity : a history of church reform from day one to Vatican II / Christopher M. Bellitto.
     p. cm.
   Includes bibliographical references (p. ) and index.
   ISBN 0-8091-4028-4
   1. Church history. 2. Reformation. I. Title.

BR148 .B45 2001
270—dc21

                             2001021776

Published by Paulist Press
997 Macarthur Boulevard
Mahwah, New Jersey 07430

www.paulistpress.com

Printed and bound in the
United States of America

# Contents

*v*

# Contents

*To my mother and father,*
*Joan and Anthony,*
*my first teachers*

# Acknowledgments

My thanks go first to Kathleen Walsh of Paulist Press. Several years ago at the International Congress on Medieval Studies at Kalamazoo, Michigan, she asked the question we all want to hear: "What's the book you always wanted to write?" Since then, she guided this book with an editor's careful eye, an interested reader's inquiring mind, and a coach's enthusiasm. I am equally indebted to Louis Pascoe, S.J., who introduced me to the world of reform and demonstrated by his own example that I had to bring head and heart to my research. The library staffs at Fordham University, St. Joseph's Seminary, and the member institutions of the interlibrary loan system were, as usual, extremely professional and helpful. My students and the audiences at public lectures helped me understand and explain this material with greater clarity. Many colleagues read this manuscript, in whole or in part, with generous and encouraging advice: Janet Baxendale, S.C., Gerald Christianson, Francis Corry, William Hudon, Thomas Izbicki, Gerard Rafferty, Anthony Sorgie, and Phillip Stump. Although they have saved me from many errors, I alone am responsible for this study; I hope I have done justice to their counsel. Finally, and as always, I thank Karen, my wife and my best friend. She keeps my feet on the ground, but makes sure I never stop dreaming.

Ad maiorem Dei gloriam

C.M.B.

# Abbreviations

In most cases, I have chosen to let English sources and translations predominate in the notes and suggestions for further reading. I have used the New Revised Standard Version of the Bible, except where I cite an author's own translation or use of another version; in those cases, I retained the author's preference because the choice of wording obviously influenced the interpretation. I have provided years for the reigns of kings, emperors, and popes; in every other case, I give the years for a person's birth and death.

*AHP*
> *Archivum historiae pontificae*

*CH*
> *Church History*

*CHR*
> *Catholic Historical Review*

Congar, *Vraie et fausse réforme*
> Yves Congar. *Vraie et fausse réforme dans l'Église*. 2d ed. Paris: Les Éditions du Cerf, 1968.

Jedin, *History of the Council of Trent*
> Hubert Jedin. *A History of the Council of Trent*. Translated by Ernest Graf. St. Louis: Herder, 1957.

*JEH*
> *Journal of Ecclesiastical History*

Ladner, *Idea of Reform*
  Gerhart B. Ladner. *The Idea of Reform: Its Impact on Christian Thought and Action in the Age of the Fathers.* Cambridge: Harvard University Press, 1959; reprint, New York: Harper and Row, 1967.

*LW*
  Jaroslav Pelikan and Helmut T. Lehmann, eds. *Luther's Works.* 55 vols. Philadelphia: Muhlenberg Press, 1955–86.

*RHE*
  *Revue d'histoire ecclésiastique*

*SCJ*
  *Sixteenth Century Journal*

Tanner, *Decrees*
  Norman P. Tanner, ed. *Decrees of the Ecumenical Councils.* 2 vols. Washington D.C.: Georgetown University Press, 1990.

*TS*
  *Theological Studies*

# Introduction

## The Need for Reform

Why should the church, an institution of divine origin, need to be reformed? The answer lies in the fact that the church is also a human institution. While the church has Christ's assurance that he will never abandon her, she still must make her earthly journey with human feet. This fact by definition means Christians will make mistakes along the way. Studying the history of reform movements provides examples of how others have tried to correct those mistakes and retain the church's essentials while adapting them to changing times. The fact that we are witnessing—indeed living—an age of remarkable renewal because of Vatican II gives us unique insights into past chapters in the history of reform that, in turn, offer perspective on our own.

The need for reform is well illustrated by the late church historian Robert McNally in his book, *The Unreformed Church,* an ironic title made doubly so since he published it in 1965 as Vatican II completed its sessions, ushering in an age of tremendous renewal. McNally notes the paradox of the church's high ideals and frequent failures: "For the disparity between the nobility of the faith which the Christian professes and the mediocrity of the life which he leads is reflected by history over and over again." The student of the church's history, indeed, is fascinated from the first moment by the glorious mission statement of the gospels, only to be immediately let down by the muddle humans can make of that mission as they try to live it out in diverse, challenging circumstances. The message of history is that although Christians stumble, God does not. As McNally puts it, "In spite of the aberrations of this or that individual, or groups of individuals, the church moves on through history under the protection of God to the splendid hour of the *eschata* when the Lord will come to take this beloved spouse unto himself."[1]

McNally's approach represents an open-eyed view of church history. He begins with the premise that Christians make mistakes and therefore must reform themselves and the institutional church to proceed. But not everyone is in agreement, or even comfortable, with an unglossed view of the church. A widescale willingness to admit, let alone embrace, failures as our aids in the history of reform is a relatively recent step among Catholics. Popes were not immune to resisting the idea the church needed correction. Gregory XVI (1831–46) reigned in an era when the church was assaulted by the many emerging "isms" of the nineteenth century: liberalism, nationalism, and so forth. Though it seems shocking to the modern reader, Gregory XVI responded by fighting the freedoms associated with these social, political, and economic movements, including the canons of western constitutional liberties: freedom of conscience, religion, press, and the separation of church and state.

A strict proponent of papal autocracy and a political conservative determined to preserve Europe's old guard, Gregory XVI in the defensive *Mirari Vos* (1832) reasserted the need for strict obedience to ecclesiastical hierarchy. He concluded an especially rigid passage by concluding, "[I]t is obviously absurd and injurious to propose a certain restoration and regeneration for [the church] as though necessary for her safety and growth, as if she could be considered subject to defect or obscuration or other misfortune."[2] For Gregory XVI, the church had no need to be reformed (indeed even raising the possibility seems forbidden) since she could not make a mistake. Without a mistake, reform was unnecessary.

Pope Paul VI (1963–78) stands in stark contrast to Gregory XVI. Writing in an entirely different social, cultural, and political climate, Paul VI in *Ecclesiam Suam* (1964) not only allowed the possibility of the need for reform, but canonized the act of reform and declared it an obligation. With *Ecclesiam Suam,* Paul VI encouraged Vatican II's program of snowballing renewal to the delight of many and the consternation of some who hoped John XXIII's revolution could be stemmed before it went too far. Paul identified three main tasks for his pontificate: honest self-reflection, a duty to reform, and the church's détente with the world. Reminiscent of McNally's verdict, Paul VI specifically noted in *Ecclesiam Suam* that the realities of the church frequently failed to measure up to her principles:

> A vivid and lively self-awareness on the part of the church inevitably leads to a comparison between the ideal image of the church as Christ envisaged, his holy and spotless bride, and the actual image which the church presents to the world today....But the actual image of the church will never attain to such a degree of perfection, beauty, holiness, and splendor that it can be said to correspond perfectly with the original conception in the mind of him who fashioned it.[3]

Therefore, a key correlative idea for reform is the notion that the church as an institution and Christians as individual believers will rarely "get the gospel right" completely in this life, but they can never stop trying. The famous phrase is *ecclesia semper reformanda:* "the church must always be reformed."[4] All Christians as well as the church in toto are on a pilgrim's journey: constantly on the way to restoring the church's ideals, never getting there, but never absolved from the duty to try.

## A Brief History of the Study of Reform

The study of reform is a very young branch of history that owes its increasing importance and urgency to three twentieth-century scholars: Gerhart Ladner, Yves Congar, and Hubert Jedin.

In large part, the study of reform was invented only in the middle of the twentieth century by Gerhart Ladner (1905–93), an Austrian convert to Catholicism who, along with many other European scholars, emigrated to the United States because of

Hitler's emergence. Ladner created a new field within intellectual history. He pioneered the task of looking at reform words with *The Idea of Reform: Its Impact on Christian Thought and Action in the Age of the Fathers,* first published on the eve of Vatican II in 1959 and then republished just after its conclusion in 1967.[5] In his meticulous, methodical study of the idea of reform, Ladner started at the beginning, the first few centuries of the church, and focused on reform theories and images more than on their practical applications. His doctoral students at UCLA and other scholars taking his lead pushed his foundations in two directions: chronologically into the medieval and reformation eras, and topically into how those ideas were made concrete.[6]

While Ladner provided the historical basis for the study of reform, the French Dominican Yves Congar (1904–95) explored the theological underpinnings of reform. He specifically turned his attention to ecclesiology, the study of the church, to examine how the church had related to changing circumstances during its history and had explained itself theologically in diverse cultures. What Congar was especially interested in uncovering were those aspects of the church that could never change and those aspects that could (indeed should) be adapted. He identified this adaptation as the process of renewal, thus offering a theological counterpart to Ladner's historical lens. We shall shortly explore the key aspects of his contribution to the study of reform from his seminal work on the subject. *Vraie et fausse réforme dans l'Église (True and False Reform in the Church),* like Ladner's *Idea of Reform,* was published before Vatican II (1950) and then again afterwards (1968).[7] His work was also influential on the role of the laity and in ecumenical efforts. Congar's candor and foresight led to his being silenced by Rome in 1954, but ironically he became one of the leading figures at the council itself and wrote some of its most important teachings.

The third key author for the study of reform in the twentieth century is a German priest, Hubert Jedin (1900–1980). Jedin made reform a legitimate object of study for Catholic historians. For nearly three centuries after the reformations of the sixteenth century, the writing of church history was distinguished by its polemics: Catholics and Protestants typically argued the "right" or "wrong" aspects of the sixteenth century based on their own religious allegiances and not on objective fact. For many Catholic authors, *reform* was a four-letter word that referred exclusively to a Protestant phenomenon, a revolution that rejected Catholic truth. Protestant authors, in turn, colored their depictions of Catholicism. As recently as the late nineteenth century, the Protestant Adolf von Harnack contended that Protestantism flourished because it renewed Christianity's ties with its Greek, Pauline roots, a connection that for Catholics was "a lifeless possession." Von Harnack referred to Catholic "errors" in Rome's discussion of justification, declaring that Catholicism amounts to "slavish dependence on tradition and the false doctrines of sacrament, of repentance and of faith."[8]

Jedin cut through the diatribes to discuss reform as a constant, central force in church history that particularly enlightened the church's pilgrim journey. Without fear or apology, Jedin looked at the cause of Luther's complaints: Catholic institutional and moral decadence. For Jedin, there was an instructive dialectic between late medieval reform and decadence that he chronicled in his magisterial *Geschichte des Konzils von Trient (History of the Council of Trent)* in 1949. Jedin studied Catholic reform in itself and over time. This allowed him to see Catholic reform predating Luther, thereby adding to Ladner's and Congar's insight that reform is an act of the church from her first moments and not simply a reaction to Luther.[9]

Working about the same time, Ladner, Congar, and Jedin identified reform as a task that transcends eras and Christian denominations. Freeing reform from confessional polemics, these three allowed Catholic scholars to study pre-Lutheran Catholic reform efforts unashamedly. For obvious reasons, this effort became a hot topic during Vatican II, leading scholars to look at the aggiornamento movement through the lens of historians and theologians. These viewpoints led them to examine how other eras had handled reform, especially the period 1350–1650 following

Jedin's example, in a search for some insights into how Vatican II was treating the matter.[10] Ladner and Congar were particularly influential at Vatican II. None other than Pope John XXIII read Ladner's *Idea of Reform* and marked up his copy of Congar's *Vraie et fausse réforme*.[11]

## The Vocabulary of Reform

What is the language of reform? We will encounter in this study terms that have been used throughout history with varying degrees of precision. Among these terms in their noun forms are *reform* and *reformation, renewal* and *renovation, revolution* and *evolution, amelioration* and *augmentation, aggiornamento, rebirth, renaissance,* and *development.* Other terms will appear paired off as antitheses: *tradition* and *progress, conservation* and *innovation* or *improvisation, restoration* and *accommodation.* Understanding the creative or destructive tension within each pair of terms is an instructive way of understanding reform ideas in different places, times, and circumstances.

The two most important words for our story are *reform (reformatio, reformare)* and *renewal (renovatio, renovare),* twin efforts that have often competed and continue to pull the church in opposing directions, though they are not necessarily adverse. Despite two generations of historical and theological research into reform, scholars are still working out what different people in diverse times meant precisely when they used *reform* and *renewal.* On the eve of Vatican II, Ladner offered this definition of reform: "the idea of free, intentional and ever perfectible, multiple, prolonged and ever repeated efforts by man to reassert and augment values pre-existent in the spiritual-material compound of the world." However precise this definition is, more than one of his students and readers has found it torturous and cumbersome. Ladner conceded his definition of reform must be considered provisional and incomplete because further research always brings greater clarity.[12]

Ladner's idea of reform begins with a first principle: Change is endemic to the human condition because human life is continually

6

subject to new beginnings. Christianity only heightens that first principle, given its teachings on physical life and death, spiritual life and death in sin, rebirth in baptism, and divine redemption. The very origins of the Christian idea of reform are grounded in humanity's attempts to reclaim our original creation in the image and likeness of God (*ad imaginem et similitudinem Dei,* from Gen 1:26) lost in Adam and Eve's fall. Reform, therefore, becomes a fundamental spiritual task for the Christian.

Ladner constructed his idea of reform by distinguishing four interlocking aspects of renewal. First, cosmological renewal represented a pre-Christian idea. Each year repeats itself: the world continues to turn, seasons follow one another, the death of winter is replaced by spring's new life. The cosmological cycle, however, presupposes a certain quality of repetition and therefore stagnation, an eternal recurrence of events incompatible with free will. Ladner saw freedom as a fundamental difference between pre-Christian and Christian ideas of reform.

A second aspect was vitalistic renewal, which also predates Christianity. It focuses on the spontaneous physical renewal of vegetable, animal, and human life as represented by the infinitives *to revive (reviviscere), to grow green again (revirescere),* and *to blossom again (reflorescere).* These words all connote the idea of renaissance, often applied (though narrowly so) to the Italian Renaissance, a supposed rebirth of light after the alleged "dark ages" of the medieval world. This idea focuses on rebirth, renewed growth, and the return of vital (in the case of the Italian Renaissance, Greco-Roman) elements of an institution or individual, as a phoenix rises from its own ashes.

Here again the Christian idea goes further. Christians never simply return to a carbon copy version of Adam's original state before the fall, but to a state beyond Adam's because of the work of redemption achieved by Christ, the new Adam. Vitalistic renewal, like cosmological renewal, does not include the intentionality associated with Christian free will. Paul treats both of these points when he refers to human creation in the *imago Dei,* but he stresses that a Christian's deliberate return to this image goes beyond Adam's state because of Jesus' redemptive action:

> Do not lie to one another, seeing that you have stripped off the old self with its practices and have clothed yourselves with the new self, which is being renewed in knowledge according to the image of its creator. In that renewal there is no longer Greek and Jew, circumcised and uncircumcised, barbarian, Scythian, slave and free; but Christ is all and in all. (Col 3:9–11)

The third aspect is messianic or millenarian renewal: a state of absolute, total perfection frequently associated with the thousand-year reign of bliss connected to Christ's second coming. It includes the idea that humanity is in a state of progress toward the goal of a utopian society or community, religious or not. Christians hope they are approaching perfection, but they know they cannot achieve full perfection in their earthly life. Still, the Christian strives to improve and looks toward an ultimate age of perfection described symbolically by the apocalyptic images of the Book of Revelation. Peter's speech represents the goal more moderately:

> Repent therefore, and turn to God so that your sins may be wiped out, so that times of refreshing may come from the presence of the Lord, and that he may send the messiah appointed for you, that is, Jesus, who must remain in heaven until the time of universal restoration that God announced long ago through his holy prophets. (Acts 3:19–21)

This hope for a future connected to inner renewal is again expressed in Christian terms:

> Beloved, we are God's children now; what we will be has not yet been revealed. What we do know is this: when he is revealed, we will be like him, for we will see him as he is. And all who have this hope in him purify themselves, just as he is pure. (1 John 3:2–3)

Ladner's fourth aspect is the one that is uniquely Christian: the stages of conversion, baptism, and penance. The Old Testament offers a background to the Christian discussion of a lifelong spiritual journey that includes continual transformation: "Restore to me the joy of your salvation, and sustain in me a willing spirit" (Ps 51:12) and "When you send forth your spirit, they are created; and you renew the face of the ground" (Ps 104:30). The Christian must experience a spiritual birth and conversion after his physical birth. This is seen in John the Baptist's calls for repentance (Mark 1:3–8) and in Jesus' response to Nicodemus's question as to how someone can be born again since he cannot return to his mother's womb. "No one can enter the kingdom of God without being born of water and spirit," Jesus replies. "What is born of the flesh is flesh, and what is born of the spirit is spirit" (John 3:4–6). Although baptism is instantaneous and nonrepeatable, conversion and penance represent, to use Ladner's phrase, "new starts in the long *process* of reform." Paul incessantly exhorts the first Christian communities to renew their hearts, minds, and spirits within:

> Be transformed by the renewing of your minds. (Rom 12:2)

> Even though our outer nature is wasting away, our inner nature is being renewed day by day. (2 Cor 4:16)

> You were taught to put away your former way of life, your old self, corrupt and deluded by its lusts, and to be renewed in the spirit of your minds, and to clothe yourselves with the new self, created according to the likeness of God in true righteousness and holiness. (Eph 4:22–24; see also Col 3:10)

The Christian dies with Christ, is reborn in Christ, and follows Christ in his new life. The Christian's path is one of continual sanctification with the aid of the Holy Spirit. Thus the Christian idea of reform involves multiple efforts, prolonged attempts, and repetition that intentionally strives for change, instead of mere recreation or reproduction of a prior state.

Is *reform* the only word related to these tasks? Ladner attempted to distinguish reform from renewal, but the words are affiliated with each other. One of his students, Louis Pascoe, noted Ladner placed the word *reform* under the more general idea of renewal—which was itself within the ideas of alteration, change, and becoming—without offering a definition of the idea of renewal to complement his complex definition of the idea of reform. The four aspects Ladner identified remained very theoretical and have not helped us sufficiently distinguish reform from renewal. Ladner himself concluded in his initial discussion of these four aspects of reform, "Various types of renewal ideas did, of course, mix and blend with the idea of reform." These words are closely related, as in Paul's letters to the Corinthians and Colossians where, in Ladner's pairing of foundational terms, "the renovation of the inner man is reformation to the image of God."

Pascoe suggests the words *reform* and *renewal* can be more clearly distinguished: "In a true sense, then, the idea of renewal can be seen as principally restorative and the idea of reform as primarily augmentative and ameliorative." However, I would argue Pascoe's use of the words *reform* and *renewal* in this statement ought to be reversed: reform is principally restorative, while renewal is primarily augmentative and ameliorative. We will discover in the course of this study that reform in church history has tended to lean more in the direction of going back to or restoring an original form, while renewal has connoted making that original form "new and improved." Pascoe already noted an overlap: "What is generally regarded as renewal in its restorative context can often unconsciously and unintentionally move into the realm of reform in its augmentative and ameliorative sense."[13] Renewal and not reform is closer to aggiornamento, that Italian word often translated as "updating," which should be rendered literally (though awkwardly) as "today-ing." This conveys the sense that renewal is a continual process, since today's renewal must be updated tomorrow as circumstances change.

## Reform Language in Church Councils

One way of looking at the nuances between reform and renewal language is to examine how these words were used in the church's twenty-one ecumenical councils. Of course, any etymological investigation must take into account the changing meanings of words and the contexts of place and time in which they were used.[14] As a way of beginning, we turn to a simple comparison of reform and renewal language, which reveals 113 examples of reform language in the ecumenical councils' documents, compared to 86 examples of renewal language. But 63 of the latter examples, nearly 75 percent of all uses of renewal language at ecumenical councils, are found in Vatican II's documents alone.

Renewal language (forms of the noun *renovatio* and the verb *renovare*) appears as early as the councils of Chalcedon (451), Nicaea II (787), and Constantinople IV (869–70). These instances, however, do not refer to renewal in the sense of Vatican II's aggiornamento, but in the technical renewal of canonical legislation that had previously been passed. Chalcedon offers the first use of a renewal word in an ecumenical council's canons: "We have driven off erroneous doctrines by our collective resolution and we have renewed *(renovavimus)* the unerring creed of the fathers." At Nicaea II, the council fathers ordered that customs previously abandoned be renewed *(renovari);* Constantinople IV renewed forms of piety that had been circumscribed.[15]

Reform language (forms of the noun *reformatio* and the verb *reformare*) does not appear in an ecumenical council before the thirteenth century despite the papacy's efforts to establish the church's freedom in naming her own bishops and patrolling clerical simony and concubinage. Three councils were held in Rome in the twelfth century, but none used reform language. This changed under Innocent III (1199–1216), who oversaw Lateran IV (1215), the first ecumenical council to use reform language explicitly in its documents. Lateran IV instructed bishops to meet in an annual synod where they must see to "the correction of excesses and the reform of morals, especially among the clergy" and appoint vicars to "carefully investigate what needs correction or reform" throughout the year.[16] Prelates were charged with exercising their "office of correction and reform" prudently and diligently, seeing especially to the correction of clerical behavior and the reform of morals.[17] Taking aim at priests with wives or concubines, Lateran

IV declared, "In order that the morals and conduct of clerics may be reformed for the better, let all of them strive to live in a continent and chaste way, especially those in holy orders."[18] After Lateran IV, councils typically began with a proclamation couched in reform language declaring the delegates would address improvements, chiefly in the clergy's moral behavior.

The Council of Trent (1545–47, 1551–52, 1562–63) and Vatican II (1962–65) offer an interesting comparison of reform and renewal language. Trent used reform language thirty times compared to only seven instances of renewal language, while Vatican II used reform language only nine times but renewal language an astounding sixty-three times.

Trent's use of renewal language did not foreshadow Vatican II's sense of aggiornamento. Three of Trent's references to renewal treated the theological issue of justification, a major sixteenth-century controversy between Catholics and Protestants:

> [A]ctual justification…consists not only in the forgiveness of sins but also in the sanctification and renewal of the inward being by a willing acceptance of the grace and gifts whereby someone from being unjust becomes just, from being an enemy becomes a friend, so that he is an heir in hope of eternal life…. Finally, the one formal cause is the justness of God: not that by which he himself is just, but that by which he makes us just and endowed with which we are renewed in the spirit of our mind…. So those justified in this way and made friends and members of the household of God, going from strength to strength, are (as the Apostle says) renewed from day to day by putting to death what is earthly in themselves….[19]

A pair of Trent's other uses of renewal language concerns the practical renewal of prior legislation, as earlier councils had done: the council reaffirmed the strict enclosure of nuns and directed that episcopal dignity be returned to its proper status. A renewal word also restored the regular meeting of provincial councils.[20] Another instance reminded bishops to visit annually the monasteries, abbeys, and benefices for which they had oversight, and generally to see that "anything needing renovation or restoration is repaired."[21]

Vatican II strongly favored renewal over reform language, choosing forms of *renovatio/renovare* seven times more frequently than *reformatio/reformare*. An interesting passage from the decree on ecumenism, *Unitatis redintegratio* (1964, no. 6), uses both types of words in the same thought:

> Every renewal of the church *(renovatio ecclesiae)* essentially consists in an increase of fidelity to the church's own calling.... In its pilgrimage on earth, Christ summons the church to continual reformation *(perennem reformationem),* of which it is always in need, in so far as it is an institution of human beings here on earth.[22]

A council that almost always explicitly emphasized renewal here selects both *renovatio* and *reformatio* to describe the pilgrim task: a return to the church's founding principles that entails a continual updating of those principles.

The emphasis on the pilgrim's journey of forward progress, hesitant decisions, and missteps is found earlier in *Unitatis redintegratio* (no. 4):

> For although the Catholic Church has been endowed with all divinely revealed truth and with all means of grace, yet its members fail to live by them with all the fervor that they should, so that the radiance of the church's image is less in the eyes of our separated fellow Christians and of the world at large, and the growth of God's kingdom is delayed. All Catholics must therefore aim at Christian perfection and, each according to their situation, play their part that the church, bearing in her own body the lowly and dying state of Jesus, may be daily more purified and renewed *(de die in diem mundetur et renovetur),* against the day when Christ will present her to himself in all her glory without spot or wrinkle.[23]

It is precisely human failure, then, that creates the need for renewal, especially in the effort to set the Catholic house in order as a prerequisite to uniting with the other Christian churches from which she is estranged. Moreover, the action of renewal is continual, a theme that pervades all of Vatican II's documents but particularly *Lumen Gentium* (1964, especially nos. 1–9), which repeatedly stressed the church's nature as an earthly pilgrim:

> Through the power of the gospel, [the Holy Spirit] rejuvenates the church, continually renewing it and leading it to perfect union with its spouse.... In order that we may be continually renewed in [Christ], he gave us a share in his Spirit.... [U]nder the action of the Holy Spirit, [the church] does not cease from renewing itself until, through the cross, it arrives at the light which knows no setting.[24]

Paul VI in *Ecclesiam Suam* reinforced Vatican II's accent on an incessant and dynamic renewal that balanced the retention of first principles with their reinvigoration:

> When we speak about renewal we are not concerned to change things, but to preserve all the more resolutely the characteristic features which Christ has impressed on his church. Or rather, we are concerned to restore to the church that ideal of perfection and beauty that corresponds to its original image, and that is at the same time consistent with its necessary, normal and legitimate growth from its original, embryonic form into its present structure.[25]

It is important to note that the act of renewing is both passive and active for Christians, a theme repeated from the patristic through the medieval periods and reaffirmed at Vatican II. *Lumen Gentium* says that the church is continually renewed by Christ and the Holy Spirit, but also mandates that the church must incessantly renew herself. Both this point and a related one—the idea that the church is simultaneously perfect and in need of perfecting—are made clear in another segment of *Lumen Gentium:* "[T]he church, containing sinners in its own bosom, is at one and the same time holy and always in need of purification and it pursues unceasingly penance and renewal."[26] These premises remind us why the image of the pilgrim church is useful when considering the church's history of reform and renewal.

## *Principles of Reform*

Having looked at the language of reform, we should also identify some principles of reform to guide our survey of the practical attempts to reform the church. We have recourse here to a pair of theologians who summarized the state of the idea just before and after Vatican II: Yves Congar, whom we have already met, and the American Jesuit Avery Dulles.

Congar identified four characteristics of reform that must be present for critical self-examination. First, criticism must be frank, sincere, and candid, thereby protecting against deception. If necessary, criticism can be radical, but changes must be accomplished without rancor. Congar stressed the act of criticizing does not equal infidelity but represents, on the contrary, an attempt to be more faithful to the church's roots since, we might add, one does not spend time criticizing what one does not love or care to see improved. Second, self-examination must be serious and focused on primary and not insubstantial, surface issues. There must be clear pastoral goals on solid intellectual and moral ground. Third, the preeminent concern of a critique must be the effect of criticism and proposed reform on the whole Christian population, especially the laity. This impact must be considered central because the church lives, in a very real sense, at its grassroots levels. As a common saying cautions, "If it's not happening in the parishes, it's not happening." Fourth, reform must be grounded in the foundations and traditions of the church; if it is a genuine effort at a return to the sources (the standard Latin phrase is *reditus ad fontes*), then reform cannot fail. Reformers must be permitted an uninhibited inquiry into those sources and history in order to renew the Christian life of faith and ritual.

Congar also catalogued four conditions in which reform could be accomplished without producing a schism. First, reform must be done in charity and pastoral service, not for intellectual play or nitpicking. Criticism must be offered to help, not harm or win; to rebuild, not destroy. Second, the reformer must strive to maintain community through dialogue, not diatribe. One way to accomplish this task is to focus on points that are shared, instead of matters being contested. The spirit of unity can be at work in both the center and periphery of a debate or community. It is indeed the creative tension between the two that can be productive: the center (typically the church's hierarchy) wants to preserve tradition and the status quo while the periphery (often the masses) wants to push those traditions forward and update them with the times. Congar cautioned, however, that after dialogue and a decision, rejection of one or the other approach should not lead to condemnation. Third, patience is necessary for reform, although reformers are frequently urgent and restless. The church moves slowly; there must be an understanding of and respect for delay. Some thinkers are simply ahead of their times and it may take decades or centuries for their ideas to be accepted, let alone championed. Even some propositions of Thomas Aquinas (c. 1225–74) were initially condemned. In our own century, the American Jesuit John Courtney Murray (1904–67) was vilified during the 1950s, yet became the primary author of Vatican II's declaration on religious freedom, *Dignitatis Humanae* (1965). Finally, Congar posited that true renewal is a return to founding ideas and traditions, a group activity of development adaptation from core principles. False renewal, by contrast, is novelty, a solo task, and an activity of innovation adaptation for its own sake.[27]

Taking a look at Vatican II's aggiornamento in historical perspective about a decade after the council ended, Avery Dulles believed the church should, as it had done in the past, focus on five tasks or types of reform: purification, adaptation, accretion, development, and creative transformation. The church must purify herself by removing corruption and correcting abuses, a stance that assumes the church was perfect at her birth. Clearing away corruptions that grew like barnacles on the church is what various Protestant reformers said they were attempting in the sixteenth century. Adaptation, which is akin to the word *aggiornamento,* should be reasonable, moderate, and gradual while it guards against excessive accommodation. When the church becomes too immersed in the secular culture that surrounds it, what is adapted takes over. Such accretion then becomes the excessive accommodation against which Dulles offered his caveat.

# Introduction

The church develops in the sense laid down by John Henry Newman (1801–90) in his *Essay on the Development of Christian Doctrine* (1844). What develops is our understanding of doctrine, scripture, and tradition, along with our ability to articulate divine mysteries and truths. In addition, because the church is the mystical body of Christ growing in the Holy Spirit, she moves ever closer (or develops) toward fulfillment in God. This idea Dulles calls "evolutionary reformism," based on a biological model of organic growth. Finally, creative transformation recalls Congar's idea of a reconstruction or development adaptation that discerns Christ in the signs of the times while remaining true to core principles. All of these tasks are applied, in Dulles's agenda, to four areas of reform: morality, discipline, structures, and doctrine.[28]

It is now time to consider how different players in church history have lived out the challenge of reform and renewal. Who embraced the ideas, and how? Who rejected the notions, and why? How did the language, principles, images, theories, practices, means, and ends of reform and renewal change in two thousand years? We must, of course, take as our guide an important point Dulles made: reform is necessary. "Those who believe in church reform, then, hold that the church can and should be changed for the better without loss of its own identity. They hold that the church exists in an imperfect but perfectible state."[29] Inquiring how various Christians have worked toward that perfectible state leads us to the beginning of the history of reform.

## NOTES

1. Robert E. McNally, *The Unreformed Church* (New York: Sheed and Ward, 1965), pp. 187–205, with quotations at pp. 187 and 193.

2. Gregory XVI, *Mirari Vos,* no. 10, in *The Papal Encyclicals 1740–1878,* ed. Claudia Carlen (Raleigh, N.C.: McGrath Publishing Company, 1981), p. 237.

3. Paul VI, *Ecclesiam Suam,* nos. 8–17, in *The Papal Encyclicals 1958–1981,* ed. Claudia Carlen (Raleigh, N.C.: McGrath Publishing Company, 1981), pp. 136–38, with quotation from no. 10 at p. 136.

4. Just before Vatican II, Hans Küng called for a history of this phrase, which he suggested could have come from Jean Calvin's circle in the sixteenth century: *The Council, Reform, and Reunion,* trans. Cecily Hastings (New York: Sheed and Ward, 1961), p. 9. No historian or theologian has yet produced a study; the phrase's origins and development remain unclear.

5. Ladner also wrote many articles, which have been collected in *Images and Ideas in the Middle Ages,* 2 vols. (Rome: Edizioni di Storia e Letteratura, 1983). His contributions were summarized and assessed by one of his students: John Van Engen, "Images and Ideas: The Achievements of Gerhart Burian Ladner, with a Bibliography of His Published Works," *Viator* 20 (1989): pp. 85–115.

6. Ladner's three leading students were Louis B. Pascoe, John Van Engen, and Phillip H. Stump. Each revised and subsequently published his doctoral dissertation: Pascoe, *Jean Gerson: Principles of Church Reform* (Leiden: E. J. Brill, 1973); Van Engen, *Rupert of Deutz* (Berkeley: University of California Press, 1983); and Stump, *The Reforms of the Council of Constance (1414–1418)* (Leiden: E. J. Brill, 1994). The present author was Pascoe's student and therefore trained in Ladner's tradition and method.

7. An anthology of Congar's writings is Jean-Pierre Jossua, ed., *Cardinal Yves Congar. Écrits réformateurs* (Paris: Les Éditions du Cerf, 1995). For his reform ideas, see especially pp. 173–247 which excerpt, among other works, *Vraie et fausse réforme.* An example of Congar's attempt to put his study of historical theology to contemporary relevance may be seen in his "Church Reform and Luther's Reformation, 1517–1967," *Lutheran World* 14 (1967): pp. 351–59.

8. Adolf von Harnack, *History of Dogma*, 3d ed., trans. Neil Buchanan (New York: Dover Publications, Inc., 1961), vol. 7, pp. 174, 256, 265–66.

9. What follows summarizes a discussion of the significance of Jedin's work published shortly after his death: Giuseppe Alberigo, "Réforme en tant que critère de l'Histoire de l'Église," *RHE* 76 (1981): pp. 72–81.

10. See, for instance, Robert E. McNally, *Reform of the Church* (New York: Herder and Herder, 1963), "The Council of Trent, the Spiritual Exercises and the Catholic Reform," *CH* 34 (1965): pp. 36–49, and "Pope Adrian VI (1522–23) and Church Reform," *AHP* 7 (1969): pp. 253–85; Nelson H. Minnich, "Concepts of Reform Proposed at the Fifth Lateran Council," *AHP* 7 (1969): pp. 163–251. John W. O'Malley produced a trilogy of articles that progressively examined what different reform ideas in their historical contexts were and how they give perspective to Vatican II's continuing scenario: "Historical Thought and the Reform Crisis of the Early Sixteenth Century," *TS* 28 (1967): pp. 531–48; "Reform, Historical Consciousness, and Vatican II's *Aggiornamento*," *TS* 32 (1971): pp. 573–601; and "Developments, Reforms, and Two Great Reformations: Towards a Historical Assessment of Vatican II," *TS* 44 (1983): pp. 373–406.

All of the studies noted so far treat isolated periods of history. The only attempt to look at the entire history of reform is a collection of focused, scholarly articles that examine reform from more than just a Catholic perspective, beginning with Augustine and proceeding through the first third of the twentieth century: *Renaissance and Renewal in Christian History*, ed. Derek Baker, *Studies in Church History*, vol. 14 (Oxford: Basil Blackwell, 1977). See also Roger Aubert, ed., *Progress and Decline in the History of Church Renewal* (New York: Paulist Press, 1967) [= *Concilium*, vol. 27]. Paul Amargier offers part of reform's history in *Une Église du renouveau: Réformes et réformateurs, de Charlemagne à Jean Hus 750–1415* (Paris: Les Éditions du Cerf, 1998); half of this work contains French translations of Latin reform documents.

11. In his memoirs, Ladner recounts how he had sent John XXIII a copy and received a note from a papal secretary thanking him in the pope's name and mentioning that the pope had been consoled and stimulated by his ideas. These anecdotes are cited by Phillip H. Stump, "Gerhart Ladner's *The Idea of Reform* Forty Years After," in *Reform and Renewal in the*

*Middle Ages and the Renaissance,* eds. Thomas M. Izbicki and Christopher M. Bellitto (Leiden: E. J. Brill, 2000), p. 11, n. 28.

12. These paragraphs abstract Ladner, *Idea of Reform,* pp. 1–62, 425–32, with his definition of reform on p. 35.

13. Louis B. Pascoe, "Gerhart Ladner's *The Idea of Reform:* A Critique," unpublished paper read at the American Catholic Historical Association conference, Washington D.C., January 1999, pp. 10, 11. Gerd Tellenbach observed there is a diverse reform vocabulary that lacks accepted starting points: *The Church in Western Europe from the Tenth to the Early Twelfth Century,* trans. Timothy Reuter (Cambridge: Cambridge University Press, 1993), p. 158.

14. For this task, we have as an excellent resource, the *Thesaurus conciliorum œcumenicorum et generalium ecclesiae catholicae. Series A: Formae* (Turnhout: Brepols, 1996), which provides an index of the words (in all their forms) used in the church's councils. This thesaurus is keyed to the edition of conciliar texts by Giuseppe Alberigo, et al., eds., *Conciliorum œcumenicorum decreta* (Bologna: Istituto per le scienze religiose, 1973). However, for the rest of this section we refer to Tanner, *Decrees* because that collection offers Alberigo's edition of the conciliar texts in their original languages with facing translations. For concerns about the altered meanings of words and contexts over time, see Alberigo's notice on the thesaurus's publication: "Per l'analisi delle decisioni dei concili ecumenici e generali," *Cristianesimo nella storia* 19 (1998): pp. 399–403.

15. Tanner, *Decrees,* vol. 1, pp. 83, 145, 160. This collection translates the passage from Constantinople IV, "a universal synod which...has revived the established forms of right conduct," but the Latin text uses a form of the verb *renovare,* not *reviviscere: "pietatis terminos renovavit".* At Constantinople I (381), the fathers used the word *renovavimus* in their remarks to the emperor Theodosius, but this referred to renewing peace among themselves, not renewing earlier canons or traditions: Ladner, *Idea of Reform,* pp. 298–99.

16. Tanner, *Decrees,* vol. 1, p. 236: *"...de corrigendis excessibus et moribus reformandis, praesertim in clero...."; "...investigent quae correctione vel reformatione sint digna...."*

17. Tanner, *Decrees,* vol. 1, p. 237: *"...praelati ad corrigendum subditorum excessus, maxime clericorum, et reformandum mores prudenter et diligenter intendant..."; "...correctionis et reformationis officium...."*

18. Tanner, *Decrees*, vol. 1, p. 242: "*Ut clericorum mores et actus in melius reformentur, continenter et caste vivere studeant universi, praesertim in sacris ordinibus constituti....*"

19. Tanner, *Decrees*, vol. 2, pp. 673, 675: "*[I]ustificatio ipsa consequitur, quae non est sola peccatorum remissio, sed et sanctificatio et renovatio interioris hominis per voluntariam susceptionem gratiae et donorum, unde homo ex iniusto fit iustus et ex inimico amicus, ut sit haeres secundum spem vitae aeternae....Demum unica formalis causa est iustitia Dei, non qua ipse iustus est, sed qua nos iustos facit, qua videlicet ab eo donati renovamur spiritu mentis nostrae (Eph 4:23)....Sic ergo iustificati et amici Dei ac domestici facti, euntes de virtute in virtutem, renovantur (ut Apostolus inquit) de die in diem (2 Cor 4:16), hoc est, mortificando membra carnis suae....*"

20. Tanner, *Decrees*, vol. 2, pp. 761, 777, 794.

21. Tanner, *Decrees*, vol. 2, p. 731: "*...quae renovatione indigent aut restauratione, reficiantur....*" This edition translates the passage, "anything needing repair or restoration is put in order."

22. Tanner, *Decrees*, vol. 2, p. 913.

23. Tanner, *Decrees*, vol. 2, p. 912. The reference to 2 Cor 4:16 echoes Trent's use of the passage concerning justification.

24. Tanner, *Decrees*, vol. 2, pp. 851, 853, 856: "*Virtute evangelii iuvenescere facit ecclesiam eamque perpetuo renovat et ad consummatam cum sponso suo unionem perducit.... Ut autem in illo incessanter renovemur, dedit nobis de spiritu suo....[S]ub actione spiritus sancti, seipsam renovare non desinat, donec per crucem perveniat ad lucem, quae nescit occasum.*"

25. Paul VI, *Ecclesiam Suam*, no. 47, in *The Papal Encyclicals 1958–1981*, p. 145. This volume reprints the English translation of the encyclical from *The Pope Speaks* 10 (1965): pp. 253–92, which in nearly every case rendered *renovatio/renovare* words as "reform." I have amended this translation, bringing *reform* into conformity with its original renewal language, following the Latin text found in *Acta Apostolicae Sedis* 56 (1964): pp. 609–59.

26. Tanner, *Decrees*, vol. 2, p. 855: "*...ecclesia in proprio sinu peccatores complectens, sancta simul et semper purificanda, poenitentiam et renovationem continuo prosequitur.*"

27. Congar, *Vraie et fausse réforme*, pp. 42–46, 55–56, 227–317.

28. Avery Dulles, "The Church Always in Need of Reform. *Ecclesia Semper Reformanda,*" in *The Church Inside and Out* (Washington D.C.: United States Catholic Conference, 1974), pp. 37–50.

29. Dulles, "The Church Always in Need of Reform," p. 39. More recently, Robert Bireley observed the church has throughout her history been subject to "periodic refashioning" and "recurring accommodation": *The Refashioning of Catholicism, 1450–1700: A Reassessment of the Counter Reformation* (Washington D.C.: Catholic University of America Press, 1999), pp. 1, 201.

# Chapter 1
# Patristic Period and Carolingian Renaissance

The idea of reform is grounded in the age of the fathers (ca. 100–500). During this patristic period the church emerged from its Judaic roots and very slowly began to grow into the fairly organized institution of the Middle Ages. Reform for the fathers meant personal reform: the reform of the individual members of the church's body. The idea of an institutional, comprehensive reform of the body of the church itself does not appear until after the year 1000. What occurs between the patristic period and the "Gregorian Reform" of the Middle Ages is an important development known as the Carolingian Renaissance (ca. 750–850). Along with biblical precedents, these are the periods on which later reform movements will build.

## The Patristic Period

The fathers in the eastern and western parts of the Roman empire agreed that reform could only be conceived in individual terms, but they held a variety of ideas about personal reform. Though diverse, these conceptions of personal reform shared an optimistic idea of a human nature created by God according to the divine image.[1]

In the east, the Greek fathers tended to focus on a return to Adam's state in paradise: a recovery of the image and likeness of God *(imago Dei)* that had been lost in the fall. This recovery was typically described in mystical and ascetical terms, as in a moment of insight when the Christian understands what life will be like in the kingdom that will come. Paul's account of a person who had been "caught up to the third heaven—whether in the body or out of the body I do not know; God knows" (2 Cor 12:2) is an example.

Origen (ca. 185–254) believed that at the end of time, Christians would be returned to the original bliss of the garden before the fall. A human being journeys toward this destination, but if he lives without sin, he receives a measure of paradise on earth: "We travel toward perfection," Origen wrote, "if stretching forth ourselves to the things that are before, we forget those that are behind; the kingdom of God being in us, the final height will be at hand for those who ceaselessly progress toward the kingdom...." Gregory of Nyssa (ca. 331–94) linked reform more closely to life on earth, that is, a reformed corporeal state: "It is indeed possible for us to return to the original beatitude, if we now will run backward on the same road which we had followed when we were ejected from paradise together with our forefather [Adam].... The definition of human beatitude is the assimilation to God."

Among the eastern fathers especially, an important element in renewal was the Holy Spirit's action within the heart of a human being open to the Spirit's aid. Basil the Great (ca. 330–79) and Cyril of Alexandria (ca. 376–444) stressed this aspect of personal reform. The Spirit is the human being's companion on the journey to God, the vivifying element that makes the trip to perfection more perfect and helps to ensure the recapturing of the *imago Dei*. Like Origen, Basil believed this goal can partially be achieved on earth. The Holy Spirit's role in personal reform is one that will be repeated throughout the Middle Ages, reiterated at the Council of Trent, and reasserted at Vatican II.

The Latin, or western, fathers also focused on a return to Adam's previous condition, but they saw something more at work. Tertullian (ca. 160–220) was the first father to express the belief that the Christian receives a fuller measure of grace than Adam received because Adam lived before Christ. Tertullian and others considered this achievement a *reformatio in melius,* a reform for the better. Baptism in Christ was a spiritual rebirth and a birth greater than Adam's, reflected in Paul's statement: "And all of us, with unveiled faces, seeing the glory of the Lord as though reflected in a mirror, are being transformed into the same image from one degree of glory to another; for this comes from the Lord, the Spirit" (2 Cor 3:18). In the west, personal reform was conceived as a return to Adam's state in paradise as well as the attainment of a higher state beyond Adam's through Christ. Jesus' resurrection brings humanity to a state beyond Adam's; Adam could never have reached this better state without Christ's redemptive death and resurrection.

So, unlike the Greek fathers' primary emphasis on a reform that turns backward to Eden, the Latin fathers looked forward. The western idea of reform entailed a return to a past state *plus* a renewal of that former state aimed at a future existence in the fullness of Christ's resurrected life. In the west, then, the movement of reform looks both backward to Eden and forward to Christ's second coming and heaven. The future state will return to the prior existence, but remake it anew. As one reform scholar recently noted, reform is like the Roman god Janus who had two faces, each gazing in a direction opposite to the other. Janus saw past and future simultaneously.[2] Like Janus, the church will often be at odds with herself as she seeks to follow the Latin patristic tradition of considering past and future at the same time.

The main proponent of the western concept of a forward-looking *reformatio in melius* was Augustine of Hippo (354–430). He taught this state would be achieved through a spiritual body that Adam would have received had he not sinned and brought on the death of his earthly body. Augustine's spiritual state would occur at the end of time, but the inner renewal begins to take place during a Christian's life and reaches a certain, though not full, degree.

> ...[W]ho would be so utterly out of his mind as to say that we
> are or shall be similar to God through our body? In the inner
> man, therefore, is the similitude.... And the more we progress
> in His knowledge and in charity, the more similar shall we
> become to Him.... And still, how ever high a man may be
> [spiritually] borne up in this life, he will be far removed from
> the perfection of similitude which would be apt for a vision of
> God...from face to face (1 Cor 13:12).

According to Augustine, a very few (including Moses and David) may in this life receive insight into the beatific vision "from face to face" through a mystical revelation akin to that which Paul refers to in 2 Corinthians 12:2. For Augustine, humanity had lost its way and must not only return to, but go beyond, its original state. A human being's recovery of God's image is a type of deification according to Augustine, although a deification by grace and adoption that will always be inferior to Christ's divine nature.

Although humanity's reformation in the image and likeness of God would ultimately be accomplished by God and not man, said the fathers, this fact did not resign human beings to passivity. For Augustine, as with any eastern or western father who considered reform before the eleventh century, all reform is tied to an individual's active self-sacrifice to God. Part of Gerhart Ladner's definition of reform, it will be recalled, included humanity's free, intentional, and repeated efforts. Only the Christian who dies to himself and the world can live in God. As Augustine put the matter in *City of God:*

> A true sacrifice then is every work which is done in such a way
> that we may adhere to God in a holy society.... Thus man
> himself, consecrated in the name of God and devoted to God,
> is a sacrifice, in as much as he dies to the world so that he may
> live to God.... If then the body...is a sacrifice, how much more
> does the soul itself become a sacrifice, when it returns to God,
> so that, inflamed by fire of love for Him, it may lose the form
> of worldly concupiscence and, subject to his immutable form,

may be reformed to him and please him because it has taken on something of his beauty. This very same thing [Paul] says...: "And be not conformed to this world; but be reformed in the newness of your mind..."(Rom 12:2).

It is on account of this intentional effort that the city of man approaches and begins to achieve the city of God on earth.

## Personal Reform and the Monastery

The fathers in east and west believed the best manner of earthly life, one that would approach citizenship in the city of God, was monasticism. For Gregory of Nyssa, for example, the goal of assimilation to God could only be accomplished if the Christian turned himself almost entirely into a purely spiritual being by withdrawing from the world and refraining from marriage, sexual pleasure, and physical labor. Through the monastic disciplines, the Christian would achieve the goal of personal reform by imitating the life of Christ, especially his purgative suffering.

Monasticism for over a thousand years was presented as the best way to pursue a detached, inner, and spiritual reform of the human being who was on a journey to recover and then go beyond the lost *imago Dei*. Physical detachment made particular sense in a world that had lost the stability of the Roman Empire and the safety of her cities. This withdrawal turned the monk inward: The ideal Christian pilgrimage included virginity, poverty, contemplation (emphasized by the eastern fathers), and a life of charity and activity (favored by the western fathers). That life of charity and activity, however, took place within each soul and monastic community; it rarely engaged the outer world. The ultimate goal was the personal conversion of a person's life and actions—indeed his very being and soul—represented by the familiar Greek term *metanoia* and Benedict of Nursia's Latin phrase *conversatio morum*.

Monasticism from its roots was an ascetic, individual, and largely lay movement that sought to provide the environment within which a Christian man or woman could pursue his or her inner, personal reform. Benedict of Nursia directed that priests should not receive any special consideration in the community, must follow the rules just like everybody else, and would be judged along with the other community members according to when they entered and how they lived (chapters 61–63). But this emphasis on individual progress did not make monasticism a selfish path. The lifestyle presupposed an important point: only when a monk had settled his own spiritual life could he then transmit the flame within his own heart to others.

Personal reform is closely allied with monasticism's spiritual starting point: the severe asceticism of the earliest desert fathers, especially in the east, who favored an eremitical (solitary) life to a coenobitical (communal) path. As Christianity became tolerated and then favored in the crumbling Roman Empire, the solitary holy man replaced the martyr as the archetypical church hero. Eastern monks were examples for the west. The Egyptian hermit Anthony (ca. 251–356) became a model for the lone ascetic; his life was publicized through his biography written by Athanasius (269–373), the bishop of Alexandria who was exiled from his see because of his opposition to the Arian heretics. Athanasius traveled progressively in the west, including visits to Aquileia, Rome, and as far north as Trier.

Traveling in the other direction, the Roman-educated Rufinus (345–410) visited monks in Egypt and Jerusalem, established a monastery at the Mount of Olives, and translated eastern monastic literature. In northern Italy, Ambrose (339–97), bishop of Milan, strongly encouraged the monastic life in his diocese, serving as a spiritual director to many such groups though he was not a monk himself. His fourth-century colleague Eusebius (the bishop of Vercelli, not the historian of Caesarea), traveled to Egypt, Palestine, and Cappadocia for nearly a decade, then introduced the monastic ideals to his diocesan clergy back home in Italy. He himself lived a common life with his own priests, sharing table, property, and spiritual exercises. Soon many hermitages were settled in the Alps and the Dolomites, their inhabitants finding there the solitude eastern monks discovered in the desert.

Southern Italy also introduced the west to eastern asceticism since the lower half of Italy was still under Byzantine control.

Like Athanasius, Rufinus, and Eusebius, John Cassian (360–435), a native of the Balkans, encountered eastern ideals of personal asceticism on his travels and communicated them to the west. Cassian was attracted to the desert experience in the east as a young man, spending time in Bethlehem and at least ten years in Egypt. Since he knew Greek well, Cassian collected much material that he brought with him in 395 to Marseilles, where he established separate monastic communities for men and women. From his direct contact with the eastern desert fathers and his specific fascination with their puritanical and detached spirituality, he compiled the *Conferences* (ca. 420–28), sayings and stories of Egyptian hermits, and the *Institutes* (ca. 417–18), a collection of a dozen books on the coenobitical life.

The characteristic disciplines of the ascetical movements that these writers brought from the east to the west fed into the patristic desires for personal reform, as we can hear from several excerpts taken from a popular anthology of the time: *Sayings of the Fathers*. Reading like a fifth-century *Poor Richard's Almanack,* the *Sayings* listed very brief proverbs, ideas, and advice from the Egyptian holymen or elders (often called abbas to denote their role as spiritual fathers) that served as slogans and ideals for western ascetics.[3]

Ascetics' diciplines allowed them to abandon outward, earthly concerns so they could focus on inner, spiritual matters. Here we divide these disciplines into three areas: ascetics intended to curb the desires of body, mind, and spirit. The ascetic first tried to deny his body by combatting his physical desires: lust, food, drink, comfort. Abba Evagrius taught, "The beginning of salvation is to contradict yourself," but Abba Theonas was even more direct: "Our mind is hindered and held back from contemplating God because we are imprisoned in our bodily passions." Another abba promised, "If a man is earnest in fasting and hunger, the enemies which trouble his soul will grow weak." So important was physical suffering for spiritual progress that one ascetic who had almost always been ill lamented that God abandoned him because he experienced a year of good health.

Second, the desert fathers wanted to curb the desires of the mind: mental distractions that hindered prayer, silence, patience, and meditation. One abba reported that he prayed to God, "Lord, show me the way to salvation," and heard a voice respond: "Be solitary, be silent, be at rest. These are the roots of a life without sin." When a fledgling ascetic asked an abba for advice, the sage answered, "Go and sit in your cell, and your cell will teach you everything." Another ascetic who had difficulty learning to keep quiet held a pebble in his mouth for three years to practice, while another asked Jesus to "protect me from my tongue." These practices were designed to predispose the ascetic to his fundamental goal of prayer. As one father expressed this discipline: "No one can see his face reflected in muddy water and the soul cannot pray to God with contemplation unless first cleansed of harmful thoughts."

A third characteristic was the effort to curb desires of the spirit: The ascetic had to learn to follow God's will and not his own. He could seek out a spiritual director or his fellows for advice and fraternal correction, on the premise that God spoke through the director or other ascetics. The point was to cultivate obedience, as explained by one abba: "A brother who entrusts his soul in obedience to a spiritual father has a greater reward than the brother who retires alone to his hermitage." This abba reported that another father had a vision where the highest rank in heaven was reserved for those under obedience to another. This spot was even higher than that alloted to hermits. When this father asked why, a celestial being told him, "Hermits have followed their own will in withdrawing from the world. But the obedient have cast away their self-will, and depend on God and the word of their spiritual father: that is why they shine the most." One striking and certainly fictional story recounts a struggling ascetic who visited the son he had left behind, then presented the son to his abba. Asked if he loved this son, the father told the abba he did with all his heart. So the abba commanded him to throw the son into a red-hot baker's oven, which the father did without hesitation. The oven instantly cooled and the ascetic was praised for imitating Abraham's obedience in nearly sacrificing Isaac. When these desires had successfully been curbed and ascetics acted like this father, spiritual rewards would follow. "If a man wills," Abba Allois promised, "in one day he can come by the evening to a measure of divinity."

This path to personal reform via self-abnegation became more structured, less severe, and increasingly communal in the late patristic and early medieval periods under the premier abbot of western monasticism. Benedict of Nursia (ca. 480–550) wrote his foundational *Rule* about 530. Personal conversion is the bedrock of his *Rule,* which synthesized several centuries of monastic developments and became the blueprint for medieval monastic and then lay spirituality.

From the first two sentences of the prologue, the *Rule* devotes itself to guiding an individual back to God through a spiritual journey:

> Son, listen to the precepts of your master; take them to your heart willingly. If you follow the advice of a tender father and travel the hard road of obedience, you will return to God, from whom by disobedience you have gone astray.

About two-thirds of Benedict's *Rule* came directly or derivatively from an earlier source and was influenced by eastern monastic practices. But under the hand of Benedict, these practices became westernized, organized, and tempered. His guide is marked especially by a tendency toward *mediocritas,* a Latin word that is not captured by the limp English pejorative "mediocrity," but rather represents a constructive moderation that adapts ascetic discipline to individual temperaments. For Benedict of Nursia, an even keel is a companion on the monk's journey.

Benedict emphasized an abbot's discretion and intuition into each monk's strengths and weaknesses. It is the abbot's job to know when to steer a middle course between disciplines that are too strict or too lax, which would inhibit, rather than facilitate, the monk's individual spiritual progress and personal reform. The earliest monks did not take vows in a formal sense as they would in later periods; poverty, chastity, and obedience were not codified until thirteenth-century scholastics made such distinctions. The first monks and nuns were typically lay men and women essentially living these goals, but at this point in history simply promising to be stable (rooted within the same monastic community), to be obedient, and to work toward the change of heart and soul captured by the Benedictine *conversatio morum*. The nun or monk must truly want to undergo these tasks. Benedict regulated that anyone seeking entrance should actually be turned away as a test. "If he is importunate and goes on knocking at the door, for four or five days, and patiently bears insults and rebuffs and still persists, he shall be allowed to enter" (chapter 58).

What Benedict set out to establish was a regular, patterned structure: a rhythm within which monks and nuns could without distraction set straight their individual relationships with God. An important contribution to the practice of personal reform was his movement away from the radical solitary life of the desert fathers toward a more communal life. The monk was an individual within a community: His subject was his own soul, to be sure, but the abbot and the community at large acted as guides in his individual spiritual journey, tempering some of the extremes of the east. The importance of communal support is underlined by the fact that the greatest penalty for the recalcitrant monk is excommunication: to be cut off from the lifeblood of the community. Benedict devoted several short chapters to the topic (chapters 23–29), noting that in the final case the abbot must sacrifice one bad monk for the sake of the community, brandishing "the surgeon's knife...[to] sever the infected member from the community" (chapter 28).

Benedict's spirituality of personal reform falls into three parts: prayer, *lectio divina,* and manual labor. Benedict's contribution to prayer was to make regular the eight hours when the monk or nun would pause to pray. The idea of the *opus Dei* is that the very "work" of God is continual prayer. This routine established the daily plan around which all other monastic exercises were placed. His framework was organized into the divine office of readings, psalms, selections from the fathers, and hymns. The *opus Dei* became the official prayer of the church, representing the *ecclesia orans:* the Christian community that never ceases to pray. Singing was essential, since the monks and nuns were to sing with the love and respect of the cherubim and seraphim who give eternal praise to God. The monk or nun's mind, soul, and voice were to be in perfect balance—in the case of singing, in harmony—just as the spiritual state was to be in tune with God's mission for the individual. These public prayers overshadowed private prayer, which receives much less attention in the *Rule:* Benedict states simply private prayer should be spontaneous, frequent, short, and unregulated.

*Lectio divina* was comprised of gleaning lessons from scripture and the fathers to guide personal reform. Prayerful, reflective reading took about four hours in the monastic day and proceeded in stages. After the Roman practice of reading aloud *(lectio aperta),* the monk read silently *(lectio tacita)* and then engaged in a reflection on the text *(meditatio),* moving on to a raising of the mind to God in prayer *(oratio).* The fruits of prayer were often shared *(collatio)* with the community or the abbot as spiritual director.

Benedict placed manual labor in a central position for monastic discipline while making its nature spiritual. Where the Greco-Roman world considered physical labor a menial task suitable only for slaves and the roaming Germanic tribes considered agricultural tasks to be women's work and therefore degrading for men, Benedict represented a much richer evolution. Since God had made the world as its creator *(Deus faber),* when man tilled the soil he became a sort of cocreator with God. As a *homo faber,* the farmer, artisan, or builder imitated God's action in Genesis. Benedict thereby sanctified work with a much more positive attitude. Physical labor aided the monk or nun's growth in holiness, helping along the man or woman's spiritual progress within.

The monastery was not the only setting for the Christian seeking to concentrate on his own reform. A significant number of elite laymen and laywomen with commitments tying them home could not completely withdraw into a monastic setting. But they knew their baptism represented only the first step in a lifelong spiritual path. These were the postbaptismal *conversi,* according to Ladner's identification, who were particularly treated by Augustine. They were generally wealthy individuals who could afford a certain degree of withdrawal from the world, which was sometimes referred to as holy leisure or a cultured retirement. There was a tradition of such a life in Rome, where wealthy women, some of them encouraged by Jerome's spiritual direction through his letters, gathered to read the Bible and pray. Augustine believed this would be his path once he abandoned his public career in Italy, achieved his final conversion in August 386, and established life with like-minded friends at a villa in Cassiciacum several weeks later.[4] They were living proof that one could be a good Christian outside the monastic life, but the monastery remained the ideal. The monastic disciplines and practices were frequently adapted as spiritual exercises by the *conversi* in their daily lives; many entered monasteries and convents in their final years.

Whether the Christian was living in the world or in a monastery or convent, his goal remained to achieve a change in his life *(mutatio vitae)* and to transform himself back into the image and likeness of God *(reformatio ad imaginem Dei).* Augustine knew this to be a daily exercise:

> Indeed, this renovation does not occur in the one moment of conversion itself, as that baptismal renovation occurs through the remission of all sins.... Of this fact [Paul] most clearly spoke when he said: "But though our outward man is corrupted, yet the inward man is renewed day by day" (2 Cor 4:16).[5]

According to Augustine, this action followed a cyclical path: After learning about the faith, the Christian proceeds through prebaptismal conversion to rebirth in baptism, then embarks on a continual process of reformation and postbaptismal conversion that includes the handing on of the faith to others who are just starting the process of personal reform according to the fathers' teaching and examples.[6]

## Carolingian Renaissance

The next important stage in the history of reform and renewal is the Carolingian Renaissance. The term *renaissance* is typically used to denote Italian literary and artistic movements around the fourteenth century, but those events were predated by other renaissances, in this case half a millennium earlier.

During the long reign of Charlemagne (768–814) and his successor Louis the Pious (814–40), governmental structures with inseparable civil and ecclesiastic elements flowered. These structures aimed at organizing a diverse group of people in central Europe under a monarchy that had both secular and religious elements. During this period, the idea of a sacred kingship or Carolingian theocracy that blurred the modern line separating church *(sacerdotium)* and state *(regnum)* flourished. Religion became a way of uniting the empire. The *sacerdotium* not only legitimated the imperial claim to authority; it also offered ideas and intellectual manpower for the religious reform that the church desired and the *regnum* had the force to implement. The Carolingian Renaissance represents a top-down reform led by the *regnum,* but fueled by the *sacerdotium.*

Royal leadership in religious affairs did not originate with Charlemagne; other rulers had previously taken up their quasi-religious role, starting with the Roman emperor Constantine in the early fourth century. In Spain, King Recared similarly told a church council in Toledo in 589:

> We should provide for those things which are God's, and increase our hope and take care of the races God has given us.... [I] have been impelled by the Lord, that, putting aside the obstinacy of infidelity and the fury of discord, I might lead this people, which served error under the name of religion, to the knowledge of the faith and to the fellowship of the Catholic church.[7]

But the Carolingians encouraged several important developments of this leadership role. Whether these developments were formation movements, renaissances, or reforms is a question that can enlighten our understanding of reform and renewal in the early Middle Ages.

Elements of the Carolingian Renaissance recall our working definition of renewal: a making new or updating of prior forms. One element was the Roman imperial ideology with which Charlemagne wrapped himself after his imperial coronation by Pope Leo III (795–816) on Christmas Day 800. Charlemagne believed he was a defender of the faith, metaphorically descended from Constantine, who first favored Christianity in 313. Charlemagne contended that the Roman Empire had been transplanted into his own. He employed almost every symbol possible to promote these ideas visually and verbally.[8] After 800, Charlemagne's seal identified him as emperor and carried a picture of Rome's city gates with a cross. The imperial motto was *renovatio Romani imperii* (renewal of the Roman Empire). Coins struck after his imperial coronation depicted Charlemagne dressed as a Roman emperor with a band of laurels on his head and the words *religio Christiana* (Christian religion). Equestrian statuary pictured him in a pose like that of Marcus Aurelius (161–80), Rome's philosopher king. Charlemagne viewed his capital of Aachen as a new or third Rome, after Rome and Constantinople.

By virtue of his quasi-ordination as emperor, Charlemagne believed he was God's vicar, the overseer of Christian society, rector of Christian people and the true religion, both priest and king. His titles proclaimed him as a new Moses and David sent to protect God's people. Charlemagne also built on Germanic traditions emphasizing the divine aspects of kingship and the king's role as lawgiver. The Franks were the new people of God, chosen as Israel had been. Charlemagne was promoted as a reforming king like Josiah who "did what was right in the sight of the Lord, and walked in all the ways of his father David; he did not turn aside to the right or to the left" (2 Kgs 22:2).

Another element of renewal developed when the Carolingian Empire sought to renew a golden era of Constantinian Christianity. Charlemagne tried to transform his society into an incarnation of Augustine's city of God. This attempt took as its organizing principles the inheritance of Roman leadership Charlemagne embraced, a written Latin culture, and Christianity. Charlemagne's imperial intentions and the papacy's goals of evangelizing northward were closely related in this incarnation, especially because each side needed the other. The church legitimated Charlemagne's claim to have taken on Constantine's mantle, while a series of popes depended on Carolingian peace and material support to spread the gospel.[9]

At the center of these efforts stood the attempt to give institutional guidance and direction to personal reform: to establish structures within which individuals could in safety and security walk the path of *metanoia*. This goal did not touch the monastic communities only, however, because the Carolingian codes aimed at a communal transformation of society, as well, a system whereby individuals living the Christian life would contribute to the Christian fabric of the empire. The church found in the Carolingian Empire a mutually beneficial partner in its task of personal reform and contributed people, ideology, and a hierarchical framework that also helped Charlemagne glue his empire together.

Reform became an engine for papal and imperial agendas. Carolingian documents frequently employed the words *renovare, reformare, emendare, renasci, renovatio,* and *regeneratio* to describe the establishment of Charlemagne's Christian empire. The Carolingian Renaissance was very pragmatic, a means to the end of the total reform of society: person by person, group by group. This pragmatic reform was promulgated through legislation called the capitularies, which often began as verbal replies to questions sent to Aachen: These were implemented by imperial delegates known as the *missi dominici*.

Any organized movement needs texts: gathering documents on reform was essential for the Carolingian Renaissance, whose scribes invented the careful handwriting and distinctive manuscript style of Carolingian minuscule. This literary renaissance was directed by Alcuin (735–804), who had been educated at York, traveled in Italy, and began to work for Charlemagne after they met in Pavia in 780. Alcuin pestered Charlemagne, whom he called King David, to continue helping the effort to find and correct texts, which would allow the empire's inhabitants to learn more about the Christian faith that would save their souls by reforming their lives: "[Y]ou diligently strive to correct those entrusted to you by God and lead souls long blinded by the darkness of ignorance to the light of the true faith." But Alcuin also criticized Charlemagne, telling him that he must do more to improve "unscholarly statements or unorthodox expressions."[10]

Carolingian scholars focused themselves on biblical and patristic writings. After compiling these texts, they commented on them, used them as model sermons, and compiled *florilegia,* volumes of excerpts on specific topics selected from the fathers along with monastic and classical sources.[11] Paul the Deacon (ca. 720–800), a Lombard historian who had spent time at Benedict of Nursia's central monastery of Monte Cassino, produced a collection of the fathers' homilies for Charlemagne, who directed that it be considered authoritative and free of errors. Canon law was another concern, since ecclesiastic and imperial legislation were virtually indistinguishable. When Charlemagne wanted to establish a law code, Pope Hadrian I (772–95) personally handed him a collection that included standard sixth-century canons plus conciliar legislation and papal decrees from Siricius (384–99) to Anastasius II (496–98).[12] Charlemagne's scholars used this collection in addition to a mid-seventh-century collection from the Iberian peninsula to organize the Carolingian church, setting out the duties and relationships of priests and clergy while establishing diocesan and provincial administrative structures.

Canon laws instructed people how to act, but Christians must also pray for personal reform. Assembling liturgical texts was an important aspect of reform because liturgical rituals mark the soul's progress. The Carolingian church derived its liturgy from Roman customs. A series of sacramentaries nominally named for several influential popes was sent to Charlemagne (ca. 785–88): the Leonine sacramentary (for Leo I, 440–61), the Gelasian (for Gelasius I, 492–96), and the Gregorian (for Gregory I, 590–604). Paul the Deacon prepared a lectionary in addition to his homilary. Earlier, Pope Paul I (757–67) had sent Charlemagne's father, Pepin (741–68), an antiphonary for liturgical singing. Rome sent a calendar of saints' and feast days, along with an *ordines,* or book of rubrics to guide the actions and prayers of liturgical celebrants.

Monasticism, the model way of life for *metanoia,* was renewed by Benedict of Aniane (750–821), who served under Pepin, Charlemagne, and Louis the Pious. As something of a second founder of Benedictine monasticism, Benedict of Aniane focused his reform at the monastery of Inden, which became a hub. Charlemagne had received a personal copy of Benedict of Nursia's *Rule* from Monte Cassino, which he kept at Inden. Each monastery in the empire was required to send two of its monks to train at Inden. They returned home not only with a centralized experience of Benedict's program for a *conversatio morum,* but the *Rule* copied from the Monte Cassino master manuscript.

Monks were not the only people who required direction for their spiritual progress; education was supposed to make all of Carolingian society Christian. Learning was to be renewed so Christians would know the faith they should profess and the moral code they should live. Education started with Charlemagne and his own children. Einhard, Charlemagne's biographer who compiled a partisan story of his life (ca. 826–36), was trained at Charlemagne's palace school at Aachen and knew the emperor personally. He recounts the emperor "was determined to give his children, his daughters just as much as his sons, a proper training in the liberal arts which had formed the subject of his own studies." Despite his own faltering efforts, Charlemagne admired and supported learning with finances and enthusiasm:

> He learned Latin so well that he spoke it as fluently as his own tongue; but he understood Greek better than he could speak it.... He paid the greatest attention to the liberal arts; and he had great respect for men who taught them, bestowing high honors upon them.... Under [Alcuin] the emperor spent much time and effort in studying rhetoric, dialectic and especially astrology.... He also tried to learn to write. With

this object in view he used to keep writing tablets and notebooks under the pillows on his bed, so that he could try his
hand at forming letters during his leisure moments; but,
although he tried very hard, he had begun too late in life and
he made little progress.[13]

In a famous letter to Abbot Baugulf (ca. 780–800), Charlemagne moved beyond his private circle toward the education of
others, starting with monks. He was particularly concerned with
imparting discipline both in a person's spiritual life and in the pur-
suit of education. It was his hope that the proper form of education would help improve the understanding of its content. This
understanding, in turn, would lead to Christian conduct in the
Carolingian territories because most texts treated spiritual and
moral subjects. Charlemagne in this letter directed that:

> ...[B]ishoprics and monasteries...ought also to be zealous in
> the cultivation of learning and in teaching those who by the
> gift of God are able to learn, according to the capacity of each
> individual. Thus just as the observance of [Benedict's] rule
> imparts order and grace to their conduct, so also zeal in
> teaching and learning may do the same for their sentences, so
> that those who desire to please God by living rightly should
> not neglect to please him also by speaking correctly.... For
> although correct conduct may be better than knowledge, nev-
> ertheless knowledge precedes conduct.

Charlemagne's advisers paid particular attention to writing
since they were dismayed to discover poor Latin grammar in letters sent to Aachen from monasteries:

> ...[W]e began to fear lest perchance, as the skill in writing
> was less, so also the wisdom for understanding the holy scrip-
> tures might be much less than it rightly ought to be. And we
> all know well that, although errors of speech are dangerous,
> far more dangerous are errors in understanding. Therefore,
> we exhort you not only to avoid neglecting the study of liter-
> ature, but also with most humble mind, pleasing to God, to
> study earnestly in order that you may be able more easily and

more correctly to penetrate the mysteries of the divine scriptures.... For we desire you to be, as it is fitting that soldiers of
the church should be, devout in mind, learned in discourse,
chaste in conduct and eloquent in speech, so that whosoever
shall seek to see you out of reverence for God, or on account
of your reputation for holy conduct, just as he is edified by
your appearance, may also be instructed by your wisdom,
which he has learned from your reading or singing, and may
go away joyfully giving thanks to omnipotent God.[14]

Charlemagne did not overlook reforming the faith lives of
the masses, as this last excerpt already indicates in its attention to
people who come looking for spiritual guidance. One of his capitularies stipulated all laypeople should know the creed and Our
Father. He sent out a statement of orthodox faith that also
exhorted Christians to act civilly toward one another, to live a virtuous life according to God's commands, and to defend the faith.
Other capitularies spelled out what was pagan and to be avoided,
and what was Christian and to be practiced. Charlemagne, capi-
talizing on his Constantinian role as defender of the faith, laid
down rules of behavior and jurisdiction for bishops, abbots and
abbesses, monks and nuns, and priests.

These directives trickled down to laity on the local level,
where Carolingian bishops like Theodulf of Orléans directed his
priests to oversee their lay flocks diligently. Priests were to establish schools in villages and hamlets where children could learn to
read and write. As Charlemagne directed, Theodulf reiterated the
requirement that every Christian be able to recite the creed and
Our Father. The bishop added they must pray at least twice a day
(morning and night), attend mass but do no work on Sunday, give
shelter to the homeless, refrain from perjury and false testimony,
be fair in business, and go to confession, where they must especially note their failure to avoid the eight vices, which Theodulf
didactically listed for his priests. For the salvation of souls, Bishop
Theodulf particularly directed his priests to teach their parishioners and explain scripture to them. The capitularies had also

stipulated frequent sermons in the vernacular language so every listener, whether literate in Latin or not, could understand.[15]

## Perspectives

One of the distinct features of the Carolingian Renaissance is its direction from above, a trend in what can be called Christian legislation beginning with the later Roman emperors in the fourth century and culminating under Charlemagne and his immediate successors into the ninth century. This perspective marks a significant change in the history of reform and one that foreshadows the top-down nature of the institutional reforms to follow in the High Middle Ages. We have seen Charlemagne and his clerical advisers set up legislation that, in essence, laid out a program for inner reform. These capitularies instructed inhabitants of the empire by telling them what they should know about the Christian faith and how they should behave according to its precepts. These actions would lead to their inner reform, but the impetus for that reform appears to have come from outside the inhabitants themselves, specifically from above in the form of enforced imperial legislation. One may rightly ask, then, how deeply these reform intentions penetrated people's hearts, even allowing for the obvious sincerity a bishop like Theodulf demonstrated toward the pastoral needs of his flock.

Though a concern for individual reform is clear in the capitularies, the extent to which Christians changed within because of legislation simply cannot be measured—and this difficulty goes beyond the normal problem for the historian that the typical Carolingian mother did not leave a journal of her spiritual life.[16] Inner spiritual progress is not something that can be quantitatively measured or even qualitatively expressed, given its very personal and often intangible nature. The Carolingian church, led by the emperor more than the pope, appears to have tried to establish a system within which personal reform could take place. But it seems likely that the systems and institutions could well have overshadowed individual attempts. Inner movements of the spirit cannot be commanded from the outside. When an institution strives to take over and direct individual reform, does individual reform lose its individuality? Do top-down reforms and magisterial dictates inhibit or facilitate inner, personal reform such as that urged by the fathers? Do codes and commands produce a *conversatio morum* or just make sure people follow the rules? Indeed, the historian may ask whether the Carolingians were sincerely trying to aid individual spiritual progress or to build an empire of subjects obedient to crown and miter. Education was a means to the end of forming decent, moral citizens of empire and church. Surely the Carolingians sought a sense of unity, justice, and loyalty not only for the sake of binding Christians together and facilitating their spiritual progress. The empire also benefited from the peace and security such unity, justice, and loyalty were intended to produce.

Was the Carolingian "Renaissance" aptly named? Ladner referred to this era as "the so-called Carolingian Renaissance," labeling it instead among "all great reform periods."[17] It is very clear Charlemagne saw his role as emperor and his kingdom as an empire in terms of an intentional renewal of Constantine's Christian Roman empire. The recovery of Latin classical and religious texts represented a literary renaissance: a gathering of old texts being made new with Carolingian minuscule manuscripts that were copied and disseminated. In addition, the focus on individual reform represented a continuation of the fathers' goals, although we have noted hierarchical direction and force were departures from the patristic idea that reform would spring from within a Christian's heart and soul.

To the extent the Carolingians tried systematically to Christianize an empire, however, we see under Charlemagne, his predecessors, and his successors more formation than renaissance or reformation. The marriage of church and state took a shape under Charlemagne that was to a certain degree different than under Constantine. True, Charlemagne was seeking to renew an imperial Christianity that had existed under Constantine. Charlemagne was attempting to organize an empire after several centuries of Christianity's growth. Christianity had spread further since the early fourth century, and its nexus had moved to Europe's western and northern sections. Charlemagne's empire represented a moment of critical mass and synthesis for Christianity and the heart of Europe. The Carolingian Renaissance helped create the tense symbiosis that would characterize the relationship between the medieval "church" and "state." To this degree, it represented both a renewal of Latin culture and a formation of Christian society that would itself require reform in the coming centuries.

## NOTES

1. This section rapidly summarizes Ladner, *Idea of Reform*, pp. 63–283, with quotations from Origen at p. 74, Gregory of Nyssa at pp. 76–77 and 90, and Augustine at pp. 191–92 and 280. See also Eugenio Garin, "La *'Dignitas hominis'* e la letteratura patristica," *Rinascita* 4 (1938): pp. 102–46. On Augustine and the *imago Dei,* see also Bernard McGinn, "The Human Person as Image of God: Western Christianity," in *Christian Spirituality: Origins to the Twelfth Century,* eds. McGinn, John Meyendorff, and Jean Leclercq (New York: Crossroad, 1985), pp. 316–21.

2. Phillip H. Stump, *The Reforms of the Council of Constance (1414–1418)* (Leiden: E. J. Brill, 1994), p. 206.

3. Owen Chadwick, ed., *Western Asceticism* (Philadelphia: Westminster Press, 1958), translates the *Sayings* along with Cassian's *Conferences* and Benedict's *Rule.* The examples cited from the *Sayings* are found at pp. 40, 42, 49, 51, 55, 94, 132, 143, 151–52, 154–56, 160.

4. Augustine pictured his life from just after his conversion to his ordination as priest in 391 as this sort of leisurely retirement, even though he stayed at Cassiciacum less than a year. On this stage of his career, see Peter Brown, *Augustine of Hippo: A Biography* (Berkeley: University of California Press, 1967), pp. 115–27.

5. Ladner, *Idea of Reform,* pp. 198–99.

6. Ladner, *Idea of Reform,* pp. 366–77.

7. J. N. Hillgarth, ed. *Christianity and Paganism, 350–750: The Conversion of Western Europe,* rev. ed. (Philadelphia: University of Pennsylvania Press, 1986), pp. 90, 91. For other examples of pre-Carolingian rulers serving as protectors of Christianity, especially as they codified Christian morality in legislation from the late fifth through the eighth centuries, see pp. 76–83, 93–97, 107–16.

8. Gerhart Ladner, "Religious Renewal and Ethnic-Social Pressures as Forms of Life in Christian History," in *Theology of Renewal,* ed. L. K. Shook, 2 vols. (New York: Herder and Herder, 1968), vol. 2, pp. 335–40.

9. Walter Ullmann's discussion of these developments informs this section: *The Carolingian Renaissance and the Idea of Kingship* (London: Methuen, 1969), pp. 1–42.

10. Paul Edward Dutton, ed., *Carolingian Civilization: A Reader* (Peterborough, Ontario: Broadview Press, 1993), pp. 106–9. Charlemagne built on earlier scholarly developments at his grandfather's and

father's courts: Pierre Riché, *Education and Culture in the Barbarian West: From the Sixth through the Eighth Century,* trans. John J. Contreni (Columbia: University of South Carolina Press, 1976), pp. 439–46.

11. Many of the earliest manuscripts of Roman classical literature date not to the Roman republic and empire but are the products of Carolingian monks.

12. Walter Ullmann, *The Growth of Papal Government in the Middle Ages* (London: Methuen, 1955), p. 89.

13. Einhard, *Vita Caroli,* chapters 19 and 25, as found in Einhard and Notker the Stammerer, *Two Lives of Charlemagne,* trans. Lewis Thorpe (London: Penguin Books, 1969), pp. 74, 79.

14. Dutton, *Carolingian Civilization,* pp. 79–80.

15. Dutton, *Carolingian Civilization,* pp. 58–69, 94–105.

16. Suzanne Fonay Wemple shines some light on the masses' experiences in *Women in Frankish Society: Marriage and the Cloister 500–900* (Philadelphia: University of Pennsylvania Press, 1981); on the spiritual life, see especially pp. 143–74.

17. Ladner, *Idea of Reform,* p. 303.

# Chapter 2
# The High Middle Ages, 1050–1300

The next important chapter in the history of reform begins about 1050 with a series of reform-minded popes; it ends about the time the papacy moved to Avignon in the first decade of the fourteenth century. This period frames a distinct stage in hierarchical, top-down reform reminiscent of the Carolingian Renaissance and the structural aspects that made it more formation than reformation. But as the head of the church attempted to direct—even dictate—reform goals, reform was bubbling up from the body of the church, as well. This bottom-up reform was most notable in revived monasteries and the poor men's movement that would culminate in both the Waldensian heresy and the new mendicant friars. Bottom-up reform among the laity and innovative religious orders would outlast and achieve more success than the papal reform efforts, which flagged significantly in the fourteenth and fifteenth centuries. The glue that held these two reform movements (top-down and bottom-up) together was the Twelfth-Century Renaissance: a rich combination of humanism, educational developments, spirituality, popular piety, and personal reform in the tradition of the fathers.

# Gregorian Revolution

Most scholarship in the twentieth century, and even earlier, referred to this period as the Gregorian Reform and focused primarily on the investiture struggle (alternately, contest or controversy) between Pope Gregory VII (1073–85) and the Holy Roman Emperor Henry IV (1056–1106). This identification, however, is very limited and fails to take into account a standard aspect of reform movements: precursor characters and issues building up to the key person or conflict that embodies the reform. This conflict is itself followed by a fallout where the various issues take decades and centuries to play themselves out. Such is the case with the Gregorian Reform, a wide-ranging development whose very name has largely been changed to Gregorian Revolution by recent scholarship that places the conflict between Gregory VII and Henry IV into a much wider chronological, organizational, and ideological context.[1] Several features distinguish the Gregorian Revolution from earlier reform movements.

## Characteristics and Goals

The Gregorian reforms were institutional and structural, as were the efforts of the Carolingian Renaissance, but the protagonist of high medieval reform was generally the pope, not the emperor. In addition, this institutional and structural reform had a broader focus than the fathers' goals. Even though the Carolingian capitularies attempted to transform society as a whole, their focal point remained the individual Christian. By contrast, the Gregorian reformers took a new direction with their comprehensive plan to transform the entire church, the *Ecclesia* herself, from the top down.

Gerhart Ladner identified the Gregorian movement as the first comprehensive, institutional, and structural reform in the church's history, one that nearly pushed aside a millennium of personal reform efforts urged by the fathers. The Gregorian reformers addressed the church's structures, though clearly not as radically as the Protestants would.[2] They viewed the *Ecclesia* in corporate terms and her reform as proceeding through officials in the church's head *(in capite)* down through the church's members or the parts of her body *(in membris)*.[3] Their reform goals were catalysts for the organization of the curias, college of cardinals, and canon law. It is this widespread impact that made the Gregorian reforms more formation and revolution than reformation, strictly speaking.

Still, the Gregorian reforms were attempts at a self-conscious restoration of a prior, allegedly golden age in the church's life. Gregory VII did not see himself as adding anything to the church: he believed his role was to return the church to her previous, pristine state. Gregorian reformers denied pure innovation, building on a statement by Pope Stephen I (254–57): "Let nothing be innovated except that which is part of tradition." The challenge for the Gregorian reformers was determining whether a custom conformed to tradition. If it did not, then it was in need of reform. If there was no tradition in the first place to which the custom could be reformed, then the custom must be abandoned. The Gregorian reformers, therefore, sought to discover original traditions and establish them as standards for the church of their age.[4] Gregory VII himself rarely used forms of the noun *reformatio* and the verb *reformare,* selecting the verb on only four occasions in 350 letters. He preferred *renovare, restaurare* (to restore), and *corrigere* (to correct), among others.[5]

This prior golden age to which Gregorian reformers aimed was the *ecclesia primitiva* comprised of the earliest Christian communities scattered throughout the Mediterranean basin with some relationship to Rome. A major issue for the high medieval church and the Gregorian reformers was the discrepancy between the moral behavior of Christians in the *ecclesia primitiva* and their own centuries.[6] A specific issue for the Gregorian reformers concerned priests who were married, officially or not. The lack of clerical celibacy added another problem in need of reform. Priests often treated a local church as their own property, passing it and the rights to its revenues along to a son, just as fathers in other professions passed their family businesses down to the next generation. This tended to blur the lines of authority between a parish and a diocesan bishop or, in larger cases, between a diocese and Rome.

Papal reform propaganda may have exaggerated the extent of these moral problems. One scholar of the period notes that the idea of a horrible moral age in the tenth and eleventh centuries allowed medieval popes and modern historians to praise the reforms that followed. But it is hard to say if moral behavior was any better or worse in the tenth and eleventh than in prior centuries. There is no special reason to think tenth- and eleventh-century priests were any worse with respect to concubinage and marriage than their predecessors. What changed was not the calls for celibacy, but the enforcement of reforming actions against transgressors for a variety of theological, political, and economic reasons.[7]

Medieval reforming popes concerned themselves with simony, the buying and selling of church offices, and the practice known as lay investiture whereby local rulers named bishops and abbots within their territories. The theory behind this proprietary system was that if a property owner built a parish church on his land or if a cathedral sat in his circle of authority, then that property owner had a right to name those who worked in the parish church or cathedral. Many priests and bishops received the symbols of their authority from this property owner and, given the feudal system of economy, pledged an oath of fealty, promising to provide services and/or funds as his half of the feudal relationship in return for his job, home, and workplace.

Working up the power ladder, more powerful rulers had for centuries named abbots, bishops, archbishops, and even popes. This relationship was cemented most visibly in dioceses when the local ruler physically invested the bishop with the symbols of his spiritual authority (episcopal ring and crozier) and his temporal authority (scepter and sword). In what must have been a dramatic ceremonial moment, the Frankish kings and emperors in the first millennium had handed these symbols to bishops with the pronouncement, *"Accipe ecclesiam"* ("Accept the church"). Such a scene surely confused the Christian population, who must have seen the bishop as the lord's inferior. Consequently, the reform issue of lay investiture was not so much one major investiture controversy between Pope Gregory VII and Emperor Henry IV in one decade of the late eleventh century as many investiture controversies that had been building across Europe for centuries. All of these problems restricted the freedom of the church or, to use what became a rallying cry or reform slogan for the high medieval church, the *libertas ecclesiae.*

## Papal Monarchy and Reform

Efforts to reform these many problems did not begin with Pope Gregory VII but predated his pontificate by a generation. Leo IX's reign in the middle of the eleventh century was the impetus for the papal revolution in reform, but ironically he came to the see of Peter through a synod called by the Holy Roman Emperor Henry III (1039–56). The emperor, exercising the traditional Constantinian-Carolingian role of defender of the faith, stepped into the heat of ecclesiastical politics at the highest level to make sense of a difficult situation.

Because of a potent brew of Roman family politics and the desire for reform, there were in 1046 three men who claimed to be pope. Benedict IX (1032–44, 1045, 1047–48) was an immoral man hated by the Romans, who chased him from the city and put Sylvester III (1045) in his place. In a raucous few months in early 1045, Benedict excommunicated Sylvester and returned to Rome. Six weeks later, however, Benedict IX decided to get married and sold his papal claim to his godfather John Gratian, who took the name Gregory VI (1045–46). John Gratian was a reformer who may have seized a chance to get rid of the unlikable and corrupt Benedict IX, but he committed simony in the process. Then the former Benedict IX tried to renege on the deal. At Sutri and Rome, the emperor Henry III deposed Sylvester III, Benedict IX, and Gregory VI. The emperor then named the next four popes. Although his efforts infringed on the church's freedom to choose her own bishops, Henry III consistently selected as pope reformers who worked against the very action the emperor was taking in naming them. Clement II (1046–47), Damasus II (1048), Leo IX (1049–54), and Victor II (1055–57) took the names of early popes to signal their desire to return to a prior age of purity. This trend continued for centuries.

Gregory VII, who had already been working for most of these reforming popes, came to the papal throne in 1073. Like his predecessors of the previous quarter century, Gregory VII aimed at reform on a more universal (that is to say, European-wide) scale. His primary reform goal was to liberate the church from secular control, since *regnum et sacerdotium* coexisted much more uneasily after the year 1000 than before. Gregory VII's greatest obstacle was the well-entrenched proprietary church system. Gregorian reformers fought this system by arguing that episcopal authority comes from God through the pope. Buying and selling a benefice represented an attempt to block the Holy Spirit's selection of the right man for a specific appointment. Simony blocked the Holy Spirit's action and frustrated the church's freedom.

The flashpoint between pope and emperor came in 1075 when both named a new archbishop of Milan. Imitating his father's actions at Sutri, Henry IV deposed Gregory VII, who responded by deposing and excommunicating the emperor.[8] The pope's action sparked a civil war in Germany. Later, Henry invaded Rome: the pope fled, then died in exile. A compromise to the investiture controversies was ultimately reached in 1122 with the Concordat of Worms between the emperor Henry V (1106–25) and the pope Callixtus II (1119–24). The emperor renounced his right to invest the bishop with the symbols of his spiritual authority, while the pope conceded the emperor could give the bishop the symbols of his temporal power.

The major battle between Gregory VII and Henry IV overshadows the full story of high medieval reform, as stereotypical clashes of titans often do. There was more to high medieval reform than papal efforts; there was more to papal efforts than just the investiture controversies. Gregorian reformers pursued their goals through a variety of means, many of them closely related to the growth of a papal bureaucracy and ideology. Reform and the growth of a papal monarchy, especially the accent on papal primacy, complemented each other.[9] One can argue that without this papal monarchy, no top-down, comprehensive, institutional reform could have taken place. Several parts of this papal monarchy functioned as means to the goal of reform: the ideology behind papal primacy; the very concept of the papacy as the central unit of the church's institutional hierarchy; and structural developments such as papal legates, the college of cardinals, and curial departments.

Medieval popes emphasized their primacy and leadership in reform in the way they interpreted the power of the keys given by Jesus to Peter in Matthew 16:18–19: "And I tell you, you are Peter, and on this rock I will build my church, and the gates of Hades will not prevail against it. I will give you the keys of the kingdom of heaven, and whatever you bind on earth will be bound in heaven, and whatever you loose on earth will be loosed in heaven." Medieval popes strictly limited this power and leadership to themselves: they maintained they personally embodied Peter's exclusive power of the keys and promoted the cult of St. Peter to make their point.

In the eleventh and twelfth centuries, reforming popes typically used the title *vicarius Petri* (vicar of Peter) to underscore the link between themselves and the first pope. The title *vicarius Christi* (vicar of Christ), favored by popes after the twelfth century, went even further in stressing the source of papal authority, since it was Christ, they argued, who delegated power to Peter and his successors. Apostolic succession was also accentuated in the frequent use of the phrases "by apostolic authority" or "with apostolic blessings" in papal letters. The idea was that the current pope was, in a sense, Peter himself and therefore the popes' reform goals were Peter's reform goals at the same time. This practice reached back to earlier popes, as when the Council of Chalcedon in 451 acclaimed Pope Leo I (440–61) in this way:

> This is the faith of the fathers. This is the faith of the apostles. We all believe thus. The orthodox believe thus. Anathema to

him who does not thus believe. Peter has expressed these things through Leo....[10]

Gregory VII leaned heavily on this tradition in asserting his ultimate authority and leadership in ecclesiastical matters, including reform. In the *Dictatus papae* (*Dictate of the Pope*, 1075), a list of rubrics that may have been the outline for a book he never got around to writing, Gregory VII declared his preeminence.[11] Among the very brief twenty seven topics, he declared the pope's feet alone are to be kissed by princes; only the pope can be called universal and depose or reinstate bishops; only a pope can make new laws and no law can be considered authoritative without his approval; that he has the authority to depose emperors; that a synod called without his authority cannot be called general; and that he can judge all but be judged by no one. Gregory VII frequently emphasized the Petrine source of his own papal authority and leadership in reform by referring to Peter and the popes, who were Peter's successors, instead of those fathers who were not. He stressed that Rome, the center of Christianity and the site of Peter's body, was the mother of all churches and that Peter (and Gregory himself, by extension) was *paterfamilias*.[12] This stance is summed up in what can be considered the keystone of the *Dictatus papae,* number 23: "That the Roman pontiff...indubitably becomes holy through the merits of Blessed Peter...."

Gregory VII put these Petrine ideas of leadership and preeminence into practice. Writing to Henry IV in 1074 before their animosity exploded, the pope nevertheless stressed his own authority by referring several times to Peter's merits, wrath, faith, and authority. Gregory soon sent a harsher letter, calling the emperor to a greater degree of obedience and deference to the papacy. Again, the pope repeatedly referred to his apostolic authority and the figure of Peter.

> Gregory, bishop, servant of God's servants, to King Henry, greeting and the apostolic benediction—but with the understanding that he obeys the apostolic see as becomes a Christian king.

Considering and weighing carefully to how strict a judge we must render an account of the stewardship committed to us by St. Peter, prince of the apostles, we have hesitated to send you the apostolic benediction....

It would have been becoming to you, since you confess yourself to be a son of the church, to give more respectful attention to the master of the church, that is, to Peter, prince of the apostles. To him, if you are of the Lord's flock, you have been committed for your pasture, since Christ said to him: "Peter, feed my sheep" [John 21:17], and again: "To thee are given the keys of heaven, and whatsoever thou shalt bind on earth shall be bound in heaven and whatsoever thou shalt loose on earth shall be loosed in heaven" [Matt 16:19]. Now, while we, unworthy sinner that we are, stand in [Peter's] place of power, still whatever you send to us, whether in writing or by word of mouth, [Peter] himself receives, and while we read what is written or hear the voice of those who speak, [Peter] discerns with subtle insight from what spirit the message comes.[13]

Papal primacy as an idea needed to be exercised if it was to be more than opinion. Primacy was lived out through the reforming papal monarchy that made the theory of the papacy a formidable reality. The papal monarchy included the bureaucratic structures that developed during the High Middle Ages to run the church and administer its considerable material holdings, its sacramental system, its manpower, and specifically its reform program. Part of this centralization included a cadre of close advisers who could be counted upon to spread and police papal reform efforts, thereby tying local reform to Rome's authority and direction.

Over time, the college of cardinals became a central element of the high medieval papal monarchy and especially the implementation of its reform program. The early Middle Ages had witnessed the slow, limited growth of a group of cardinal deacons, priests, and bishops around the city of Rome whose privileged position was mainly liturgical.[14] The twelfth and thirteenth centuries saw a marked consolidation of the cardinals' power. Freely electing a pope without outside interference is the most obvious marker of the cardinals' power and the one most visibly tied to the reform goal of *libertas ecclesiae.*

Nicholas II addressed this reform goal by assigning the cardinals the leading role in choosing popes in the election decree *In nomine Domini* (1059). At that time, canon law allowed other clerics to participate and the current pope to state his preference for a successor, although his opinion was not binding. The Third Lateran Council (1179), under the reforming pope Alexander III (1159–81) who fought the proprietary church system, mandated that only cardinals could participate in the election. When two-thirds of the college of cardinals agreed on a candidate, that man would be pope. About a century later, the Second Council of Lyons (1274) laid down specific provisions for a papal conclave. This council stipulated the cardinals, and no other clerics, must gather no later than ten days in the city where the pope had died. They were to be sealed off and their rations were pared down to bread, water, and wine after eight days if they failed to elect a pope. All of these efforts were designed to reform the papal election, prevent simony, and offer a leading example of *libertas ecclesiae* for the rest of Christianity to follow.

Very often, the link between Roman headquarters and the churches in the field were the legates the popes sent out to promulgate their reforms and oversee compliance. These legates filtered papal reforms down to the diocesan and then the parish level by serving as the frontline shock troops of reform. Popes empowered their legates to speak and make decisions in their names. Not surprisingly, the leading legates were frequently cardinals who were permitted to wear papal insignia and use the title *vicarius papae* (vicar of the pope). In a number of other significant and highly visible positions, the cardinals were not only entrenching themselves in papal administration while increasing their influence, but they were strengthening the machinery of reform.[15] Cardinals became heads of papal departments, called curias: a *camerarius* oversaw the curia for papal finances, while a *cancellarius* was in charge of a huge chancery that produced and kept track of the massive, steady work of recording and promulgating papal appointments,

court decisions, relationships with religious orders, political nego-
tiations, and ordinary correspondence. The position of *cancellarius* grew to such power that four chancellors were elected pope in
the twelfth century.[16]

Pope Paschal II (1099–1118) particularly relied on cardinals
as reforming legates and put others in charge of curial departments. So important did the cardinals become that in the twelfth
century popes appointed 300 of them; their thirteenth-century
successors added another 140. As a core body of advisors, they
were able to carry the papal reforms from Rome throughout
Europe and convey back to Rome a sense of how those reforms
were being received, amended, or ignored. Cardinals soaked up
the spirit of centralized reform because almost every one of them
lived in Rome during the High Middle Ages, leaving only on missions as papal legates. Another reform aspect related to their ele-
vation: Clergy raised to the college of cardinals normally had to
resign their previous posts, typically as bishops or abbots, to avoid
offering scandalous examples of absenteeism and pluralism.[17]

## Canon Law: The Engine of the Gregorian Revolution

Popes and cardinals could not make decisions arbitrarily;
their practical reform program needed theories and case studies to
back them up. Canon law provided the necessary support. In
many ways, canon law was the engine that drove the Gregorian
Revolution and the organization of a papal monarchy.[18]

The codification of medieval canon law in the High Middle
Ages represents a reform in itself. The compilation of canon law
began with the recovery of Roman law, especially the volumes of
decisions, excerpts, and analysis that had been gathered under
the Roman emperor Justinian (527–65). Early popes modeled
their legislative functions on the Roman style, producing answers
to questions known as decretals that imitated the imperial *decretum:* a written reply an emperor gave indicating his decision in a
case, a decision that enjoyed the force of law. The earliest papal
decretal appears in 385 from Pope Siricius (384–99); later popes

used decretals to rule on doctrine, liturgy, ecclesiastical discipline, and temporal matters such as property rights. Canon law was also comprised of patristic writings, the decrees of local synods and ecumenical councils, episcopal decisions, monastic customs, and civil law.

Canon laws were collected in Africa, Gaul, and Italy from the fourth through the seventh centuries. On the Iberian peninsula, a breakthrough occurred when scholars tried to make sense of the growing body of law. After producing a chronological version of these laws that indicated how one decision built on another, in the seventh century they arranged the *Hispana Systematica* by topic, producing chapters on ordinations, sacraments and the liturgy, doctrine, heresy, and church courts. These efforts culminated in a collection Pope Hadrian I handed Charlemagne in 774 so the emperor could codify law and protect the church in his empire as part of the Carolingian Renaissance.

By the High Middle Ages, these collections had grown to be enormous and, sometimes, contradictory. The next great step in canon law, the engine of reform, was produced by Gratian, who wrote a volume in 1140 known by its shorthand title, the *Decretum*. Its actual title better describes his attempt to make sense of the confusing morass of overlapping canon laws: *Concordantia discordantum canonum (A Concordance of Discordant Canons)*.[19] Gratian attempted to organize nearly four thousand canonical texts and figure out which were authoritative, which represented competing jurisdictions, and which could be employed to decide a case in a particular situation. He also addressed the hierarchy of law by prioritizing divine, natural, and human laws.

Because the papal reform and monarchy were developing rapidly, new cases were constantly arising. What followed Gratian were volumes that collected papal decretals, conciliar canons, and other relevant decisions after 1140. These were not only gathered, but then interpreted or "glossed" in an effort to catch up with and explain the rapid expansion of the papal reform movement and its precedent-setting decisions. Johannes Teutonicus in 1215 produced the authoritative commentary on Gratian, called the *Glossa ordinaria.* In 1234, Pope Gregory IX added an extra book, the *Liber extravagantium* but also called the *Decretales,* by directing the Dominican Raymond of Penaforte to sift through recent papal letters and conciliar legislation. This collection was, in turn, glossed by Bernard of Parma. Gratian and Gregory IX's collections became the basis for the *Corpus iuris canonici,* the body or code of canon laws, upon which later canons built. Pope Boniface VIII (1294–1303) in 1298 added another book, the *Liber sextus,* that Johannnes Andreae glossed.[20]

Canon law had become a tool for the dissemination of the papal reform program. Popes could make and send out decisions restricting immoral clerical behavior, reducing simony, and fighting for the *libertas ecclesiae.* In so doing, the popes not only promulgated their reform ideas, but also asserted their centralized authority.

## Reform Synods and Councils

Medieval popes also employed synods and councils (words that in the Middle Ages were effectively synonymous) to make decisions, to promulgate legislation, and to promote their reform program in a setting that emphasized papal authority. Between 1050 and 1123, from Leo IX's pontificate to the First Lateran Council, popes oversaw dozens of synods of various sizes. Gregory VII held a synod in Rome during Lent 1078 that called for the church's *restauratio* (restoration). His synods were actually fairly collaborative meetings that witnessed discussions that informed final decisions. This collaboration allowed Gregory to implement decisions more forcefully since they had the backing of the synods' participants, the bishops.

Papal synods (ca. 1050–1123) repeatedly condemned the reform targets of simony; clerical immorality, specifically concubinage; and lay interference in ecclesiastical matters, especially the naming of abbots and bishops. Pope Urban II (1088–99) physically extended the synods and their reform goals beyond Italian soil by holding an important meeting in France at Clermont in 1095. His immediate successor, Paschal II, held sixteen papal councils. Between 1140 and 1160, however, there were almost none, which may indicate the reform machinery of legates and decretals was working so well it overrode the need for synods.[21]

Apart from the many smaller councils and synods the reform popes employed, they held four major, centralizing councils, which the church catalogs among her twenty-one ecumenical councils. All met in Rome: in 1123 (Lateran I, under Callixtus II), 1139 (Lateran II, under Innocent II), 1179 (Lateran III, under Alexander III), and 1215 (Lateran IV, under Innocent III). All legislated a top-down reform program like the smaller synods, fighting simony, concubinage, and lay investiture.

Lateran I approved the Concordat of Worms, which addressed the long conflict between papacy and empire, but otherwise ordered very general and mixed prohibitions against common problems. Lateran II followed the tradition of ratifying prior reform legislation and papal decrees. It also more specifically addressed the clergy, laying down that priests who married were not truly married and ordering the faithful to avoid their masses. The council stated the sons of these priests could not be ordained unless they joined a religious order and declared no benefice could be passed along as an inheritance.

Lateran III's attendance represented the spread of the papacy's authority. While most of the three hundred bishops who participated were French and Italian, there were nineteen each from German and Spanish territories, six each from England and Ireland, a Hungarian, a Dane, seven from the Holy Land, and several observers from Greek churches. Lateran III continued to reform the clergy by stipulating bishops and priests must have a legitimate birth, good morals, and a decent education. Bishops were ordered to step up their visitations but also to tone down the opulence of their traveling parties (relatively speaking: archbishops could not hold banquets and were restricted to fifty horses in their entourage). The council paid particular attention to the training of parish priests: Each cathedral was ordered to pay for a professor and to establish funds so that anyone wishing to study for ordination could do so tuition-free.

Lateran IV was the foremost reform council of the Middle Ages. As with Lateran III, this council represented a widening circle of papal influence. Over four hundred bishops attended, along with about eight hundred abbots and priors; royal ambassadors from Constantinople, Germany, France, England, Aragon, Portugal, and Hungary were also present. The council worked forcefully to reform clerical immorality by suspending any cleric living with a woman as well as their bishops who permitted this situation. Clergy were prohibited from jobs considered unfit for a priest: civil and military positions, working in trades or acting, loitering in inns, watching gamblers, or serving as surgeons. Their dress was to be sober and moderate: worn neither too long nor too short, clothes were to be fastened at the neck and devoid of red, green, or embroidery. The council also addressed lay reforms, notably by preventing laypeople from buying or selling church property and from taxing the clergy.

## Pastoral Considerations

All of these elements may portray high medieval Gregorian reformers as bureaucrats who followed a master plan of reform, exclusively institutional, that Gregory VII laid down full-blown on the first day of his pontificate. Thanks to H. E. J. Cowdrey's massive reappraisal of Gregory VII, we can come to a more nuanced understanding of the man, his reform ideas, his impact, and the nature of the structural, top-down reform that followed his pontificate.[22]

Although he had been a major player in previous popes' reform efforts, as pope himself Gregory VII did not come into office with a blueprint for reform. His ideas were not formulaic: Gregory VII was not a systematic thinker with a predetermined plan, but a much more adaptable, flexible, and spiritual figure than previously presented. Gregory VII's reform thought, although based on several decades of experience, continued to develop in response to concrete situations. From this perspective, Cowdrey sees the Dictatus papae as a set of first steps and not final conclusions whose virulence was mitigated in the face of practical considerations over time. The pope's responses were also not determined solely by politics; they were often moderated to conform to pastoral concerns. For Gregory VII, reform was a work in progress—and a pastoral task at that.

Gregory VII's pastoral concerns with religion and morality were frequently evident. In his 1078 and 1080 Roman synods, for instance, the pope addressed the question: "What makes true penance?" He answered that the penitent must turn to God under the guidance of a pastor; he must make a sincere decision to trade good for sinful acts; and he must experience a personal, inner conversion. This answer reminds us of the fathers' focus on personal reform and represents, according to Cowdrey, Gregory's "wide-ranging...concern for the pastoral and moral renewal of the church and of the individual Christian." Gregory VII saw pastoral concerns in each of his many roles: administrator, rector, pastor, priest (especially with respect to liturgy), teacher, leader of the faithful, and preacher. Although this last function was most often exercised as an exhorter of kings and princes instead of the masses, Cowdrey concludes Gregory VII did not overlook pastoral concerns in the body of the church and personal reform among individual Christians. According to Cowdrey's reassessment, Gregory VII followed the pastoral tradition of Benedict of Nursia and Gregory I. He was less the "founder" of medieval papal monarchy than its "forerunner" and a more pastoral pope than the canon lawyers who would dominate the see of Peter in the coming centuries.

So a crucial but overlooked part of Gregory VII's legacy as a reformer is the flexibility with which he transmitted the fathers' attention to personal reform. That focus was not entirely buried by the rigid administrative structures of the papal monarchy. Canon law, for example, was no bureaucratic sledgehammer. Many cases dealt with sacramental and moral matters. Some of the earliest topics around which canon law collections were organized dealt with the sensitive and omnipresent topic of marriage. Ivo, the bishop of Chartres, wrote a *Decretum* that slightly predated Gratian's. In his preface, written in 1095, Ivo indicates that he considers canon law to be a pastoral science:

> Beginning with the statements of the faith which are the foundation of the Christian religion, I go on to the sacraments of the church, then to instruction on conduct and its correction.... It is, however, necessary to warn the prudent reader that, if he does not at once fully understand what he reads, or if he finds apparent contradictions, he should not immediately censure the author, but consider that there are some things that are to be understood rigorously and others with flexibility. The reason for this is that some extracts represent judgments and others are counsels that are to be interpreted mercifully. The guiding principle of the whole building is charity: that is to say, a concern for the salvation of our neighbors, which requires us to do unto others as we would be done unto. If every ecclesiastical teacher so interprets the rules to ensure that his teaching is based on this rule of charity, he will neither err nor sin.[23]

Clearly, then, there was more to the Gregorian Revolution than a power struggle between Henry IV and Gregory VII. And, as we have just seen, institutional reform efforts in the church's head were not devoid of religious, moral, and pastoral implications *in membris*. With this perspective, we must continue widening the lens through which we look for medieval reform goals and efforts.

## Twelfth-Century Renaissance

While canon law was the engine that ran the machinery of the papal monarchy and the Gregorian Revolution, the heart and soul of medieval reform was the composite of spiritual, educational, and humanistic elements known as the Twelfth-Century Renaissance. Charles Homer Haskins in 1927 laid the groundwork for the idea of a medieval renaissance that occurred before "the" Renaissance, usually taken to mean the Italian Renaissance of several centuries later, in *The Renaissance of the Twelfth Century*. Fifty years later, a group of scholars met at Harvard to reevaluate and push forward Haskins' ideas, categories, and evidence, later publishing their papers in *Renaissance and Renewal in the Twelfth Century*. This volume operates as a companion to Haskins' book by marking half a century of scholarship on the topic of medieval reform and renewal that championed the idea of a renaissance before "the" Renaissance.[24]

Three articles in the latter collection dealt with religious topics (the renewal of religious life, theology, and liturgy), but spirituality generally took a backseat to articles on renaissances and renewals in education; society and the individual; law, politics, and history; philosophy and science; literature; and art and architecture. These concerns make sense given the fact that the Twelfth-Century Renaissance occurred simultaneously with agrarian developments that allowed urban expansion since city dwellers did not have to grow their own food. There was also population growth based on increased food production and a Commercial Revolution that improved the economy. The organization of economic units into guilds and urban corporations that followed had considerable legal and political ramifications.

Society was flowering in nearly every aspect of life and people were aware of the upswings. Twelfth-century writers themselves used the word *renovatio* to describe what was going on in all spheres of human activity.[25] But although all of these topics could not fail to touch on religion in some way during the Christian Middle Ages, rarely is the Twelfth-Century Renaissance's spirituality and humanism laid side by side with the Gregorian Revolution, despite the fact that the two movements run along parallel lines and intersect at particular moments. It is important to see medieval spirituality and the Gregorian reform efforts as parts of a whole: matching steps, in a sense, of reform in the High Middle Ages.

The centerpiece of the Twelfth-Century Renaissance in terms of religious reform is the evangelical awakening that placed the gospel squarely at the heart of the everyday person's spirituality.[26] This awakening touched all Christians, leading to the radical poverty of some heretical movements as well as to the efforts of many lay Christians to care for the least of Christ's brothers and sisters (following Matt 25:42–45) in hospitals, poorhouses, and other relief activities. In modern terms, these attempts to carry the gospel's values and calls for action into the marketplace would be called social justice concerns.

The spiritual foundation of these social justice activities was an active, apostolic life *(vita activa* or *vita apostolica)*. Such actions gave personal and practical witness as they mirrored Christ's life, especially his humanity, humility, poverty, and suffering. These emphases on poverty and suffering would have been specifically attractive to those who did not profit from economic expansion or guild membership—the castoffs of the Commercial Revolution in the twelfth and thirteenth centuries. These castoffs were attracted to the preaching of the gospel in the vernacular and the identifications that itinerant, poor preachers made to their own destitute lives. Not all of these preachers were licensed by the church, however, and their proselytizing led some to condemnation and heresy (as we shall see in the next section that considers heresy and religious orders through the prism of reform).

The high medieval evangelical awakening was particularly infused with a very optimistic idea of human nature, and here the Twelfth-Century Renaissance continues the personal reform and spirituality of the fathers. One familiar aspect of the fathers' conception of personal reform was the dignity and perfectibility of human nature. Another aspect was the active nature of human beings' attempts to recover their lost *imago Dei,* an activism at the core of the *vita apostolica* that recalls Ladner's working definition of reform as "free, intentional...multiple, prolonged and ever repeated efforts." This definition of patristic reform related to another aspect of twelfth-century spirituality: the partnership between human beings and God that built on Paul's conception of the spiritual journey as a continual process of human progress toward sanctification supported by the Holy Spirit's help.

In the twelfth century, scholastic humanists inherited these patristic ideas. Scholastic humanists were not as centered on the recovery and imitation of Roman literary and rhetorical style as the humanists who followed in France and Italy in the later Middle

Ages, to whom most people refer when they speak of "Renaissance humanism." Although these earlier scholastic humanists were concerned with linguistic style, their activities were also full of spiritual matters, particularly related to patristic ideas of humanity's state and potential. According to scholastic humanists picking up on the patristic tradition, God granted dignity to humans by creating them in the divine image. God also granted human beings the free will to accept or decline the need for constant personal reform and the duty to lead a morally correct life. Human beings were not passive characters in their personal reform but were, to use historian Charles Trinkaus's evocative words, "alive, actively assertive, cunningly designing, storming the gates of heaven."

Because human beings are divine creatures, the exercise of human potential in partnership with divine grace was not the kind of humanism sometimes exalted as humanity's ability to break clear from its divine source. Twelfth-century humanism glorified the God who created human beings. While the era before 1100 had emphasized supernatural aid and humanity's dependence on God to understand the world, the twelfth century accentuated human beings' ability to figure things out for themselves, although divine aid was not disregarded.[27] Scholastic humanists of the Twelfth-Century Renaissance specifically stressed that human beings should always strive to reform themselves by reconnecting with their divine origins, a concept Trinkaus called an "anthropocentric theology" grounded in a renewed interest in the spirituality of the fathers.[28]

In addition, scholastic humanists were not the practitioners of the arid, impractical scholasticism that gave the scholastic theological method a bad name in the fourteenth and fifteenth centuries. Rather, scholastic humanists of the High Middle Ages were practical, spiritual, and content-based. They resurrected the patristic notion that human beings were able, with divine grace and help, to recapture the knowledge and relationship with God they had enjoyed in Eden before Adam's fall. Following the western patristic idea of a personal *reformatio in melius*, especially as developed by Augustine, these humanists further believed humans could go beyond Eden because of Jesus' redemptive death and resurrection.

Although scholastic humanist efforts were partially textual, as with canon law, they aimed not simply at making doctrine systematic and deciding court cases, but at providing guidance for Christian conduct. Scholastic humanists particularly recommended the study of philosophy as a way to improve human reason, freedom, and moral courage, with the ultimate goal always being the improvement of a believer's spiritual progress. One writer stated the matter of introspection especially bluntly: "The highest philosophy is the continual meditation of death."[29] These pragmatic and spiritual goals led scholastic humanists to put their ideas to a pastoral purpose. They spread their organization of dogma and morality to parishes by writing sermons, manuals, and handbooks for pastors, which allowed the pastoral aspects of the Gregorian Revolution to trickle down among the church's members.[30]

In the medieval university, study ideally consisted of hearing material explained, discussing it, and then sharing it through preaching. Peter the Chanter (d. 1197), a moral theologian and scholastic humanist with very pragmatic concerns, indicated the pastoral intent of the scholastic theological method directed toward personal reform.

> Explication is a sort of foundation or base for what follows, because upon it other uses of the text rest. Disputation is a sort of wall in this exercise, this building, because nothing is fully understood or faithfully preached unless first analyzed by disputation. Preaching, however, which the previous ones support, is a sort of roof protecting the faithful from the raging storms of vice.[31]

This effort recalls the Carolingian imperial capitularies and episcopal directives that targeted parish audiences, furnishing the principles of faith and codes of behavior that tried to help Christians achieve their heavenly rewards.

High medieval scholastic humanism and personal reform in the model of the fathers were closely aligned, especially in the optimism with which scholastic humanists tried to figure out the natural world. The study of the natural world led upwards to God. They believed that if they could understand the harmony of nature, they could also understand the harmony of humanity and divinity within themselves, thereby renewing the unique, individual relationship and partnership existing between God and each human being created in the *imago Dei*. As with canon law, music imagery helps us see what these authors were after. One author described God's creation of the world in terms of a musical instrument:

> The supreme artisan made the universe like a great zither upon which he placed strings to yield a variety of sounds, for he divided his work in two—into two parts antithetical to each other. Spirit and matter, antithetical in nature yet consonant in existence, resemble a choir of men and boys blending their bass and treble voices.… Material things similarly imitate the distinction of choral parts, divided as things are into genera, species, individuals, forms, and numbers; all of these blend harmoniously as they observe with due measure the law implanted within them and so, as it were, emit their proper sound. A harmonious chord is sounded by spirit and body, angel and devil, heaven and hell, fire and water, air and earth, sweet and bitter, soft and hard, and so are all other things harmonized.[32]

All the dualities of creation—nature and humanity, male and female, reason and faith—complemented each other. Full knowledge of any one of these topics led to fuller knowledge of the other.

Just as a Christian could understand God the more he or she understood nature, Christians could also understand God the more they understood themselves and others. We see here another indication of continuity in the history of reform: the earlier patristic and monastic objective of inner, personal reform was picked up in the twelfth century. The Socratic admonition to "know thyself" was a popular feature among twelfth-century spiritual writers who used Latin versions of the phrase to recommend confession, obedience, and a general awareness of one's conscience in relationship with God. To know yourself meant to know God for the medieval monk or nun. And knowing yourself was part of a dialectical relationship among knowing yourself, others and, above all, God in a spirit of loving friendship.[33] As Richard of St. Victor (ca. 1123–73), a mystical theologian, wrote: "Let a man first understand the invisible things of himself before he presumes to stretch out to the invisible things of God.... [F]or unless you can understand yourself, how can you try to understand those things which are above yourself?"[34] Turning inward, as the earliest ascetics and monks had done, led not only to the *metanoia* or *conversatio morum* Benedict of Nursia had sought, but to turning outward to fellow pilgrims and to God.

Searching for the inner self, a penetrating exercise, became an important tool for personal reform. This exercise was aided by the twelfth century's approving stance toward aggressive questioning. As Abelard (1079–1142) described the process famously in *Sic et Non (Yes and No)*, "By doubting, we come to inquiry; through inquiring, we perceive the truth." Monastic theology was not always open to this process.[35] Scholastic humanists sometimes attacked those who resisted aggressive questioning, saying they were restricting knowledge of the world and themselves while promoting ignorance. William of Conches (ca. 1080–1160), a philosopher and theologian at Chartres, defended the age's probing intellectual activities against critics with a passionate rebuke:

> Ignorant themselves of the forces of nature and wanting to have company in their ignorance, they don't want people to look into anything; they want us to believe like peasants and not to ask the reason behind things.... But we say that the reason behind everything should be sought out....[36]

The Gregorian Revolution's institutional goals and the intellectual, educational, and spiritual dimensions of the Twelfth-Century Renaissance worked symbiotically to renew the high medieval church. The Gregorian Revolution, especially the emerging machinery of papal monarchy, required learning and manpower. The Twelfth-Century Renaissance provided both with its systematizing of theology, morality, and canon law on the one hand, and its cathedral schools (that turned into universities) where scholastic humanists produced these achievements, on the other. These schools, in turn, enjoyed the church's financial support to operate; they paid popes and bishops back by turning out an elite cadre of graduates who staffed papal and episcopal bureaucracies. How these multilayered reform developments affected, and were affected by, diverse reform movements in the body of the church leads us to consider religious orders and lay spirituality as complements, correctives, and challenges to medieval reform *in capite*. What we will find is that the Twelfth-Century Renaissance had an impact on reform both *in capite et in membris,* but not always with a similar result.

## Religious Orders and Reform

The same period that created the papal monarchy and Twelfth-Century Renaissance also produced a renewal of the religious life. Tremendous variety characterized this renewal, giving the lie to the notion of medieval Christianity as an era of cookie-cutter spirituality marching lockstep with the papacy. The High Middle Ages witnessed a series of reforms of the monastic life: each wave usually reacted against or in support of the former change. At the same time, innovators such as Francis of Assisi (1181–1226) and Dominic Guzman (ca. 1170–1221) radically adapted monastic ideals, applying them via their new mendicant orders to the exigencies of the Commercial and Gregorian Revolutions.

This great growth in the number and diversity of male and female religious orders represents additional aspects and nuances of high medieval reform. Here we will concentrate on Cluniacs, Carthusians, Cistercians, Franciscans, and Dominicans as representative. However, there were so many new orders of monks and nuns that Pope Innocent III at Lateran IV in 1215 stipulated all new orders had to ally themselves with an earlier tradition of religious life, rather than strike out on their own. As one author writing about 1140 poetically described the explosion, monks

> are seen to flower again *[reflorere]* and, after having been almost overwhelmed by the winter frost and desiccated by

the constant northern winds, are restored *[revertuntur]* to their pristine state by the new sun and warmed by the favoring breezes…. In the cloisters, as in trees, a rare fruit grew ripe. A workshop of total sanctity was set alight by the fire sent from above and fanned by violent winds.[37]

## Cluny

The Cluniacs were a large branch of reformed Benedictines spread throughout Europe who took their name from a founding monastery in the French town of Cluny in Burgundy. This monastery's charter represents the first step in what became the Gregorian goal of *libertas ecclesiae* because the monastery was free from outside influence. The Cluniac precedent *in membris* was influential on Gregory VII and those who followed his efforts *in capite.*

In 909, Duke William the Good of Aquitaine chose an abbot named Berno and endowed the monastery at Cluny with land and money. William probably took this unusual step for two reasons. First, he had no heir. But second, and certainly more importantly for himself, William had committed a murder that weighed heavily on his conscience. In Cluny's founding charter, William is at least honest when it comes to these self-serving intentions:

> To all right thinkers it is clear that the providence of God has so provided for certain rich men that, by means of their transitory possessions, if they use them well, they may be able to merit everlasting rewards. As to which thing, indeed, the divine word, showing it to be possible and altogether advising it, says: "The riches of a man are the redemption of his soul" (Prv 13). I, William, count and duke by the grace of God, diligently pondering this, and desiring to provide for my own safety while I am still able, have considered it advisable—nay, most necessary, that from the temporal goods which have been conferred upon me I should give some little portion for the gain of my soul.[38]

Regardless of his personal motives, William's actions promoted monastic reform. Key provisions of the charter William granted to Cluny represent its reform nature. Cluny was to be free from secular authority as well as episcopal authority because of the cozy relationship that had often existed between a local landlord and the bishop who was a relative or sycophant. The monastery was placed under the direct control of the papacy and was responsible to the pope alone. The monks would be left free to choose their own abbot in an election unhindered by outside influence. This model was quickly adopted by new monasteries founded under Cluny or older monasteries that embraced the reform.

By 1100, three hundred monasteries were allied with Cluny; a century later, that number had multiplied five times to fifteen hundred monasteries.[39] This astounding growth testifies to the need for monastic reform and the theme of *libertas ecclesiae* that dialectically supported Cluniac expansion and the papacy's reform goals. Indeed, Cluny itself was dedicated to Peter and Paul. The founding charter specifically noted that the monastery was placed under papal protection, symbolically represented by William's requirement that the Cluniac monks should send money to Rome every five years in payment for candles the papacy would provide in return. When this arrangement is multiplied exponentially so that fifteen hundred Cluniac monasteries were bound to the papacy by 1200, the mutual support is clear. The monasteries through their close ties with Rome were able to augment and spread the papacy's use of the cult of Peter to emboss its authority and propagate the reform goal of *libertas ecclesiae*.[40]

Cluniac reform touched more than a monastery's juridical status. The Cluniac reform most visibly reimagined the exercise of prayer. Cluniac prayer and liturgy are immensely important for later groups reacted against these Cluniac reforms. These other monastic communities tried to counter what they saw as accretions: in essence, they found themselves reforming a reform.

For Benedict of Nursia, prayer was simple. Cluny's modifications, which spread quickly throughout Europe as more monasteries affiliated with the abbot of Cluny, increased the splendor of prayer and liturgy in many tactile ways. The *opus Dei,* which typically had taken five hours, consumed about eight hours in a Cluniac monastery. Cluniac art and architecture were notable for their rich decorations, intricate sculpture, and size. Cluniac monasteries were self-contained cities with hundreds of monks, a far distance from Benedict's small communities of one or two dozen monks operating at a subsistence level. The liturgy became increasingly grandiose, since Cluniac monks saw themselves as serving with the angels in a heavenly court as feudal vassals to God. The monastic choir anticipated the heavenly choir of seraphim and cherubim who did nothing but sing praises around God's throne and altar. The monastery, choir, and cloister were depicted as a type of paradise. Vestments and vessels were made of the finest materials: silk, brocade, and gold threads were sewn into altar cloths and chasubles; chalices, crucifixes, and candlesticks were made of gold and silver.

The Cluniac reforms also reconfigured the emphasis on manual labor, a distinct component of Benedictine spirituality. The physical and material asceticism that imbued Benedict's *Rule* was, in a Cluniac setting, placed within the context of the liturgy. Long stretches of prayer replaced work in the fields as causes of ascetic fatigue and monotony. Manual labor's spiritual aspects gradually became lost, along with the sanctification of labor, which Benedict had promoted. The *opus Dei* replaced manual labor in the Cluniac time commitment. This change led to the introduction of lay brothers *(conversi),* as opposed to the more literate choir monks, who appear in almost every religious order around the eleventh century. *Conversi* were generally drawn from the lower classes: they performed tasks in support of the monastery's physical needs (especially agricultural) and were prevented from becoming monks.[41]

The introduction of the *conversi* represents a departure from Benedict of Nursia's plan for personal reform for the monks. The issue is not the presence of laity, since Benedictine monasticism was largely a lay movement. But the tiered population of choir monks and *conversi* produced just the sort of hierarchy within a monastery against which Benedict had specifically written, as when he stressed that the priest who enters the monastery should enjoy no special privileges. Cluniac choir monks were dispensed from manual labor because their frequent celebration of masses, often to fulfill a benefactor's bequest, was considered their task for the community. But this practice of using *conversi* distanced the monk from the spirituality of labor that aided personal reform and was important for the Benedictine monastic tradition.

## Cistercians

As with the Gregorian Revolution, the Cluniac monasteries, in seeking to reform by withdrawing from secular influence and worldliness, ended up creating a parallel of that worldliness. The Cluniac reforms came under attack as additions and dispensations that did not conform to the spirit or the letter of Benedict's foundational *Rule*. Thus arose the Cistercian monks who aimed at reforming the Cluniacs, who saw themselves as reformed Benedictines. It is hard to understand the Cistercians apart from Cluny.

The Cistercians did not achieve the striking growth of the Cluniacs, but the number of Cistercian monasteries rose from 7 in 1187 to 525 in 1200, reaching 742 in 1500. The simultaneous popularity of the Cistercians and Cluniacs indicates the urgent recognition of the need for reform as well as the variety of ways to pursue competing concepts of reform.

The Cistercians took their name from Cîteaux, the site of their first monastery south of Dijon established in 1098, nearly two centuries after Cluny's founding. An abbot named Robert of Molesme (1028–1112) was a restless monk dissatisfied with his monastic experiences. With about twenty other like-minded monks, he founded a small monastery in an isolated spot where the group sought to recreate the asceticism of the desert fathers, substituting a heavily wooded area for sand and caves.

In a brief document justifying their intentions, this first group made clear they wanted to return to monasticism's original sources *(reditus ad fontes),* especially Benedict of Nursia's *Rule.* In the first words of this *Exordium Parvum,* these original Cistercians described the hard road they were laying down for themselves, so their successors

74

may pray for us who have, unflagging, borne the burden of the day and the scorching heat; and that they too, on the straight and narrow path traced by the *Rule,* may sweat it out until they breathe their last and, having laid down their mortal load, repose happily in everlasting rest.[42]

The Cistercians pursued a fourfold *reditus ad fontes,* much of it in reaction to Cluny. First, the Cistercian monks returned to the purity of the *Rule,* getting rid of any dispensations that had, to their eyes, mitigated it. Bernard of Clairvaux (1090–1153), an early Cistercian, protested in detail against the dispensations he believed were destroying the virtuous monastic life. "Who would have dreamed, in the far beginning of the monastic order, that monks would have slid into such slackness?" an exasperated Bernard asked in *An Apologia for Abbot William* (1125). "What a way we have come from the monks who lived in Anthony's day!"[43]

In contrast, the Cistercians rigorously adhered to the *Rule,* even to the point of regulating clothing (to the barest necessities, and these were not to be fancy) and meals (only two hot dishes were permitted at table). But the Cistercians also feared a literalist approach to the *Rule.* They believed literalism would degenerate into a legalistic adherence that would prevent the *Rule* from facilitating spiritual progress. Cistercian abbots followed Benedict's pastoral principles of balance and discretion: they continued to make decisions that would not compromise spiritual progress and were reasonably based on individual cases and local customs.

Second, the Cistercians returned to poverty and simplicity, and here the reaction against Cluny is marked. Their recovery of simplicity is clearest in terms of the liturgy. The Cistercians stripped the liturgy down to its essentials, in part because they believed the centrality of prayer and the eucharist had been lost amid what some considered the ornate theatrics of Cluniac liturgy.[44] Significantly, liturgical simplicity is treated with minute detail in the *Exordium Parvum,* the very first document of the reforming Cistercian order. The plan seems designed to institute a liturgy that avoided exactly those elements that distinguished Cluniac liturgy.

...[T]o ensure that God's house, in which they desired to serve him devoutly day and night, was empty of anything redolent of pomp or superfluity, or tending to corrupt the poverty—guardian of the virtues—which they had unconstrainedly embraced, they settled that they would keep neither gold nor silver crosses, but only ones of painted wood, nor more than one branched candlestick, and that of iron, nor censers, save of copper or iron, nor any but fustian or linen chasubles without silk or gold or silver, nor albs or amices except of linen, and likewise without silk, gold or silver. As regards all mantles, copes, dalmatics and tunics, these they eschewed entirely. They did, however, keep chalices, not gold but silver ones, or preferably silver gilt.... And they laid down, too, that the altar cloths should be made of linen and have no ornamentation, and that the wine cruets should be without gold or silver.[45]

Bernard was not content to praise simplicity and went on the attack against churches with extensive decorations.

What is this show of splendor intended to produce? Tears of contrition or gasps of admiration? O vanity of vanities, but above all insanity! The walls of the church are ablaze with light and color, while the poor of the church go hungry. The church revets its stones in gold and leaves its children naked. The money for feeding the destitute goes to feast the eyes of the rich. The curious find plenty to relish and the starving nothing to eat. As for reverence, what respect do we show for the images of the saints that pattern the floor we tread beneath our feet? People often spit on angels' faces, and their tramping feet pummel the features of the saints.... [W]hat possible bearing can this have on the life of monks, who are poor men and spiritual?[46]

Third, the Cistercians returned to the spirituality of manual labor by restoring the balance among work, public prayer, and private meditation. They went back to a simpler, shorter *opus Dei* than that sung at Cluniac monasteries, and they reenergized the concept of physical labor as a positive means of sanctification. They particularly wanted to restore subsistence farming and to avoid the trappings of feudal materialism that had immersed the Cluniac monasteries. However, the Cistercians would become well known for their own huge agricultural complexes, called granges, staffed by illiterate *conversi* as opposed to choir monks, just like the Cluniac monasteries.

Finally, the Cistercians returned to the spirituality of solitude and the earlier monastic goal of withdrawing from society. (The famous phrase is *contemptus mundi:* contempt for the world.) Bernard particularly decried worldly abbots, asking in his *Apologia:*

> [W]hat evidence is there of humility when one solitary abbot travels with a parade of horseflesh and a retinue of lay-servants that would do honor to two bishops? I swear I have seen an abbot with sixty horses and more in his train. If you saw them passing, you would take them for lords with dominions over castles and counties, not for fathers of monks and shepherds of souls....[47]

Personal conversion was the Cistercians' primary goal; their aim clearly returned to the patristic and ascetic roots of monasticism.[48] The theory behind their fourfold *reditus ad fontes* was precisely that if the monks observed the original *Rule* fully by following its true spirit and intent, their hearts would be purified. This purity would lead to charity, contemplation, and *metanoia*. The *Exordium Parvum* makes specific mention of Benedict of Nursia's goal: to effect an individual *conversatio morum* in the life of each monk.

> And thus, drawing the integrity of the *Rule* over the whole tenor of their life—liturgical observance as well as daily living—they followed faithfully in its track, and, having stripped off the old self, they rejoiced to have put on the new.[49]

Bernard repeated the patristic and twelfth-century theme of self-knowledge that leads to God by frequently paraphrasing Augustine's prayer, "God, let me know you and know myself." Bernard, along with many other monastic leaders, continued another patristic and twelfth-century theme by discussing the reformation of man in the *imago Dei* through the correct action of human free will supported by divine grace.[50] The Cistercians, then, represent a twelfth-century continuation of the patristic ideal of personal reform even as they acted in the context of, and reaction to, Cluniac monasticism, which had been a reform movement itself.

## Carthusians

The Cistercians and Cluniacs were not the only monastic reform movements of the High Middle Ages. One other group stands out among many. The Carthusians mainly avoided the tensions between the Cluniacs and Cistercians by ignoring them. The Carthusians radically embraced monasticism's ascetic roots more than any other medieval group. The Carthusians were highly contemplative, but extremes of individualism in the Carthusian monasteries were tempered by community activities, as Benedict's *Rule* intended. Their founder, Bruno (ca. 1032–1101), who lived for a time as a hermit under Robert of Molesme's spiritual direction, took up a highly individual and eremitical life about 1084 with a few followers. The order grew very slowly, with thirty six houses in 1200 and barely seventy a century later. But those numbers, small especially when compared to Cluny and Cîteaux, probably do not indicate a lack of interest as much as the inability of most monks to live as austerely as the Carthusians dictated.

Carthusian austerity is indicated by the layout of their monasteries, which were built to promote individual more than communal action. Each cell had a private garden and workshop for manual labor, a supply of water, and a fireplace; a second floor offered a study, bed chamber, and oratory for private prayer. The monk's cell and the cloister became sacred ground that, one imagines, often turned the monk's thoughts to the original garden of Eden and mankind's creation in the *imago Dei*. One prior led about a dozen monks in each monastery; this small scale insured that the abbot would know his monks and provide the discretionary spiritual direction Benedict's *Rule* stipulated as crucial for individual progress.

Carthusian activities emphasized personal reform and simplicity. Unlike Cluniac monasteries, prayers and liturgies at Carthusian monasteries were stark and mainly solitary; with the Cistercians, Carthusians saw the Cluniac changes as nonessential accretions and distractions to a monk's spiritual journey within. Unlike the Cistercians and their large granges, Carthusian manual labor consisted of small, individual tasks the monks performed in their private workshops and gardens. Meals and recreation were generally taken alone, although the monks met for spiritual conferences. Each monk directed himself to the primary goal of contemplating God in solitude and silence. Almost all travel and correspondence, even for an apostolic purpose, was forbidden, and few guests were permitted within the Carthusian monastery. Only rarely did the house distribute alms or food to the poor in the surrounding countryside. Carthusians essentially contracted with *conversi*, no more than twenty per house, who raised the crops necessary for the monks' survival and acted as liaisons with the outside world.

The Carthusians upheld the monastic ideals so well that their supporters, though not the humble Carthusians themselves, could boast *non deformata, non reformata:* because the Carthusian order had never been deformed, it never needed to be reformed. The Carthusians represented a hard-core monastic spirituality by recreating and living fully the origins of monasticism, especially the movement's strict attention to the absolute necessity of personal reform.[51]

## Poor Men's Movement

Francis of Assisi's mendicant vision did not spring from nowhere. He must be placed within the twelfth-century backdrop of the poor men's movement before we can comprehend him as a high medieval reformer. The poor men's movement, which produced heretics along with orthodox believers like Francis, began from a reform perspective. The movement was centered in France in Lyons and in northern Italy in Lombardy, places where the Commercial Revolution had increased both wealth and poverty—

a medieval version of the rich getting richer and the poor, poorer. Some members of what might be called a middle class combined their moderate incomes with simple, charitable activities. In Lombardy, these people and some who were poorer were known as the *Humiliati* and the Poor Men of Lombardy; the Poor Men of Lyons rallied around a man named Waldo.[52]

A married man with children who did well as a cloth merchant, Waldo appears late in the twelfth century. He was struck one day by the radical call to poverty of Matthew 19:21 where Christ tells the rich young man to sell his possessions, give the money to the poor, and follow him. Waldo was also influenced by the story of St. Alexis, a fifth-century Roman patrician who converted to Christianity, left his wife, and begged alms. Determined to follow Matthew 19:21 and St. Alexis's example literally, Waldo became a wandering, mendicant preacher. He quickly attracted a crowd who read or heard the Bible that he had someone translate into the vernacular language.[53]

Since he gathered distrust along with adherents, Waldo and his followers appealed to Lateran III in 1179 for approval. Pope Alexander III was open to their call for poverty but distinguished between doctrinal preaching, which required a church license and therefore was forbidden to Waldo, and exhortatory preaching, which the pope permitted to the laity. Within several years, however, many local synods condemned Waldo and the poor men's groups. In 1184, Alexander's successor Lucius III (1181–85) formally declared the Waldensians and others heretics in the document *Ad abolendum*. From this point on, the Waldensians became increasingly virulent in their criticism of the church's worldliness and clerical immorality.[54]

The poor men's movement anticipated Francis by emphasizing poverty as an ideal of the virtuous Christian life. Waldensians saw themselves as the poor of Christ *(pauperes Christi)* and did not believe the evangelical life was restricted to a life lived within a religious order. The early church was held up as the model to be restored, especially the description of the *ecclesia primitiva* in Acts 4:32–35. This is a key passage for reformers throughout the church's life and describes a community of equals that shared its resources:

> Now the whole group of those who believed were of one heart and soul, and no one claimed private ownership of any possessions, but everything they owned was held in common. With great power the apostles gave their testimony to the resurrection of the Lord Jesus, and great grace was upon them all. There was not a needy person among them, for as many as owned lands or houses sold them and brought the proceeds of what was sold. They laid it at the apostles' feet, and it was distributed to each as any had need.

Other Waldensian beliefs were also reform-oriented and saw the *ecclesia primitiva* as normative, an interesting twist since Gregory VII, who pushed the papal revolution against which the Waldensians reacted, had also turned to the *ecclesia primitiva* as a model. For the Waldensians, as for many reformers who would follow, the *ecclesia primitiva* started to lose its purity in the early fourth century when Constantine endowed the church with land, money, prestige, and temporal trappings. The church's subsequent power, they alleged, corrupted her. In addition, Waldensians dismissed many ecclesiastical customs and traditions, which they viewed as external trappings of religious piety, urging instead a simplification of religious exercises. Any practice that they claimed could not be traced to the early church should be dismissed. Waldensians rejected tithing, fasting, feast days, vigils, miracles, indulgences, excommunications, processions, images, and icons. They kept only the Lord's Prayer. Waldensians also largely rejected the sacraments, purgatory, the church's role in biblical interpretation, and the intercessory power of the saints.

Although the Waldensians were condemned as heretics, it is instructive to see their ideas in the broader light of the Gregorian Revolution and the twelfth century's evangelical awakening. The gospel's centrality was a frequent reform theme of the poor men's movement that placed them in line with orthodoxy and tradition. One of these poor men early in the twelfth century told his fellow *pauperes Christi* that if anyone asked what religious order they belonged to, "tell him the order of the gospel, which is the basis of all rules." Peter the Chanter noted Anthony the hermit had handed some followers the gospels when they asked him for a rule. Francis of Assisi would soon tell Innocent III, "I do not come here with a new rule; my only rule is the gospel."[55]

At least initially before *Ad abolendum* in 1184 radicalized many Waldensians, as such an action is bound to do, they were in some ways more supportive of papal reform goals like celibacy than their parish priests. While this sometimes led to animosity toward individual priests, it did not always lead to the idea that getting rid of priesthood as an institution and status was necessarily a reform goal—despite the Waldensian claim, "It is better to confess to a good layperson than to a wicked priest." Among other reasons, this kind of criticism against married priests and worldly bishops won the Waldensians animosity between 1179 and 1184. However, many of the *pauperes Christi* often gained greater credibility among the laity because, unlike some of the parish priests they criticized for greed or immorality, these poor laypeople were practicing what they were preaching. This easily led to the dangers of zealotry and a holier-than-thou attitude. Still, their dynamic embrace of the Bible is evidence that the poor men's movement grabbed fiercely onto the twelfth century's evangelical awakening and invitation to personal reform. They read or heard the gospels and tried literally to act as Christ had acted.

The Waldensians and other poor men interpreted the Gregorian reform slogan *libertas ecclesiae* differently than the church's hierarchy. The Gregorian reformers discussed the church's freedom to name her own leaders and conduct her own business without outside influence. The Waldensians and other poor men's groups believed the church's freedom ought to refer to disentangling the church from the creeping worldliness and secularism that had become an ironic byproduct of the reforming papal monarchy. For them, *libertas ecclesiae* was spiritual freedom and reform that reacted against the legalism and worldliness of the Gregorian Revolution. Some writers stressed that the spirit of God was more important and liberating than the flood of ecclesiastical ordinances accompanying the Gregorian Revolution, following 2 Corinthians 3:17, "...where the spirit of the Lord is, there is freedom."[56] They sought a return to the gospel and early church's purity.

Two orthodox theologians agreed. The Cistercian Bernard of Clairvaux complained to his former student, now Pope Eugenius III (1145–53), that the papal curia had become a worldly court: "I am astonished that you, a man of piety, can bear to listen to lawyers dispute and argue in a way which tends more to subvert the truth than to reveal it. Reform this corrupt tradition." Telling the pope that ministry, not dominion, had been given to him, Bernard instructed Eugenius, "Go out into [the world], not as a lord, but as a steward." He recalled the first pope's example.

> This is Peter, who is known never to have gone in procession adorned with either jewels or silks, covered with gold, carried on a white horse, attended by a knight or surrounded by clamoring servants. But without these trappings, he believed it was enough to be able to fulfill the Lord's command, "If you love me, feed my sheep." In this finery, you are the successor not of Peter, but of Constantine.[57]

Likewise, a scholastic theologian like Peter the Chanter, who may have taught the future Pope Innocent III and whose career at Paris flourished because of the Gregorian Revolution, critiqued the ill effects of what he considered the church's over-regulation.

> ...[W]hen [traditions] are numerous they weigh heavily upon those who uphold them and upon those who transgress them; unless such traditions are kept brief and few and have been instituted for the most obvious and useful reasons, they become an obstacle to obeying divine precepts. *They restrict the liberty of the gospel....*
>
> We are oppressively burdened with a multitude of contrived practices, although authority speaks, because even some useful things have to be tossed aside or we get borne down by them. We ought rather to teach and work to get the gospel observed, since so few now observe it....[58]

The criticisms of Bernard of Clairvaux and Peter the Chanter are reminders that the Twelfth-Century Renaissance influenced reform *in capite et in membris*. The Twelfth-Century Renaissance supported reform *in capite*. But *in membris*, especially as it inflamed the poor men's movement and the extreme poverty of the evangelical awakening, the Twelfth-Century Renaissance simultaneously represented a corrective and challenge to the Gregorian Revolution. Perhaps a better way of seeing this dichotomy is to view the Twelfth-Century Renaissance's influence *in membris* as a complement to the Gregorian Revolution, and here is where Francis of Assisi, viewed in the context of high medieval reform, is so helpful.

## Franciscans

While monastic life was being renewed in multiple ways and the poor men's movement was correcting and challenging the Gregorian Revolution, a new form of religious life was being invented, indicating religious orders during the High Middle Ages represented both traditional and innovative approaches to reform. The best example is Francis of Assisi, who essentially invented a new type of religious order: the mendicants. A problem with referring to Francis is the fact that he has become a saint who transcends time. Francis has been taken out of historical context and adopted by environmental, social justice, peace, and political activists. Whether or not their adoption is valid, such an ahistorical approach frequently fails to see Francis as living during the late twelfth and early thirteenth centuries, when the papal monarchy and evangelical awakening had been progressing side by side for some time. Presentism obscures the idea of Francis as a high medieval reformer. Francis strode barefoot through several medieval worlds: the material wealth and poverty created by the Commercial Revolution, the papal curia and bureaucracy driven by a series of canon lawyer–popes, the scholastic theology he avoided but his contemporary and partner in the mendicant explosion, Dominic Guzman, embraced, the spirituality of the *vita apostolica,* and the radical imitation of Christ that marked the Twelfth-Century Renaissance, especially in its humanistic aspects.

Like Waldo, Francis was a man of some wealth who experienced a personal conversion and then wandered around trying to find a way to exercise his inner religious feelings. After his capture during a battle between Assisi and Perugia in 1202, followed by a year of illness as a prisoner, Francis grew in apostolic consciousness but lacked direction. In Assisi, Francis began working with the city's poor while living and dressing as a hermit. He increasingly turned his personal reform outward to a *vita apostolica* after his experience at San Damiano in 1205. According to his first biographer, Francis

> was walking one day near the church of St. Damian, which had nearly fallen to ruin and was abandoned by everyone.... [S]omething unheard of before happened to him: the painted image of Christ moved its lips and spoke. Calling him by name it said: "Francis, go, repair my house, which, as you see, is falling completely to ruin."[59]

Francis took this directive literally, as Waldo had done when he heard the story of St. Alexis and Matthew 19:21. Francis began to rebuild physically the San Damiano church building, selling some of his father's cloth and begging money from the people of Assisi to pay for materials. He later took this order to apply in a broader reform context to the whole church.

Francis's second major reform experience came at the Portiuncula three years later when he heard the mass gospel of Matthew 10:1–10, where Jesus sends his disciples out on mission to Israel's lost sheep. They are ordered to preach the good news, heal the sick, clean lepers, raise the dead, and cast out evil spirits. Jesus directs his disciples to act in the context of poverty, carrying neither pack nor staff nor second coat, wearing no shoes, carrying no money and accepting none. Jesus sends the twelve as itinerant preachers. Changing from an eremitical life to that of the itinerant preacher, Francis, like other *pauperes Christi,* walked barefoot and devoted himself to apostolic activities.

Francis's complementary reform role is demonstrated by his dealings with Innocent III, who could justifiably be seen as Francis's antithesis: the worldly canon lawyer–pope presiding over a papal monarchy. Despite recent problems with the Waldensians, Innocent III recognized something special in Francis, especially because of a dream he had in which his own Lateran basilica was falling down. This dream seems to parallel Francis's own understanding of the San Damiano voice as directing him, first, to repair that particular church building, but then to help restore the entire church. Innocent III

> recalled a certain vision he had had a few days before, which, he affirmed, under the guidance of the Holy Spirit, would be fulfilled in this man [Francis]. [The pope] had seen in his sleep the Lateran basilica about to fall to ruin, when a certain religious, small and despised, propped it up by putting his own back under it lest it fall. "Surely," [Innocent III] said, "this is the man who, by his works and by the teaching of Christ, will give support to the church."[60]

Perhaps trying to recoup some of the Waldensian enthusiasm that had been dampened and driven away since *Ad abolendum,* the pope allowed Francis and his early disciples to live their apostolic lives under ecclesiastical authority.

Though the Franciscans' reform stance complemented the papal monarchy, the push for regulation so characteristic of the Gregorian Revolution may have worked against Francis. His first *Rule,* now lost, apparently was not the legal document with which Innocent III usually worked, although he approved it in 1210. It contained not much more than a series of relevant scriptural quotations justifying the Franciscan lifestyle. As the order grew beyond Francis's ability to manage, he resigned as minister general but wrote another *Rule* in 1221. This document was like the first *Rule*—scriptural, not legalistic—and for this reason was rejected by the pope's advisers.

The papacy approved a more structured, legalistic *Rule* in 1223, but many have wondered if its legal nature weakened the charisma of Francis's apostolic vision. He himself may have felt that way because he wrote a *Testament* near his death urging his many followers to adhere to the radical poverty, humility, simplicity, and personal witness he had offered in imitation of Christ, especially his physical suffering and service. He did not reject the *Rule* of 1223, but he did stress his original purpose:

> When God gave me some friars, there was no one to tell me what I should do; but the Most High himself made it clear to me that I must live the life of the gospel. I had this written down briefly and simply and his holiness the pope [Innocent III] confirmed it for me. Those who embraced this life gave everything they had to the poor.[61]

To prevent the interpretation that the *Testament* was intended to subvert or replace the *Rule* of 1223, Francis stressed the two documents were to be taken in tandem and ordered that both be followed obediently.[62]

This insistence on obedience is important to Francis as a reformer. He preached in the wake of the Waldensians and was initially distrusted because of the taint their extremism placed on evangelical preaching. Yet he shared their reform perspective. Francis and his followers embraced poverty radically, as did the Waldensians, and both reached out to imitate Christ, especially in his suffering and service to medieval society's outcasts. Both groups preached in the vernacular, telling the gospel stories simply to the everyday Christian.

But Francis did not join the poor men's progressive rejection of the sacramental system and episcopal authority. Francis did not reject the Gregorian Revolution, as some of his contemporaries did when interpreting *libertas ecclesiae* as freedom from ecclesiastical authority; instead, he complemented *in membris* the papal reform program *in capite*. His apostolic vision captured in an orthodox manner the spirituality that led others into heresy. For those who felt alienated and burdened by the Gregorian Revolution's machinery, Francis offered an alternative that fell within that machinery's purview without being crushed by it.[63]

During an era of papal monarchy and Gregorian Revolution, Francis promoted the patristic emphasis on personal reform, starting with himself. In the papal bull *Mira circa nos* that canonized Francis only two years after his death, Pope Gregory IX (1227–41) portrayed Francis as a great reformer. Gregory IX many times cited passages from Paul's letters to describe Francis as a model of the perfected *imago Dei* precisely because he had conformed himself so closely to the life of Christ.[64] Francis's practice of living the gospel's values is captured in his alleged statement, "Preach the gospel. Use words if you must." There is no record of his saying these words, but his personal witness gave him the kind of credibility that first attracted followers to Waldo and others in the poor men's movement. That credibility was specifically bolstered by Francis's embodiment of Jesus, so much so that he was seen, then as now, as another Christ *(alter Christus)* and bore the stigmata. Francis's life, especially in physical suffering, since Francis was tough on his own body, mirrored his era's fascination with the human, historical Christ of the gospels as a model to be imitated.

## Dominicans

If the Franciscans sometimes nudged the legalistic papal monarchy despite their support and complement of the Gregorian Revolution, then the Dominicans linked high medieval reform *in capite* and *in membris* by drawing on all aspects of the Twelfth-Century Renaissance. Dominic Guzman put both the learning and the spirituality of the twelfth century to the service of the church, particularly with respect to bringing heretics back into the fold. As a young priest, he established communities of women and men whose example of a simple, ascetic, penitential, and apostolic life grounded in the age's evangelical awakening matched those of nearby heretics without joining their rejection of orthodoxy. His goal was to establish an order of friars not unlike the Franciscans in their obedience and orthodoxy, but one whose organization avoided the debates about poverty that troubled the Franciscans almost from their first days. While the Dominicans, like the Franciscans, focused on Matthew 10:1–10, they saw poverty as a means to the end of personal reform via preaching, while some Franciscans saw poverty as a reform value in itself.

Dominic's evangelical ideal of itinerant preaching within the context of poverty and humility not only places him with Francis but, like the Franciscans, gave Dominicans credibility among their audiences. Dominic's reform achievement was in marrying scholastic humanism's pastoral intentions, often expressed in learned treatises designed to trickle down to pastors through handbooks, with the everyday lives of Christians on the local level. While Dominic had great respect for his personal friend Francis, he took a different approach to the mendicant life. This difference is represented very simply but clearly in the names of the head of each order. The Franciscans' head is called the minister general while the Dominicans are led by a master general, which derives from the name of a university doctor *(magister)*. For the Dominicans, the doctor of theology was also a doctor of souls who administered God's medicine through his preaching.

Dominic put university learning to the service of personal reform *in membris,* thereby personifying the way in which the Twelfth-Century Renaissance functioned as the fulcrum between the institutional Gregorian Revolution *in capite* and the individual Christian's evangelical awakening *in membris.* He believed a solid theological foundation was the best way to achieve effective preaching and to promote personal reform. Dominic envisioned a dynamic dialectic at work among study, preaching, and contemplation. As with the monastic idea, personal reform would naturally direct the Christian to share his insights with others. The Dominicans' intellectual study nourished prayer and action. Study was therefore integral to a Dominican friar's personal sanctification and his ultimate pastoral goal: promoting personal reform within other Christians.

## Perspectives

Having explored reform in the period roughly bordered by 1050 and 1300, it is appropriate to ask what insights can be drawn about the nature of high medieval reform in itself and with respect to earlier developments. We can draw several conclusions relating to the Gregorian Revolution, the Twelfth-Century Renaissance, the diversity of reforming religious orders, and the relationships among these three major areas.

The Gregorian Revolution was an attempt at trickle-down, institutional reform that considered the reform of the entire body of the church on a scale larger than the Carolingian Renaissance. One of the Gregorian goals was to establish the clergy as an elite class whose authority was spiritual, not temporal. This reform goal related primarily to the problem of lay investiture at the highest echelons of society, represented most dramatically by the conflict between Pope Gregory VII and Emperor Henry IV. But there were many investiture controversies on the local levels that caused the Gregorian reformers to operate *in membris,* as well. Ironically, as we have seen, in the attempt to separate the church from the world that had invaded it prior to 1050 or so, the church after that time herself grew worldly in the development of the papal monarchy that paralleled secular monarchies and their courts. This development, in turn, required reforming.

The Gregorian reformers created a revolution in the sense that their efforts produced structural growth aimed at regulating the entire life and body of the church. This growth is seen in the establishment of the papacy as an institution, Roman curias, the college of cardinals with their specific duties and privileges, synods and councils on the ecumenical and diocesan levels, canon law that codified and disseminated the Gregorian reforms, and universities. All of these developments may be seen with the Carolingian Renaissance as more formation than reformation, since the church after the Gregorian Revolution looked and operated much differently than before.

One can argue about the extent to which a top-down revolution took root among the masses, a question that has already been applied to Charlemagne's efforts. The Gregorian Revolution was not without critics. Peter the Chanter and the poor men's movement, stirred by the evangelical awakening of the Twelfth-Century Renaissance, argued against excessive regulation of individual faith lives. They interpreted *libertas ecclesiae* as a reform goal very differently than the Gregorians, who used the phrase as a reform slogan against lay interference in church matters. It seems fair to conclude that, as with the Carolingian Renaissance, the Gregorian Revolution tried to impose reform and may have run into problems because of this attempt. Indeed, the multiple heretical and orthodox movements of the high medieval church *in membris,* especially those exercising the apostolic life in imitation of Christ and the poor *ecclesia primitiva,* seemed to challenge, correct, and complement the Gregorian Revolution's attempts to direct moral behavior by precept from above.

The diversity and plurality of reform movements as part of the Twelfth-Century Renaissance demonstrate reform in the High Middle Ages was not restricted to the Gregorian Revolution *in capite.* A creative tension existed within the church, a tension some scholars see as a pull between tradition and progress in the Middle Ages.[65] In fact, the Twelfth-Century Renaissance illustrates how a dynamic sense of tradition can be grounded in the past as it moves forward into the future. This idea recalls the usefulness of the Roman god Janus as an image of ecclesiastical reform, for the church continually looks to the past and the future at the same time.

A dynamic sense of tradition, demonstrated by the innovative mendicant movements, was grounded in obedience to the church's authority. But it also complemented a more static sense of tradition, illustrated by the Cistercian and Carthusian return to monasticism's original *contemptus mundi.* We see in the twelfth century's many reform movements a marriage, sometimes rocky, between conservation and innovation. The idea of continual progress was embraced by the scholastic humanists and even the canon lawyers, who joined innovative methods of scholastic theology to the church's essential pastoral task: guiding souls to heaven. Yet scholastic humanism was sometimes opposed, typically by the practitioners of a less aggressive monastic theology, precisely because its methods were new. Gregory VII himself stressed that he was not adding anything new to the church, but only reiterating her traditions. Others, building on Christ's dictum that one must take from the old and the new (Matt 13:52), defended their innovative theological methods. Peter of Blois (ca. 1135–1211) described these tasks as the renewal of forgotten treasures:

> We are like dwarfs standing on the shoulders of giants; thanks to them, we see farther than they: busying ourselves with the treatises written by the ancients, we take their choice thoughts, buried by age and the neglect of men, and raise them, as it were, from death to renewed life.[66]

This marriage of backward- and forward-looking reform, of conservation and innovation, is what makes the High Middle Ages such a rich moment in the history of reform. Diverse reform efforts complemented one another even as they sometimes competed. The same age that witnessed the structural Gregorian Revolution *in capite et in membris* also continued the patristic goal of personal reform among the Cistercians, the Carthusians, and the poor men's movement. There was a multiplicity of monastic reforms, with Cluny reacting against lay interference and then Cîteaux reacting against Cluny. The mendicants added their riff to religious life, moving from the monastic withdrawal from the world to its embrace while avoiding the Waldensians' heretical rejection of papal authority. The very idea of a "religious life" expanded beyond religious orders to revitalize the active faith lives of the laity, many of whom adapted the orders' charisms to their everyday circumstances through third orders. The same Pope Innocent III who personified how canon law had become the engine of the papal monarchy and bureaucracy allowed the Franciscans and Dominicans to flourish and, at Lateran IV, directed monastic orders to meet frequently in general chapters to reform themselves. *Libertas ecclesiae* meant different things to different people *in capite et in membris,* but both saw the phrase in terms of reform and renewal while they disagreed about its proper objects and activities. High medieval reform movements not only recovered and revitalized past traditions, they progressively pushed the church forward.

# NOTES

1. See principally Harold J. Berman, *Law and Revolution: The Formation of the Western Legal Tradition* (Cambridge Mass.: Harvard University Press, 1983), especially pp. 99–107, where he identifies four key characteristics of what he labels the medieval "papal revolution": its totality, rapidity, violence, and duration. Berman's enthusiastic assessment claims the papal revolution "introduced into western history the experience of revolution itself. In contrast to the older view of secular history as a process of decay, there was introduced a dynamic quality, a sense of progress in time, a belief in the reformation of the world" (p. 118). Because Gregory VII's birth name was Hildebrand, some scholars have called this period the Hildebrandine, instead of the Gregorian, reform.

2. Ladner, *Idea of Reform*, p. 277, n. 14, quoting Congar, *Vraie et fausse réforme*. See also Ladner, "Religious Renewal and Ethnic-Social Pressures as Forms of Life in Christian History," in *Theology of Renewal*, ed. L. K. Shook, 2 vols. (New York: Herder and Herder, 1968), vol. 2, p. 341: "…[F]or the first time in Christian history[,] more than personal or monastic reform, indeed a structural reform of the church as a whole had to be envisaged."

3. The phrase *reformatio in capite et in membris* recurs often in the history of reform. It originally described the legal relationship between a bishop (head) and the priests attached to his cathedral (members). The first appearance of the phrase yet found is in one of Innocent III's decretals from 1206; the first time it is used at a council is in 1311 at Vienne. A proposal at Vienne used *in capite et in membris* to discuss the legal relationship between the pope and his bishops, in addition to papal leadership in reform. See Phillip H. Stump, *The Reforms of the Council of Constance (1414–1418)* (Leiden: E. J. Brill, 1994), pp. 237–39 and, more completely, Karl Augustin Frech, *Reform an Haupt und Gliedern: Untersuchungen zur Entwicklung und Verwendung der Formulierung im Hoch- und Spätmittelalter* (Frankfurt: Peter Lang, 1992).

4. Ladner, "Two Gregorian Letters: On the Sources and Nature of Gregory VII's Reform Ideology," *Studi Gregoriani* 5 (1956): pp. 221–42. One of Ladner's later articles repeats key parts of this study almost verbatim: *"Reformatio,"* in *Ecumenical Dialogue at Harvard*, eds. S. Miller and G. E. Wright (Cambridge Mass.: Harvard University Press, 1964), pp. 172–90. According to Ladner, Gregory VII was distinguishing bad new customs from good old customs.

5. Gerd Tellenbach, *The Church in Western Europe from the Tenth to the Early Twelfth Century,* trans. Timothy Reuter (Cambridge: Cambridge University Press, 1993), p. 160, claims Gregory VII never used forms of the noun *reformatio* and offers the four citations for *reformare* forms. With Ladner, Tellenbach notes a pervading sense of the reform of the *Ecclesia in toto* throughout Gregory VII's writings. Ladner lists Gregory VII's reform vocabulary in "Two Gregorian Letters," p. 221, n. 4.

6. On the reform concerns that follow, see H. E. J. Cowdrey, *Pope Gregory VII 1073–1085* (Oxford: Clarendon Press, 1998), pp. 536–53. This work reassesses a seminal reforming pope, summarizes decades of scholarship, and proposes fresh interpretations.

7. Tellenbach, *The Church in Western Europe,* pp. 161–67. On celibacy as a reform goal, see Michael Frassetto, ed., *Medieval Purity and Piety: Essays on Medieval Clerical Celibacy and Religious Reform* (New York: Garland, 1998).

8. Gregory VII, for his part, believed it was the pope's job as God's mouthpiece to call civil rulers to task, as the prophet Samuel had done to Saul (1 Sam 15:22–23). Pope Gregory I, in his *Moralia* (595), had discussed this passage in terms of obedience; Gregory VII referred to this incident twenty two times in his letters: Cowdrey, *Pope Gregory VII,* pp. 556–58. Cowdrey presents Gregory's idea of the proper relationship between *regnum* and *sacerdotium* at pp. 608–58.

9. Ladner, "Two Gregorian Letters," p. 224.

10. Quoted in Ladner, *Idea of Reform,* p. 300.

11. The *Dictate of the Pope* is translated in *Readings in Western Civilization,* vol. 4, *Medieval Europe,* eds. Julius Kirshner and Karl F. Morrison (Chicago: University of Chicago Press, 1986), pp. 142–43.

12. Cowdrey, *Pope Gregory VII,* pp. 514–29. Cowdrey considers Gregory's treatment of the power of the keys at pp. 572–76.

13. Ephraim Emerton, trans., *The Correspondence of Pope Gregory VII: Selected Letters from the Registrum* (New York: Columbia University Press, 1932), pp. 56–58, 86–88.

14. On the development of the college of cardinals, see Stephan Kuttner, "*Cardinalis:* The History of a Canonical Concept," *Traditio* 3 (1945): pp. 129–214; Michel Andrieu, "L'origine du titre de cardinal dans l'Église romaine," *Miscellanea Giovanni Mercati* 6 (1946): pp. 113–44; Joseph Lecler, "Le cardinalat de l'Église romaine: Son évolution dans l'histoire," *Études* 330 (1969): pp. 871–79; and Peter A. B.

Llewellyn, "Le premier développement du collège des cardinaux," *Recherches de science religieuses* 67 (1979): pp. 31–44.

15. I. S. Robinson lays out what follows in *The Papacy, 1073–1198: Continuity and Innovation* (Cambridge: Cambridge University Press, 1990), pp. 90–120; see also Colin Morris, *The Papal Monarchy: The Western Church from 1050 to 1250* (Oxford: Clarendon Press, 1989), pp. 165–69.

16. They were Gelasius II (1118–19), Lucius II (1144–45), Alexander III (1159–81), and Gregory VIII (1187).

17. John F. Broderick, "The Sacred College of Cardinals: Size and Geographical Composition (1099–1986)," *AHP* 25 (1987): pp. 9, 12, 19–20.

18. Uta-Renate Blumenthal identifies canon law as the "origin, inspiration, and source for the renewal and reform of the church in the eleventh century, particularly with regard to reform of and by the papacy": "The Papacy and Canon Law in the Eleventh-Century Reform," *CHR* 84 (1998): p. 202. For a description of the administrative developments of the papal monarchy and their connections with canon law, see Walter Ullmann, *The Growth of Papal Government in the Middle Ages* (London: Methuen, 1955), pp. 310–43 and 359–81, and Berman, *Law and Revolution,* pp. 199–254, especially his helpful (if idealized) schematic of the medieval church's administrative structures and jurisdictional lines of authority at pp. 210–11. Cowdrey describes the Gregorian "ordering" of the church: *Pope Gregory VII,* pp. 584–607.

19. The musical image works even better in Stephan Kuttner's small but extremely helpful explanation of the medieval canonists' efforts: *Harmony from Dissonance: An Interpretation of Medieval Canon Law* (Latrobe Pa.: The Archabbey Press, 1960). On Gratian's tasks and achievement, see Berman, *Law and Revolution,* pp. 143–48, and R. W. Southern, *Scholastic Humanism and the Unification of Europe,* vol. 1, *Foundations* (Oxford: Basil Blackwell, 1995), pp. 283–310.

20. There were a number of additions to canon law between the Avignon papacy and the Council of Trent in the late sixteenth century, when canon law was again synthesized. In 1918, Pope Benedict XIV (1914–22) repeated the effort, gathering everything since the late sixteenth century into a new *Corpus iuris canonici* that was itself revisited as part of Vatican II's aggiornamento. That last effort produced the *Revised Code of Canon Law,* promulgated in 1982 by Pope John Paul II.

21. *Dictionary of the Middle Ages,* 3:632a–39b, s.v., "Councils, Western (869–1179)," by Robert Somerville; Cowdrey, *Pope Gregory VII,* pp. 589–91.

22. This and the next two paragraphs rely on Cowdrey, *Pope Gregory VII,* pp. 495–513 (with quotation at p. 513), 564–83, 688, and 695–97. On the religious side of Gregory VII's personality and pontificate, a topic prior generations of scholars would have found surprising even in suggestion, see Cowdrey, "The Spirituality of Pope Gregory VII," in *The Mystical Tradition and the Carthusians,* ed. James Hogg (Salzburg: Institut für Anglistik und Amerikanistik, 1995), vol. 1, pp. 1–22.

23. Quoted in Southern, *Scholastic Humanism,* p. 258.

24. Charles Homer Haskins, *The Renaissance of the Twelfth Century* (Cambridge Mass.: Harvard University Press, 1927); Robert L. Benson and Giles Constable with Carol D. Lanham, eds., *Renaissance and Renewal in the Twelfth Century* (Cambridge Mass.: Harvard University Press, 1982; reprint, Toronto: University of Toronto Press, 1991).

25. Benson and Constable, *Renaissance and Renewal,* p. xvii.

26. See generally M.-D. Chenu, *Nature, Man, and Society in the Twelfth Century,* eds. and trans. Jerome Taylor and Lester K. Little (Chicago: University of Chicago Press, 1968), especially pp. 239–69, on the evangelical awakening. Chenu did not separate everyday spirituality from elite theology, however, as is clear from the title of the original French edition: *La théologie au douzième siècle* (Paris: J. Vrin, 1957). *Nature, Man, and Society* does not translate every chapter of *La théologie au douzième siècle.*

27. R. W. Southern put it neatly: "There was a profound sense of the littleness and sinfulness of man" in the earlier Middle Ages: *Medieval Humanism and Other Studies* (Oxford: Basil Blackwell, 1970), p. 32.

28. Charles Trinkaus, *In Our Image and Likeness. Humanity and Divinity in Italian Humanist Thought,* 2 vols. (Chicago: University of Chicago Press, 1970), vol. 1, pp. xiv–xxiv, and vol. 2, pp. 761–64; Paul Oskar Kristeller, *Renaissance Thought and Its Sources,* ed. Michael Moony (New York: Columbia University Press, 1979), pp. 169–96.

29. Quoted in Giles Constable, *The Reformation of the Twelfth Century* (Cambridge: Cambridge University Press, 1996), p. 274.

30. Southern, *Scholastic Humanism,* pp. 1–57, and *Medieval Humanism,* p. 29–60.

31. Quoted in Chenu, *Nature, Man, and Society,* p. 253 n. 19.

32. Quoted in Chenu, *Nature, Man, and Society,* p. 8.

33. Constable, *The Reformation of the Twelfth Century,* pp. 275–78.

34. Quoted in Southern, *Scholastic Humanism,* p. 28.

35. Jean Leclercq compares monastic and scholastic theology: "The Renewal of Theology," in Benson and Constable, *Renaissance and Renewal,* pp. 68–87.

36. Quoted in Chenu, *Nature, Man, and Society,* p. 11.

37. Quoted in Giles Constable, "Renewal and Reform in Religious Life: Concepts and Realities," in Benson and Constable, *Renaissance and Renewal,* p. 43. Constable delineates the variety of new and reformed religious orders in *The Reformation of the Twelfth Century,* pp. 44–124. Adam S. Cohen argues abbots and abbesses had a strong self-awareness of their own reform intentions and offers visual images that placed the abbess, not the bishop, at the center of a particular reform program: "The Art of Reform in a Bavarian Nunnery around 1000," *Speculum* 74 (1999): pp. 992–1020.

38. Brian Tierney, ed., *The Middle Ages,* vol. 1, *Sources of Medieval History,* 5th ed. (New York: McGraw-Hill, Inc., 1992), p. 139.

39. Part of this spectacular growth can be attributed to the unusually long, stabilizing reigns of three abbots who oversaw Cluny and their affiliated monasteries for 155 years: Maieul (954–94), Odilo (994–1048), and Hugh (1049–1109). By contrast, during this same 155-year period, there were ten times as many popes. Abbot Hugh, in an interesting twist of history, was godfather to Henry IV, the Holy Roman Emperor who was Pope Gregory VII's nemesis. During one of their frequent confrontations, it is highly likely Hugh brokered a temporary truce between them.

40. H. E. J. Cowdrey traces the close ties between the Cluniac reform movement and the papacy's goals in *The Cluniacs and the Gregorian Reform* (Oxford: Clarendon Press, 1970). One example of influence, again ironic, is the fact that Henry III visited Cluny during the abbacy of Odilo.

41. Constable, *The Reformation of the Twelfth Century,* pp. 77–80.

42. Pauline Matarasso, ed. and trans., *The Cistercian World Monastic Writings of the Twelfth Century* (London: Penguin Books, 1993), p. 5.

43. Matarasso, *The Cistercian World,* p. 50.

44. Chrysogonus Waddell believes Cluny lost the unifying, essential intent of worship that justified the monasteries' lavish liturgies. When this happens, "the marvelously choreographed liturgy degenerates into ritualism. The newer religious communities of the twelfth century, with their mystique of poverty and simplicity, had difficulty understanding Cluny…. [E]ven Cluny no longer understood Cluny.": "The Reform of the Liturgy from a Renaissance Perspective," in Benson and Constable, *Renaissance and Renewal*, pp. 103–4.

45. Matarasso, *The Cistercian World*, p. 8.

46. Matarasso, *The Cistercian World*, pp. 56–57. Bernard, however, was not a simple enemy of art, as Daniel Marcel La Corte demonstrated in "Bernard of Clairvaux: On Art and Beauty," *Cistercian Studies Quarterly* 29 (1994): pp. 451–70.

47. Matarasso, *The Cistercian World*, p. 55.

48. The Cistercians did have an impact on reform beyond their monasteries' walls by influencing bishops and priests who worked for social unity and each Christian's personal reform: Martha G. Newman, *The Boundaries of Charity: Cistercian Culture and Ecclesiastical Reform, 1098–1180* (Stanford: Stanford University Press, 1996).

49. Matarasso, *The Cistercian World*, p. 6.

50. Basil Pennington, "The Cistercians," in *Christian Spirituality: Origins to the Twelfth Century*, eds. Bernard McGinn, John Meyendorff, and Jean Leclercq (New York: Crossroad, 1985), p. 210; Gerhart Ladner, "Terms and Ideas of Renewal," in Benson and Constable, *Renaissance and Renewal*, p. 14.

51. See generally Dennis D. Martin, trans., *Carthusian Spirituality: The Writings of Hugh of Balma and Guigo de Ponte* (New York: Paulist Press, 1997). Although they were *non deformata*, Carthusians were concerned with improving themselves, as Martin explained in *Fifteenth-Century Carthusian Reform* (Leiden: E. J. Brill, 1992).

52. His name is alternately given as Valdès; sometimes Peter or Pierre is added as a first name, though there is no textual evidence to support this.

53. Gregory VII had prohibited translating the liturgy and readings into the vernacular because he feared those who read the Bible on their own would misunderstand it: "It is obvious to those who consider the matter thoroughly that God was rightly pleased for holy scripture to be veiled in some places, lest, if it were freely accessible to all, it would grow cheap and subject to contempt, and lest, perversely understood by

99

the unskilled, it might lead them into error." Quoted in Karl F. Morrison, "The Gregorian Reform," in *Christian Spirituality,* p. 190.

54. Primary sources related to the Waldensians are provided in Edward Peters, ed., *Heresy and Authority in Medieval Europe. Documents in Translation* (Philadelphia: University of Pennsylvania Press, 1980), pp. 139–63, 170–73. For similar writings from other groups, see R. I. Moore, *The Birth of Popular Heresy* (Toronto: University of Toronto Press, 1995).

55. Chenu, *Nature, Man, and Society,* pp. 239, 256.

56. Constable, *The Reformation of the Twelfth Century,* pp. 261–62.

57. Bernard of Clairvaux, *Five Books On Consideration: Advice to a Pope,* trans. John D. Anderson and Elizabeth Kennan (Kalamazoo Mich.: Cistercian Publications, 1976), pp. 44 [=Book I, 10.13], 60 [=Book II, 6.12], 117 [=Book IV, 3.6].

58. Quoted in Chenu, *Nature, Man, and Society,* pp. 256–57 (emphasis added).

59. Marion A. Habig, ed., *St. Francis of Assisi, Writings and Early Biographies: English Omnibus of the Sources for the Life of St. Francis* (Chicago: Franciscan Herald Press, 1973), p. 370 (Thomas of Celano, *The Second Life of St. Francis,* bk. 1, ch. 6, no. 10).

60. Habig, *St. Francis of Assisi,* p. 377 (Thomas of Celano, *The Second Life of St. Francis,* bk. 1, ch. 11, no. 17). Giotto painted this scene as part of his cycle depicting Francis's life in the Assisi basilica.

61. Habig, *St. Francis of Assisi,* p. 68.

62. Habig, *St Francis of Assisi,* p. 69: "The friars should not say, this is another *Rule.* For this is a reminder, admonition, exhortation, and my testament which I, Brother Francis, worthless as I am, leave to you, my brothers, that we may observe in a more Catholic way the *Rule* we have promised to God.... [The order's officials] should always have this writing with them as well as the *Rule* and at the chapters they hold, when the *Rule* is read, they should read these words also.

"In virtue of obedience, I strictly forbid any of my friars, clerics or lay brothers, to interpret the *Rule* or these words, saying, 'This is what they mean.' God inspired me to write the *Rule* and these words plainly and simply, and so you too must understand them plainly and simply, and live by them, doing good to the last."

63. Some of Francis's followers quickly moved in another direction. These *fraticelli* or "Spiritual Franciscans" increasingly attacked the

papacy, especially when popes mitigated absolute poverty, which these splinter Franciscan groups believed could never be compromised.

64. Regis J. Armstrong, "*Mira circa nos:* Gregory IX's Views of the Saint Francis of Assisi," *Laurentianum* 3 (1984): pp. 398–405.

65. The following paragraphs take as their starting points Chenu, *Nature, Man, and Society,* pp. 310–30, and Constable, "Renewal and Reform in Religious Life," pp. 37–67.

66. Quoted in Chenu, *Nature, Man, and Society,* p. 326. Peter of Blois may have been repeating Bernard of Chartres here.

# Chapter 3
# From Avignon to Trent: The Era of Multiple Reforms

Martin Luther and Vatican II dominate the discussion of the history of reform. But, as we have been chronicling, the history of reform ideas and efforts is much larger than the life of one German professor in the sixteenth century and a four-year council held in Rome in the 1960s. We have considered the formative centuries of reform with the fathers and seen how the Middle Ages built upon those traditions. It is now time to explore what may be the richest, most paradoxical centuries of reform: the late medieval and reformation years, about 1300 to 1600.

From the start, it is crucial to discuss the parameters of reform in these centuries for this era, more than any other, is subject to preconceptions and caricatures. First, there were multiple reforms in this period. Not only can we identify reformers who can be called Protestant and Catholic, but each of these two large trees branched off into a variety of versions of Protestant and Catholic reforms. For this reason, it is best to use a lowercase *r* and the plural: *reformations* can stand not only for the major Protestant-Catholic split, but for the divisions within each of those traditions.

Second, we have to address the question of continuities and discontinuities during the period. This book's introduction noted that many studies were distinguished by polemics, especially concerning these centuries. Thus one group of scholars saw only Catholic decadence during the period from 1300 to 1600, from which Luther emerges as a phoenix; another group considered Luther a troubled revolutionary and believes the church would have held a reforming council even without the German challenges. This dichotomy has tended to identify Luther as a great wall standing between the Middle Ages and modernity, or even as the "first modern man." Such a conception of Luther cultivates the idea of the discontinuity of reform. There may be something to this: before Luther, it is redundant to say Catholic Christianity, because all western Christians were Catholics and vice-versa. Soon after Luther breaks with Rome, we must identify Christians as Protestant or Catholic.

But there may be more continuity than discontinuity at work in the 1300 to 1600 era on both the Protestant and Catholic sides. Much recent scholarship has put Luther back into the late medieval and Catholic contexts in which he grew up and developed his ideas. Some scholars, both Protestants and Catholics, have looked at Catholic reformers living before Luther in an effort to find prototypes or forerunners of the Protestant reformations. But not every reformer before Luther had the same reform ideas or goals as Luther: not every Catholic advocating reform before the *95 Theses* was a proto-Lutheran.

Historians have identified considerable vibrance in the reform ideas of the two centuries before Luther to go with the excesses, divisions, and malaise of the church during that time. Although these reforms were ineffective for the most part on the institutional, top-down level, the very fact that at least a handful of the pope's inner circle advocated reform indicates a number of well-placed Catholics before Luther recognized the need for it. Moreover, reform seems to have been at work in the body of the church despite (or maybe because of) the problems in her head, the papacy. Some Catholics therefore foreshadowed not Luther or other Protestant reformers, but the Council of Trent. We will pursue these examples to investigate the idea of continuity among Catholic reformers and find "forerunners" of the Catholic, in addition to the Protestant, reformations.[1]

We are working against a common perception that Luther's was the only Protestant reform program and that Catholics reformed only in reaction to Luther. The history of reform from 1300 to 1600, however, is far richer and more complex than this starting point. Our exploration of the continuities and discontinuities in these three hundred years will place together the Avignon Papacy (1305–77) and the Great Western Schism (1378–1417), the age of Luther (1483–1546), and the Council of Trent (which met in stages, 1545–63). Late medieval Christianity, Luther, and Trent are not separate, but are interconnected sections of one chapter in the history of reform. In order to understand Luther, one cannot take him out of the context of Catholic reform successes and failures (ca. 1300–1450). So, too, Trent in the sixteenth century cannot be considered apart from the Catholic reform failures of the fourteenth and fifteenth centuries or apart from Luther and the multitude of Protestant reformers.

We begin by looking at Catholic reform efforts in the late Middle Ages, for our purposes between approximately 1300 and 1450, in the church's head and her body. The contrast in terms of reform will be striking: not much progress will take place in the church's head, while her members kept the pace of reform going in a lively but disorganized way. The chapter's second part explores Luther in the context of these late medieval Catholic reform efforts, examining where he was and was not in line with them. We will discover he had a very different concept of reform than his Catholic counterparts. Other reformers will reveal the variety of Protestant ideas of reform, some of them quite critical of Luther himself. Finally, we will take on the debate surrounding the very name and meaning of the "Catholic Reformation" and "Counter-Reformation," again discovering a diverse group of ideas and efforts within the Catholic church of the sixteenth century. All of this aims at a general reevaluation of late medieval and reformation era reform, and specifically a reassessment of the Council of Trent, which was in some ways a progressive council that anticipated later, modern reforms but was held captive by the burden of Luther's challenge.

## The Late Middle Ages (ca. 1300–1450)

### Institutional Developments, Reform Failures

Two events dominate the church in the late Middle Ages: the Avignon Papacy (1305–77) and the Great Western Schism (1378–1417), when two, and then three, popes—each with his own curia and college of cardinals—claimed to be the true successor to Peter. These are complicated and important stories, but we will explore them quickly in order to get to the theme of this study: the implications of Avignon and the Schism for reform.

For a number of political, military, and geographic reasons, the papacy moved from its traditional seat in Rome to Avignon early in the fourteenth century. One reason for this move to France had to do with the papacy's increasing domination by the French royal family. The papacy's temporary relocation from Rome also made sense because Italy was consuming itself in a series of civil wars during the fourteenth century. In addition, the self-styled Holy Roman Emperors in central Europe twice invaded Italy. France was therefore physically more attractive and certainly safer than Rome in the fourteenth century.

The papacy further entrenched itself in Avignon as it expanded its bureaucracy and built lavish palaces. The Avignon bureaucracy has been caricatured for its corruption, and this assessment is surely deserved to some degree. Legal cases on church matters were allowed to stay open because multiple appeals brought in fees for courts and documentation, for example. The cardinals who oversaw this bureaucracy and reaped a portion of the financial benefits were overwhelmingly French and therefore inclined to keep the papacy in Avignon. The popes named 133 cardinals between 1305 and 1377: 112 were French.

Because of this high living and centralized papal monarchy, Avignon became a target for reformers. The Italian humanist Petrarch (1304–74), for example, called Avignon the "whore of Babylon." Using an Old Testament metaphor, he referred to this period as the "Babylonian captivity of the papacy." Bridget of Sweden (1303–73) and Catherine of Siena (1347–80) loudly criticized the papacy's distance from Rome and, when it finally returned there, called for continued reform. Catherine, in particular, wrote with great boldness to Pope Urban VI (1378–89), urging him to eliminate the simony and greed still plaguing the church three centuries after Gregory VII began his papal revolution:

> Most holy father, God has placed you as a shepherd over all his sheep of the Christian religion.... He has placed you in an age in which there is more wickedness among the clergy than during long ages past, both within the body of the holy church and in the universal body of all the Christian religion.... Where is charity's generous care of souls and its distributions to the poor, for the works of the church, for their needs? You know very well that they are doing just the opposite. Oh, miserable me! It grieves me to say it: your children are nourishing themselves on what they receive through the blood of Christ; they are not ashamed to play the swindler with the very hands you have sanctified and anointed—you, the vicar of Christ—without speaking of the other miserable things they do.... By arrogance, combined with great avarice, they commit simony, buying benefices with gifts, with flattery, or money, or with dissolute and vain adornments....
>
> But in all truth, most holy father, I cannot see how this can be done properly unless you totally reform the garden of your bride with good and virtuous plants. Take care to choose a company of men in whom you find virtue, holy men and unafraid of death. And do not look to their importance, but [make sure] they are shepherds who will govern their flock with solicitude. Then [choose] a company of good cardinals who will be true pillars for you and, with divine aid, will help you bear the weight of your many labors.

It is significant that, even with so many problems in the church's head, Catherine still pointed out the need for reform in the church's body as being just as important. She specifically told the pope that when the clergy reformed their personal conduct, the laity would reform their lives by following their priests' good example.

> When this happens I have no doubt that the laity will mend their ways: they will do so necessarily when they are constrained by [the clergy's] holy teaching and honest life. This is not something to sleep on, but something to strive for all you possibly can until death, with forcefulness and neglecting nothing, for the glory and praise of God's name.[2]

Although the Avignon Papacy was guilty of many of the charges Petrarch, Bridget, and Catherine leveled against it, not every Avignon pope overlooked reform. While some Avignon popes certainly promoted bureaucratic greed and malaise, others were genuine reformers. John XXII (1316–34) permitted increased absenteeism, the practice that allowed bishops to live away from their dioceses and avoid their fundamental roles as shepherds. By contrast, Benedict XII (1334–42) fought absenteeism by expelling from Avignon any prelates who had pastoral responsibilities somewhere else. Benedict XII may have been elected in part because of his successes at fighting heresy in France; as pope, he reorganized the papal administration and required more rigorous examinations for priest and bishop candidates. He strictly reduced the number and amounts of fees for documents and procedures; he also fought the practice of politicking (and bribing) for major offices. But even Benedict XII was handcuffed by the entrenched Avignon curia and atmosphere: Although he apparently considered a return to Rome and sent money to begin repairs to Roman buildings, he had the papal archives moved to Avignon and started building the papal palace there. His successor, Clement VI (1342–52), lived like a major power broker, but Innocent VI (1352–62) and Urban V (1362–70) continued some of Benedict XII's reforms, especially concerning absenteeism, examination of candidates, and improved education for priests.

The limited reform achievements of the Avignon popes stalled due to one of the most confusing moments in church history: the Great Western Schism, which lasted almost forty years. Gregory XI (1370–78) died shortly after moving the papacy back to Rome from Avignon. His successor, Urban VI, was a cantankerous pope who alienated the very men who had elected him. Several months after Urban took office, the cardinals, who were predominantly French, deemed their election of him invalid. The Romans had rioted during the conclave, screaming for an Italian pope who would stay in Rome. The French cardinals claimed this circumstance nullified the election because they chose Urban quickly out of fear for their lives. These cardinals held another election and selected the French cardinal who had lost to Urban in the prior election. He took the name Clement VII (1378–94) and, after some initial threats of physical violence were exchanged by Clement and Urban, returned to Avignon.

Christianity was split between two popes, two curias, two colleges of cardinals, and two centers of power. European countries lined up behind one or the other papacy. But this was not just a problem in the head of the church: Individual dioceses sometimes had two bishops, one appointed by the Roman and one by the Avignon pope. They competed with each other and could call on dueling priests for support. Things became so confusing in the body of the church that in the Spanish city of Toledo, the priest celebrating mass avoided backing the wrong pope by praying during the consecration "for the true pope, whoever he is."

Because confusion reigned in the head (or heads) of the church, the church's body had to look in another direction for assistance. This direction was a council, which represented the church's members through delegates: bishops, abbots, royal officials, canon lawyers, theologians, and university professors. In 1409, most of the cardinals from both the Avignon and Roman obediences abandoned each of their popes and gathered in Pisa to settle the Schism, reform the church, and provide peace. The council delegates depended for their authority on the idea of conciliarism. A complex set of overlapping ideas, the most extreme form of conciliarism, in brief, held that a universal council, not the pope, was the church's highest authority and therefore could depose popes, proclaim doctrine, and legislate reforms.[3]

Despite major abuses requiring attention, the Pisan delegates concentrated not on reform but on unifying the papacy, clearly the biggest problem. They deposed the Roman pope Gregory XII (1406–15) and the Avignon pope Benedict XIII (1394–1417), then elected Alexander V (1409–10). Alexander was supposedly the unifying pope, but he and his successor John XXIII (1410–15)[4] were not universally recognized and became known as the Pisan or conciliar popes. It was no surprise that neither Gregory XII nor Benedict XIII accepted deposition; both, along with the new Pisan pope, continued to assert that theirs was the true claim to the papacy. The church went into the Council of Pisa with two popes and emerged with three instead of one. In this environment, reform never had a chance to be considered seriously.

Reform also lost out to the pressing matter of unifying the papacy at the next council, Constance (1414–18). Constance ostensibly had three agenda items: unity, matters of faith (or heresy), and reform.[5] Delegates at Constance mainly addressed reform in 1416 while they waited for an answer from Benedict XIII, who was the most stubborn of the three contending popes. Once he refused a final attempt at reconciliation, they dropped their reform discussions and spent most of 1417 figuring out how to depose Benedict and elect a new pope without repeating Pisa's mistakes. Their choice, Martin V (1417–31), was able to hold the church together under one obedience.

Still, some reform measures were debated and adopted at Constance, if only in committee. Phillip H. Stump recently reevaluated Constance's reform ideas, which for centuries were accepted as almost complete failures. Stump asserts Constance achieved a measure of success in terms of the reform *in capite*, but pastoral reform *in membris* largely failed for two reasons. First, the great diversity of reform ideas and plans discussed at Constance precluded agreement on the many details necessary for a comprehensive program. How could delegates decide on a reform program when they could not settle on one pope? Second, the leaders at Constance believed reform would start by resolving the Schism and then trickle down to the church's members. Reform had to start with unifying the papacy.[6]

Nevertheless, Constance delegates knew the problems ran deeper than the papacy, and they discussed three areas of reform for the parish clergy: personal morality, pastoral care, and qualifications for service. They proposed that clergy with pastoral duties be well-educated, with at least a license in canon or civil law or a bachelor's degree in theology. They should be sufficiently paid for their work and maintain celibacy. The Constance committees debated a proposal whereby a priest would be required to give up his concubine within one month; if he did not, they suggested parishioners should not go to him for the sacraments—if a superior (such as a bishop) approved this extreme action. But these and other ideas never made it out of introductory deliberations in committee at Constance, let alone were they approved by the whole council and instituted in membris.

Proposals for reform in capite, on the other hand, were largely successful at Constance, at least in the short term. Starting at the top, delegates focused on simony as it related to the many fees the papacy demanded from bishops and church officials. These reforms decreased papal taxes and other abuses; some proposals sought a more efficient, streamlined, and learned curia.[7] The mere fact that many of these reform goals are familiar from the Gregorian Revolution of several centuries earlier indicates the same problems persisted. Reforming these longstanding problems took time, clearly encountering some failures along the way.

Other reform councils followed Pisa and Constance, but the major problem endured: Reform was overshadowed by the struggle for power between a papacy working to recover its authority and conciliarists continuing to assert that a council was higher than the pope. Martin V held a brief council in Siena (1423–24), but only because a decree of Constance demanded one. He took the opportunity to strengthen his own power by reorganizing the curia, increasing the collection of taxes from his lands, and signing private treaties with different countries reaffirming papal authority. As at Constance, at Siena reform *in membris* fell to the proverbial wayside.

The next reform council was a roller-coaster ride that met in different pieces in several cities off and on for almost twenty years. The Council of Basel-Ferrara-Florence-Rome (1431–45) witnessed an increasingly radical conciliarism losing out to greater papal recovery. Pope Eugene IV (1431–47) called, dissolved, and then approved the Council at Basel (1431–33). When the meeting moved to Ferrara and then Florence several years later the major issue for the pope consisted of trying to reconcile with the Greek churches, in part because this union would be another reassertion of papal supremacy and restoration. The shaky agreement between East and West quickly collapsed. Meanwhile, a few extreme conciliarists who maintained their own competing council in Basel fought Eugene and elected another pope in his place, but eventually recognized Eugene's successor and voted to dissolve itself. In these contexts, as at Constance and Siena before, reform struggled to remain on the agenda, especially in the church's body.

In the late Middle Ages, conciliarism largely eclipsed reform, even though reform and councils had been closely allied in the four Lateran Councils from 1123 to 1215. Fifteenth-century popes and councils postponed most reforms, particularly in the church's body, as they fought each other for power. While many reform ideas were discussed and even urged on the delegates by preachers in their frequent sermons calling for reform, most were not translated into legislation and action.

As Stump pointed out with reference to Constance, there was also the problem of the variety of reform ideas. Some ideas cancelled each other out. Others could not be integrated in the context of the Schism, the papal-conciliar power struggle that followed Constance, and the fact that so many of these ideas were promoted and debated by people with competing loyalties. Even when a fifteenth-century council did legislate reform, it tended to be in the church's head, which was undergoing its own tumult, and not her members. In addition, a council's reform decrees could not be implemented and policed for compliance without the papacy's participation. Given the papal-conciliar battles, popes did not wish to acknowledge the implication that the church's head was deformed and required reform.

In the fifteenth-century councils, the papacy had become the target and not the agent of reform. This key development may explain why, even though reform decrees were legislated for the church's head, they were not always implemented. Because of this failure, reform *in capite* was postponed. Bad situations grew worse, and reform faltered within the top echelons of the church.[8]

## Popular Developments, Reform Progress

What happens when institutional reform *in capite* fails? The late medieval period demonstrates that reform does not always require an impetus and direction from above in order to survive. Institutional malaise did not translate into popular malaise: despite incredible confusion in the church's head, Christians in the church's body did not give evidence that they despaired. The spirit of reform lived in the church's body with tremendous popular enthusiasm, optimism, and hope that these difficult times would soon improve.[9]

While the Avignon papacy, the Schism, and the papal-conciliar battles roared above them through the fourteenth and fifteenth centuries, Christians on the parish level looked to their own individual reforms. Their everyday spirituality focused itself on personal reform, representing a return to reform's roots. Late medieval spirituality was not so much original as a continuation of high medieval spirituality and the Twelfth-Century Renaissance that was grounded in the fathers. In the late medieval context of institutional chaos and malaise, however, the twelfth century's personal and patristic elements of reform became more pronounced and urgent.[10]

Late medieval religious practice is distinguished by several characteristics tied to personal reform: interior piety, self-knowledge in solitude that often led to very active lay spirituality (the marriage of action and contemplation), a personal identification with the suffering Christ, and humanism.[11] There were more personal penitential activities, such as pilgrimages. Attention to Jesus' passion resulted in an increase in the stations of the cross, passion plays, and, in the extreme, public self-floggings. A popular genre of devotional literature guided readers and sermon audiences through an intimate, meditative encounter with scenes from Christ's life so they could follow his model of service and sacrifice in order to renew themselves.[12] Mysticism, especially among women, flourished in the late Middle Ages as another example of an intense, inner spirituality.

Humanism, an element of personal reform already encountered during the twelfth century, also flourished during the late Middle Ages. Writers and preachers championed the partnership between humanity and divinity, reminded people of their dignity as made in the *imago Dei,* and emphasized human beings' God-given potential to act on the principles of Christian faith. Humanists led the charge in recovering the fathers' original texts, recognizing in them not only persuasive rhetoric, but values of personal reform that would counteract institutional failures.

By focusing on practical concerns, humanism encouraged lay Christians working in professions and at home to act morally and to reform their lives without necessarily withdrawing from the world. This was a bit different from their monastic predecessors, who sought personal reform within the walls of their monasteries during Christianity's first millennium. This self-conscious role in improving one's religious state again points to reform continuities. It recalls the emphasis on action, intention, freedom, and personal reform Ladner identified as the hallmarks of the patristic idea of reform, which we have seen at work through the medieval evangelical awakening.[13]

As was the case with high medieval personal reform *in membris,* which challenged and complemented the institutional Gregorian Revolution, during the Schism of the late Middle Ages individual Christians continued to focus on their own spiritual progress. And, again, like their high medieval precursors, some of them were orthodox and others became heretical even though their motivations were frequently reform. The most helpful example of late medieval inner, grassroots reform that could be taken as both supportive of and a challenge to the institutional church *in capite* is the *devotio moderna* (modern devotion).[14]

This popular movement began with the Dutch religious leader Gerard Grote (1340–84) who, like Francis of Assisi, was the son of a cloth merchant. Grote dabbled in the arts, law, medicine, and theology at the University of Paris. When he was nearing thirty five, he experienced a conversion and spent four years at a Carthusian monastery. There he became acquainted with that order's radical return to Benedictine monasticism's roots: silence, manual labor, and prayer all ordered to a monk's personal reform. Grote did not have a monastic vocation nor did he ever rise to mystical heights in prayer, but he read extensively in John Cassian's *Institutes* and *Conferences* as well as the twelfth century's spiritual writers. There he found the origins and rediscovery of the patristic idea of personal reform.[15]

Back home in Utrecht Grote was ordained a deacon and preached a reform program reminiscent of the Gregorian Revolution. He especially denounced immorality and simony among parish priests, which brought him unwelcome attention from the diocesan bishop. Grote soon gathered around him like-minded men and women who met informally in his home each evening to pray, to read and discuss the Bible, and to support one another's efforts. Soon some of the men and women were living in separate homes where they led a common life, but not a formal monastic one of vows and a habit. Members of a loose fellowship more than an established order, they shared property, a dormitory, meals, chores, and brought money in through their trades.[16]

*Devotio moderna* piety is marked by its strong interior attention to personal reform. The movement's aim was to be present with God in daily life through spiritual exercise, which one member called "true inwardness" and which we can identify as an inside-out reform. An internal disposition to good must accompany actions, else they might become devoid of spiritual meaning. Constancy was praised and frequent exhortation given to conform one's will to God's so all actions, however humble, would be for God. Simple tasks and lives were held up as examples: spinning or sweeping a small courtyard were identified as paths to God. It was a simple, popular piety for clergy and laity, though laypeople seemed to account for most of the movement's adherents.

*Devotio moderna* spirituality was less a doctrinal program than an attempt to live a devout life in a materialistic climate, especially in the Low Countries, where the textile industry was rapidly exploding in an early capitalistic culture. Many found this climate a distraction or obstacle to God. "If such people of the world begin to discuss vain and worldly stuff," a female *devotio moderna* leader advised, "interrupt their talk, if you can, with good matter concerning the Lord Jesus and his saints." Indeed, their everyday spirituality of living in the world while maintaining a Christian focus sounds remarkably like Vatican II's call for Catholics to bring Christianity into the workplace—but six hundred years early. It also reached back to the late Roman postbaptismal *conversi,* who could not fully withdraw from society but who nevertheless wanted to imbue their daily lives with Christian faith and action.

Building on the twelfth-century evangelical awakening, *devotio moderna* followers focused on the historical, human, suffering Jesus. They tried to identify with him through their own purgative trials, such as confession, asking others to point out their faults, or fasting and abstinence. Leaders wrote imaginative manuals for guided meditation: Grote suggested using scriptural imagery as "a kind of sensible conversation and direct communication with the saints." The famous *Imitation of Christ* may have come from a *devotio moderna* author; it was certainly influenced by the movement's spirituality. This manual helped readers place themselves as witnesses to scenes of Christ's life from the gospels, especially his passion, death, and resurrection. The manuals encouraged readers to identify and imitate Christ's actions, most notably his humility, service, and obedience, in so doing reforming themselves by literally conforming to their original image and likeness of God.[17]

*Devotio moderna* piety was a lived spirituality dedicated to reforming individual Christian lives one day at a time in the knowledge that conversion is a daily, continuous activity. Followers attracted some criticism because they rejected many externals of religion that they complained had replaced true, inner piety. As reformers, they opposed overuse of statues, vigils, pilgrimages, relics, the rote exercise of prayers and devotions, and a mathematical approach to totaling up indulgences. They contended that these kinds of faithful exercises had lost their place as means to the end of salvation. Too many Christians, the *devotio moderna* adherents argued, were concerned with how many rituals they performed, not why they did so.

Of course, as human beings, *devotio moderna* followers were as susceptible to excess as anyone else. One leader advised that one should confess blindness if he did not know what to confess; another told his sister to accept blame even if she were innocent. A brother sought criticism of his actions on his deathbed, while a sister extolled colleagues who were so compliant that if ordered to set one of their houses on fire, "they would do so without objection."

Their reform goal was personal progress in the virtues and an affective, emotional relationship with God. But the *devotio moderna* did not abandon all learning, only very high-end, scholastic arguments that had become divorced from pastoral applications. They read scripture, parts of the mass, homilies, and saints' lives translated into their own Dutch vernacular as part of their private meditation, not academic disputation. Grote called advanced study the devil's work, but he respected education that led one closer to God. He urged his followers to be "constant and studious in reading that we [may] withstand the subversion of ignorance and foolishness, the seedbed of many evils." They kept prayer journals and notebooks of gospel passages and their thoughts on them, marking their progress up the spiritual ladder toward God.

About the same time that the *devotio moderna* represented orthodox reform *in membris,* other reformers (whom the church condemned as heretics) reiterated some of the complaints Waldensians had made against immoral priests who bought church offices and ignored their pastoral responsibilities. John Wycliffe (ca. 1330–84) in Oxford and Jan Hus (1369–1415) in Prague attacked simony and immorality. Their increasingly radical complaints led them away from reforming a broken church system and toward abolishing certain aspects altogether. Wycliffe's followers (called Lollards) and some other groups ended up denying the real presence of Christ in the eucharist, the entire system of sacraments, the idea that the church contains both saints and sinners, the church's role in interpreting scripture, and the papacy's validity, because it had become rich and therefore divorced from the poverty of the *ecclesia primitiva*.[18]

Late medieval criticism and reform sometimes went together, as had happened several centuries earlier. Followers of Hus and Wycliffe, among others who remained orthodox, were like the early Waldo in agreeing with some of the Gregorian Revolution's goals. Their stances have often been called anticlerical, but this is unfair to their positions; the very word *anticlericalism* dates not from the late Middle Ages but the nineteenth century. Indeed, these groups were decidedly proclerical since they held clerics to the highest standards and pointed out shortcomings for correction. As Grote once put it in a sermon to priests, "I honor and greatly love the 'priest.' I hate and properly abominate the 'fornicator.'"[19]

Orthodox and heretical reformers *in membris* during the late Middle Ages also criticized what can be called arithmetical piety: devotions performed over and over so good deeds could pile up and buy a person's way into heaven. The devotions were not the problem; the simplistic multiplication of prayers and actions was. Two Hail Marys were twice as good as one, but only half as good as four, and so on. People prayed to saints for nearly every illness. This preoccupation with death led some to gross and literal imitation of Christ's passion; dances of death were intended to ward off epidemics. The rote recitation of prayers and rosaries was a common abuse, as was the tolling up of indulgences from visiting relics and churches. Some Christians purchased deathbed absolutions in advance, just in case they could not find a priest at the moment of death; others made financial provisions for masses to be said for their souls in perpetuity.

The goal was to whittle down with indulgences the number of days a Christian might have to spend in purgatory before gaining heaven, a practice against which Hus complained. One of the great ironies is that Martin Luther's own protector, Frederick the Wise, kept a relic collection worth nearly two million days of indulgences. A German cardinal even topped this, claiming his relics brought almost forty million days, which translates into over 107,520 years.[20] One wonders what they had done to work off so much time.

Though these practices clearly needed to be reformed, arithmetical piety does at least give evidence of great faith, even if it is admittedly misdirected. Clearly, Christians were focusing on their own spiritual states, however obsessively, and especially so on the local level during the late Middle Ages. There was evidently a great vitality of faith. Apart from the pious activities, they gave money to their parishes, filled the pews, and staffed hospitals and orphanages. Their valid criticisms of the clergy grew louder and more impassioned because of rising, not lowered, expectations for clerical conduct—a sign of the desire for reform from below born of love, not hate, for the church. Nor was the church behind the times: She embraced humanism and used the printing press, churning out manuals for pastors, model sermons, and books to guide confessors and penitents during the sacrament of penance.[21] While three popes and a variety of conciliarists *in capite* fought themselves and rendered reform stillborn, the spirit and practice of reform was alive and well *in membris* in the late medieval church.

## Protestant Reformations

### Martin Luther

Luther was a Catholic priest and scholar who saw the church's problems, was bound by some of the conventions of his time, and suggested ways to improve the late medieval church in which he lived. He did not set out to create a revolution or leave the church—indeed, it was surely his position the Catholic church had left him, not the other way around. So, we must take Luther first as a Catholic seeking to help the church from within and then as the herald of a Protestant revolution. For his own part, Luther did not think of himself as a reformer because he thought only God could reform the church. Only rarely did he use the word *reformatio*, although he demonstrated some pride in his reform accomplishments. "I must praise myself for once.... I think I have made...a reformation to make the papists' ears ring," he wrote, adding elsewhere, "Thanks be to God, I have done more reforming with my gospel than [the papists] have been able to do in five councils."[22]

Part of Luther's early education was in a school run by the *devotio moderna;* as a teenager, he studied for a law degree until a fierce storm led him to call out for St. Anne's protection, promising to become a monk if he wasn't struck by lightning. Luther survived and kept his promise: In 1505 he joined a reformed branch of the Augustinian order in Erfurt, where the monks rigorously pursued an ascetic path to spiritual progress and fought to maintain their freedom from Roman oversight. Luther progressed in his ecclesiastical career: He was ordained a priest and went on to a theology doctorate in 1512. The next year, he started his career as a scripture professor at Wittenberg.

Luther's reform ideas start with many of the same complaints others voiced about the late medieval church: arithmetical piety *in membris,* greed *in capite.* He stepped into the history of reform with his *95 Theses.* These were written to respond to what Luther saw as a crude trade in indulgences, as seen in the list's alternate title, *Disputation on the Power and Efficacy of Indulgences.*[23] Luther's criticism was sparked when Johann Tetzel peddled indulgences nearby. Not only was Tetzel collecting money to help build St. Peter's in Rome; more perniciously, perhaps, he was also helping to repay the debt incurred by a German archbishop who held three diocesan sees simultaneously.

These problems—papal grandeur and the pluralism/absenteeism that prevented pastoral service—would have been high on any orthodox reformer's agenda. Luther did not mean to start a battle with his propositions, only to outline a number of points (in this case, 95) he thought should be debated at Wittenberg. His list was just like the many other memos professors had posted for consideration for years. In Luther's case, word got back to the archbishop who, angered for obvious reasons, sent the list to Rome. The pope initially gave the matter little attention, but Tetzel and others pressed for action. Tetzel may have been angered especially by theses 27 and 28:

> 27: They preach only human doctrines who say that as soon as the money clinks into the money chest, the soul flies out of purgatory.
> 28: It is certain that when money clinks in the money chest, greed and avarice can be increased; but when the church intercedes, the result is in the hands of God alone.

With the *95 Theses,* Luther had intended to fight the mathematical approach to faith that placed the purchase of indulgences before true and inner contrition, but he also criticized papal greed, bureaucracy, and worldliness. It became clear rather quickly that the church would not respond favorably to his criticisms. The *95 Theses* turned out to be an unintended spark. Luther's calls for reform grew increasingly strident in the three pamphlets he published in rapid succession during the summer and autumn of 1520, where he explained his ideas on justification by faith.

In the first pamphlet, Luther laid the duty of reform on every Christian person, especially the princes, because he contended there was a priesthood of all believers. This appeal *To the Christian Nobility of the German Nation Concerning the Reform of the Christian State* (August 1520) aimed to tear down what he called the three "walls" of Roman Catholicism: only the pope could validly interpret scripture, only the pope could summon a general council, the papacy's spiritual authority was greater than the state's temporal authority.[24] He advocated change in the church's structure by replacing a hierarchical spiritual authority with one that was relatively more egalitarian (given the contemporary social classes).

In the first part of this pamphlet Luther especially attacked financial abuses *in capite* that had been building since the high medieval papal revolution. These abuses had become particularly burdensome during the Avignon papacy and had resisted reform during the Great Schism with its accompanying period of papal recovery from conciliarism's challenge. After recounting the many ways Roman avarice collected fees to grant dispensations and allot church offices, Luther concluded, exasperated: "It seems as though canon law were instituted solely for the purpose of making a great deal of money."[25]

Luther was also concerned with reform *in membris,* especially arithmetical piety: The system of devotional actions and consequences he believed distanced the church from her origins. He held that the church should help herself by getting rid of what he saw as accretions to the church's structure—a strategy of addition by subtraction. The most striking example is found in his second pamphlet, *The Babylonian Captivity of the Church* (October 1520), which relied on scriptural principles to reduce the number of sacraments from seven to three: baptism, eucharist, confession. Luther also called for the abolition of all vows, including those made by members of religious orders, apart from the original baptismal vow.[26]

In essence, Luther wanted to substitute the movement of the Holy Spirit and the church's original organization for the current structures and hierarchical authority of the medieval church. In *Babylonian Captivity* he focused his opposition on the idea of development of doctrine, structures, and sacraments. This approach was a strict *reditus ad fontes* (return to the sources), with the source being the original church. He took as his norm the actions of Christ: The mass, for example, should resemble Jesus' last supper without any nonscriptural additions. The apostles (or their successors, the bishops) could not add any sacrament not instituted by Jesus.[27]

No ecclesiastical authority could change the early church's model, according to Luther. In *To the Christian Nobility,* he explained the New Testament does not distinguish episcopal from sacerdotal authority, nor delineate any other offices: "But of bishops as they now are the scriptures know nothing.... I am not referring here to popes, bishops, canons, and monks. God has not instituted these offices. They have taken these burdens upon themselves...." In the same section of that pamphlet, he declared celibacy to be another innovation—and a diabolical one, at that:

> But the Roman see has interfered and out of its own wanton wickedness made a universal commandment forbidding priests to marry. This was done at the bidding of the devil, as St. Paul declares in 1 Timothy 4 [:1, 3], "There shall come teachers who bring the devil's teaching and forbid marriage." Unfortunately so much misery has arisen from this that tongue could never tell it....
>
> I want to speak only of the ministry which God has instituted, the responsibility of which is to minister word and sacrament to a congregation, among whom they reside. Such ministers should be given liberty by a Christian council to marry to avoid temptation and sin. For since God has not bound them, no one else ought to bind them or can bind them, even if he were an angel from heaven, let alone a pope. Everything that canon law decrees to the contrary is mere fable and idle talk.

Later Protestant reformers built on these ideas to conclude any action or authority that had not been explicitly instituted by Jesus was a human invention that distanced the contemporary church from the original church and therefore must be discarded.[28]

Luther had also given details of his idea of reform by subtraction in *To the Christian Nobility.* He advocated stripping away all feast days except Sunday: "...[S]ince the feast days are abused by drinking, gambling, loafing, and all manner of sin, we anger God more on holy days than we do on other days." The number of cardinals should be restricted to a dozen; the pope should abolish 99 percent of his court. Pilgrimages, while not inherently bad, should be curtailed because people used them to get into heaven while ignoring their Christian duties, even to the extent of spending money on the trip that would have been put to better use. A man, Luther explained, "permits his wife and child...to suffer want back home. And yet the silly fellow thinks he can gloss over such disobedience and contempt of the divine commandment with his self-assigned pilgrimage, which is really nothing but impertinence or a delusion of the devil." Luther also wanted to get rid of masses for the dead or at least restrict them. Too many were being said and these irreverently: "What pleasure can God take in wretched vigils and masses which are so miserably rattled off, not read or prayed. And if they were prayed, it would not be for God's sake and out of love, but for the sake of money and of getting a job finished."[29]

In the third of his early pamphlets, *The Freedom of a Christian* (November 1520), Luther referred to the reform of the inner human being made in God's image and likeness, recalling the fathers' emphasis.[30] He repeatedly attacked the accumulation of outer actions by which many Christians thought they would earn their way into heaven. His concern was with an individual's own spiritual journey; his fear was that Christians would misinterpret both what he was advocating and criticizing.

> There are very many who, when they hear of this freedom of faith, immediately turn it into an occasion for the flesh and think that now all things are allowed them. They want to show that they are free men and Christians only by despising and finding fault with ceremonies, traditions, and human laws; as if they were Christians because on stated days they do not fast or eat meat when others fast, or because they do not use the accustomed prayers, and with upturned nose scoff at the precepts of men, although they utterly disregard all else that pertains to the Christian religion. The extreme opposite of these are those who rely for their salvation solely on their reverent observance of ceremonies, as if they would be saved because on certain days they fast or abstain from meats, or pray certain prayers; these make a boast of the precepts of the church and of the fathers, and do not care a fig for the things which are of the essence of our faith. Plainly, both are in error because they neglect the weightier things which are necessary to salvation, and quarrel so noisily about trifling and unnecessary matters.

Orthodox Catholics would have agreed with a fair number of Luther's criticisms, but in 1520 his impatience began to show. The history of reform had until Luther been marked by evolutionary change and a slow (even glacial) pace. Luther sometimes advocated rapid, fairly revolutionary change, as if encouraging his growing group of followers to offend Catholic sensibilities deliberately:

> [The Christian] will meet first the unyielding, stubborn cere-monialists who like deaf adders are not willing to hear the truth of liberty but, having no faith, boast of, prescribe, and insist upon their ceremonies as means of justification.... These he must resist, do the very opposite, and offend them boldly lest by their impious views they drag many with them into error. In the presence of such men it is good to eat meat, break the fasts, and for the sake of the liberty of faith do other things which they regard as the greatest of sins.

But Luther also counseled against implementing too much reform too quickly.

> How much better is the teaching of the apostle Paul who bids us take a middle course and condemns both sides when he says, "Let not him who eats despise him who abstains, and let not him who abstains pass judgment on him who eats" (Rom 14:3). Here you see that they who neglect and disparage cere-monies, not out of piety, but out of mere contempt, are reproved, since the apostle teaches us not to despise them. Such men are puffed up by knowledge. On the other hand, he teaches those who insist on the ceremonies not to judge the others, for neither party acts toward the other according to the love that edifies.... As a man is not righteous because he keeps and clings to the works and forms of the ceremonies, so also will a man not be counted righteous merely because he neglects and despises them.

Luther was aware that when teaching the Christian in the pew, a reformer must move slowly and carefully explain what a particular reform is and why it is being done. In language that seems bound by a certain condescension of the times, Luther continued to discuss how to implement reforms:

> The other class of men whom a Christian will meet are the simple-minded, ignorant men, weak in the faith, as the apostle calls them, who cannot yet grasp the liberty of faith, even if they were willing to do so (Rom 14:1). These he must take care not to offend. He must yield to their weakness until they are more fully instructed. Since they do and think as they do, not because they are stubbornly wicked, but only because their faith is weak, the fasts and other things which they consider necessary must be observed to avoid giving them offense. This is the command of love which would harm no one but would serve all men. It is not by their fault that they are weak, but by that of their pastors who have taken them captive with the snares of their traditions and have wickedly used these traditions as rods with which to beat them....
>
> For this reason, although we should boldly resist those teachers of traditions and sharply censure the laws of the popes by means of which they plunder the people of God, yet we must spare the timid multitude whom those impious tyrants hold captive by means of these laws until they are set free. Therefore fight strenuously against the wolves, but for the sheep and not also against the sheep.[31]

So although Luther seems at times an impatient reformer, he actually advocated unhurried progress. In eight *Invocavit* sermons (so named because they started on the first Sunday of Lent) he offered at Wittenberg in March 1522, he actually advised his more enthusiastic followers to slow down. Some of them had rapidly and nearly completely renounced anything reminiscent of Roman Catholicism.[32]

Led especially by Andreas Karlstadt (ca. 1480–1541) during Christmas 1521, while Luther was away from Wittenberg, they introduced changes that some congregants found unsettling and shocking: masses celebrated in the vernacular and without vestments, communion received without fasting and under both species, very public marriages of priests, and the destruction of images. Luther's concern, once more reminiscent of the theme of personal reform, was that outer changes would be made without the necessary inner change that was far more meaningful. Luther did not think simple iconoclasm would accomplish his reform ideas; in fact, some reformers seemed to be acting without thinking about their actions—precisely what Luther had criticized about late medieval Catholic devotions.

Change based on the gospel's precedents and the principle of love, Luther preached, should come gradually so it may be understood, received, and embraced for the right reasons.

> Dear brother, if you have suckled long enough, do not at once cut off the breast, but let your brother be suckled as you were suckled. I would not have gone so far as you have done, if I had been here. The cause is good, but there has been too much haste.

In particular, Luther clearly stated his opposition to the Roman idea of the sacrifice of the mass. But he also stressed that if it were just snatched away from Christians, they would not be allowed to decide for themselves if it should be abolished in the freedom Luther considered essential.

> ...[I]t should be preached and taught with tongue and pen that to hold mass in such a manner is sinful, and yet no one should be dragged away from it by the hair....
>
> Now if I should rush in and abolish it by force, there are many who would be compelled to consent to it and yet not know where they stand, whether it is right or wrong, and they would say: I do not know if it is right or wrong, I do not know where I stand, I was compelled by force to submit to the majority. And this forcing and commanding results in a mere mockery, an external show, a fool's play, man-made ordinances, sham-saints, and hypocrites. For where the heart is not good, I care nothing at all for the work. We must first win the hearts of the people....
>
> In short, I will preach it, teach it, write it, but I will constrain no man by force, for faith must come freely without compulsion. Take myself as an example. I opposed indulgences and all the papists, but never with force.[33]

Luther was not the only Christian calling for change, but those who followed his lead were sometimes less circumspect and more virulent than he was (at least in his earliest writings). His actions sparked others to take up his call in diverse ways that demonstrate that the Protestant movement was no more monolithic than the late medieval Catholic reform efforts preceding Luther.

## Jean Calvin

From his first efforts, Jean Calvin (1509–64) was more intentional a reformer than Luther, but Calvin wanted to reform not only Roman Catholicism, but the early Protestant changes, too. A French humanist and civil lawyer who became a Protestant in 1533, Calvin's training in these fields provided much of Protestantism with its enduring form and purpose. His *Institutes of the Christian Religion*, first published in 1536 but revised eight times to deal at great length with emerging situations and questions, established what is sometimes called Reformed Protestantism, which found its home in Geneva, Calvin's base of operations starting in 1541.[34]

Going beyond Luther, Calvin expounded and made certain principles firmer. Most famously, he rigidly held that all Christians were totally depraved. Any human effort to obtain merit for salvation was useless; God alone elected (or predestined) some men and women for salvation. Calvin condemned the Catholic system of seven sacraments as "fable and lie." He upheld only two sacraments: baptism and the Lord's Supper (a phrase that began to replace *eucharist,* perhaps to indicate its connection to Jesus' original action).

Calvin believed the Christian community should be a theocracy: minister and magistrate were theoretically separate but practically the same. A church-led state should strictly regulate all behavior in order to maintain civic order and patrol the hardhearted. It was government's obligation to implement God's will in the world: Religious reform and social reform were closely intertwined. Calvin transformed the medieval religious *vita activa* into the equivalent of good citizenship in the Protestant *polis.*

Like Luther, Calvin in his reform program rejected the over-whelming reliance on external observances characterizing the arithmetical piety of late medieval Roman Catholicism. Although he did not mention Catholicism by name in the following passages from his 1536 *Confession of Faith,* Calvin was clearly alluding to some of the same problems Luther pointed out:

...[W]e think it an abomination to put our confidence or hope in any created thing, to worship anything else than [God], whether angels or any other creatures, and to recognize any other saviour of our souls than him alone, whether saints or men living upon earth; and likewise to offer the service, which ought to be rendered to him, in external ceremonies or carnal observances, as if he took pleasure in such things, or to make an image to represent his divinity or any other image for adoration.

Calvin's position largely ignored the slow progress Luther counseled in his *Invocavit* sermons, but he agreed with Luther that ultimately reformers should abolish most Catholic practices rather than keep them. Some Catholics might wish to reform certain of their practices by stripping away their multiplication to find what was original and worth rescuing from mindless repetition. For Calvin, most Catholic rituals were inventions that were not part of the early church's norms anyway and so should be destroyed, not reformed. As he put the matter when treating prayer and the sacraments in the *Confession,*

...[W]e reject the intercession of the saints as a superstition invented by men contrary to scripture, for the reason that it proceeds from mistrust of the sufficiency of the intercession of Jesus Christ....

In as much as the mass of the pope was a reprobate and diabolical ordinance subverting the mystery of the holy supper, we declare that it is execrable to us, an idolatry condemned by God....

...[A]ll laws and regulations made binding on conscience which oblige the faithful to things not commanded by God, or establish another service of God than that which he

demands, thus tending to destroy Christian liberty, we condemn as perverse doctrines of Satan, in view of our Lord's
declaration that he is honored in vain by doctrines that are
the commandment of men. It is in this estimation that we
hold pilgrimages, monasteries, distinctions of foods, prohibition of marriage, confessions and other like things.

The reform standard for Calvin was always, and strictly, the
gospel: as he set out to recreate the form and function of the first-
century *ecclesia primitiva* in Geneva in the middle of the sixteenth
century, this was the only fountain from which he drew in his *reditus ad fontes.*

> ...[T]he proper mark by which rightly to discern the church
> of Jesus Christ is that his holy gospel be purely and faithfully
> preached, proclaimed, heard and kept.... On the other hand,
> where the gospel is not declared, heard and received, there we
> do not acknowledge the form of the church. Hence the
> churches governed by the ordinances of the pope are rather
> synagogues of the devil than Christian churches.[35]

At this important moment in the history of reform, we can
witness an instructive debate between the competing Catholic and
Calvinist ideas of reform. Cardinal Jacopo Sadoleto wrote an
open letter to the Genevan city council in March 1539, admitting
the Catholic church required reform but denying that a break was
the best way to accomplish this goal. Later that year, Jean Calvin
issued his response: Christians must return to the *ecclesia primitiva,* not simply fix the Catholic way of doing things.[36]

Sadoleto was not blind to the church's problems, nor was he
immune to accusation. He was secretary to two Medici popes and
was himself an absentee bishop: named bishop of Carpentras in
1517, he did not reach his diocese until 1523, but he quickly
returned to Rome in 1524 for another three years before going
back to Carpentras. He became very interested in humanism and
reform, however, and for the next two decades played an important role in Catholic reform efforts.

Sadoleto's letter aimed to bring Geneva and Rome back together again. He included several hopeful expressions for unity, starting with his careful address to the Genevans: "Very dear brethren in Christ, peace to you and with us, that is, with the Catholic church, the mother of all, both us and you." He returned to this theme near the letter's conclusion, where he asked the council to

> be one among ourselves, and one in [Christ]. For this the Catholic church always labors, for this she strives, viz., our concord and unity in the same spirit, that all men, however divided by space or time, and so incapable of coming together as one body, may yet be both cherished and ruled by one spirit, who is always and everywhere the same. To this Catholic church and Holy Spirit those, on the contrary, are professed adversaries who attempt to break unity, to introduce various spirits, to dissolve consent, and banish concord from the Christian religion, attempting this, with an eagerness and a zeal, by machinations and arts, which no language can sufficiently express.

Sadoleto was not entirely conciliatory when detailing how "professed adversaries" disrupted unity. He objected to what he called innovations or novelties, bringing him into direct conflict with the Protestant reform principle of a return to the *ecclesia primitiva*. Sadoleto particularly believed the idea of justification by faith alone was put forward by "new men" and "inventors of novelties" who ignored the additional need of good works for salvation.

> The point in dispute is whether [it is] more expedient for your salvation, and whether you think you will do what is more pleasing to God, by believing and following what the Catholic church throughout the whole world, now for more than fifteen hundred years, or (if we require clear and certain recorded notice of the facts) for more than thirteen hundred years approves with general consent; or innovations introduced within these twenty-five years, by crafty or, as they think themselves, acute men; but men certainly who are not themselves the Catholic church?

Sadoleto derided these "acute men" who promoted innovation for lacking humility and obedience: They presumed to interpret scripture on their own and put themselves ahead of the tradition, which, with scripture, comprised the church's teaching authority according to the Catholics.

In his response, Calvin recounted the familiar financial abuses that required reform. He also described Catholic ceremonies as childish, superstitious, and too numerous. Their formality had distanced the congregation, their multiplication had lessened their significance, and their ornateness had stripped them of meaning. Had he pursued this line of thought exclusively, Calvin would have been agreeing with Sadoleto that the Catholic church only needed a good housecleaning, but was otherwise worth saving.

Instead, Calvin turned to the *ecclesia primitiva* as the exemplar of doctrine, discipline, sacraments, and ceremonies, implicitly applying to the Catholics the charge of innovation and novelty. He wanted Christianity to reform by returning strictly to its "native purity" and following only the early church's original examples, not medieval developments. If she collected more money than she required, the excess should go to the poor, as had occurred in the early church. Bishops should be examined, elected, and installed into their office according to the old way. Any liturgical practice that could not be found in scripture Calvin called "fictitious worship."

Calvin also met Sadoleto squarely on the core issue: deciding among the reform models of the original church, Catholic developments over one and a half millennia, and the "innovations" of the prior quarter century which Sadoleto had indicted.

> ...[Y]ou teach that all which has been approved for fifteen hundred years or more, by the uniform consent of the faithful, is, by our headstrong rashness, torn up and destroyed.... You know, Sadoleto, and if you venture to deny, I will make it palpable to all that you knew, yet cunningly and craftily disguised the fact, not only that our agreement with antiquity is far closer than yours, but that all we have attempted has been

to renew that ancient form of the church, which, at first sullied and distorted by illiterate men of indifferent character, was afterward flagitiously mangled and almost destroyed by the Roman pontiff and his faction.

I will not press you so closely as to call you back to that form which the apostles instituted (though in it we have the only model of a true church, and whosoever deviates from it in the smallest degree is in error), but to indulge you so far, place, I pray, before your eyes, that ancient form of the church, such as their writings prove it to have been in the age of Chrysostom and Basil, among the Greeks, and of Cyprian, Ambrose, and Augustine, among the Latins; after so doing, contemplate the ruins of that church, as now surviving among yourselves.... Will you here give the name of an enemy of antiquity to him who, zealous for ancient piety and holiness, and dissatisfied with the state of matters as existing in a dissolute and depraved church, attempts to ameliorate its condition, and restore it to pristine splendor?

There is a certain irony at work in Calvin's brand of Reformed Protestantism, which took the *ecclesia primitiva* as its guide. Calvin may fairly be seen as replacing a medieval theocracy—the papal monarchy he and Luther criticized—with another species of the same animal under the banner of "reform." Calvin, like Luther, denied the Roman church coercive spiritual authority and any temporal power at all, yet Calvin's Protestant *polis* essentially recreated this system, albeit in a less monarchical form. In addition, Calvin did not refrain from taking coercive action against those he declared heretics. He quarreled with Michael Servetus (1511–53), a Spanish academic who claimed the idea of the trinity contradicted Christ's teachings and attacked both the *Institutes* (marking up a copy and sending it to Calvin) and Catholic dogma. With the Catholics, Calvin believed Servetus's position to be heresy. When Servetus entered Calvin's church, Calvin ordered him arrested; soon after, Servetus was burned as a heretic.

The irony continues. Geneva became a "mother church," the true exemplar of Calvin's Reformed Protestantism—so much so that Geneva was sometimes known as the "Protestant Rome."

Since the *ecclesia primitiva* was the reform model for Protestant groups, in his *Ecclesiastical Ordinances* (1541) Calvin restricted Geneva's organized church to the form of the ancient church as found in scripture.

Geneva, and other communities by extension, reinstated the four ministerial offices taken from this ancient church model: Pastors preached the word, teachers researched the word, elders regulated behavior, and deacons administered charity. A consistory of ministers made decisions communally. In 1559, an Academy (later University) of Geneva was established to train Protestant pastors who then were sent abroad to establish communities. Geneva's Company of Pastors acted as a court of appeals, not unlike the papal curia, and became a center for the production of Protestant hymnals, catechisms, and apologetic materials. This process mirrored the high medieval papal monarchy's support for universities where priests and bishops trained; they then exported the Gregorian Revolution and its moral, canonical, and political goals. Protestants from different European countries similarly spent an apprenticeship in Geneva, often as refugees when their ideas were persecuted at home by the Catholic church. In Geneva they soaked up Calvin's forms of Protestantism and brought them to their native countries where they put their own spin on Calvin's structures.[37]

## The English Reformations

What happened in England during the sixteenth century is normally taken as a separate reform and this makes some sense for two reasons. First, the desire of Henry VIII (1509–47) to annul his marriage to Catherine of Aragon was a unique motive. Second, once Henry broke from Rome, the practice and doctrines of Christianity in England remained largely Roman Catholic during the rest of his reign. What followed Henry was a complicated series of religious changes and reactions lasting for decades and engaging Catholic, Protestant, and hybrid religious reforms.

In a recent book that made a dramatic impact on the debate, Eamon Duffy argued Catholicism was vibrant, lively, and fairly well informed before Henry VIII broke with Rome to "reform" Catholicism. Duffy believes the swift return to traditional Roman Catholicism under Mary I (1553–58) indicates that Henry was motivated by political, not religious, concerns and forced his Church of England onto traditional Catholics who never truly followed his "reforms." Duffy recognizes the practice of Catholicism may have been arithmetical, but it was not decadent and somehow "saved" by Henry VIII in the manner in which some say Luther "saved" Christianity from her Roman practices. He admits, however, to discontent that had led to calls for reform before Henry. John Wycliffe and the Lollards recognized clerical improprieties requiring reform, for instance, and humanists at Cambridge and Oxford read Luther, gathering in Cambridge at the White Horse Inn, which, around 1520, became known as "Little Germany."[38]

Henry did make changes considered reforms, but he retained much of Roman Catholicism. Essentially, Henry remained Catholic, at least in his own mind, while contending in the *Act of Supremacy* (1534) that as a monarch he was not subject to any other monarchs, including the pope. He considered himself head of the Church of England, but according to Henry that church was Catholic. The king's *Ten Articles* (1536) were more Catholic than Protestant: They affirmed the real presence of Christ in the eucharist, infant baptism, and the intercessory role of Mary and the saints (while noting that none were to be placed ahead of Jesus). His *Six Articles* (1539), sometimes called the "six bloody articles" because of the violence with which they were applied, legislated the death penalty against those who rejected transubstantiation and clerical celibacy.

Under Henry's son Edward VI (1547–53), England turned more Protestant, although during these decades of turmoil there were Catholics and Protestants of many shades in England. The bishops, Parliament, and the archbishop of Canterbury Thomas Cranmer (1489–1556) influenced Edward to revoke the *Six Articles,* approve the reception of both bread and wine at the Lord's Supper, and remove the ban against married clergy. These Protestant changes were then reversed under Mary, who restored

Roman Catholicism to papal obedience. Cranmer paid for his Protestantism with his life under "Bloody Mary," but the English church again moved away from Catholicism during the long reign of Elizabeth I (1558–1603), whose approach at settlement angered both Catholics and Protestants.

In retrospect, Elizabeth's solution emerges as a "middle way" that rejected papal, Roman dominance as well as the fragmentation of Protestant denominations plaguing the reform movement on the continent. The Anglican *Thirty-Nine Articles* (1563) refuted Catholic and some radical Protestant principles. Elizabeth gradually replaced Catholics with Anglicans in her government, restored her father's acts in her own *Act of Supremacy* (1559), in particular restoring the monarch as head of the Church of England, and required an oath of allegiance from her bishops.

The state of the reformed English church during the early part of Elizabeth's reign may be gauged in a treatise written by John Jewel in 1562. Jewel's *Apology of the Church of England* defended the Anglican reforms from Catholic charges of schism, heresy, and immorality. He explained the Anglican church had returned to biblical and apostolic norms, which the Roman church had abandoned. Jewel specifically complained about the "papal monopoly" on the interpretation of scripture which, he exulted, was now properly in the hands of all believers. Jewel further mandated that any charge against the Anglican church and any defense of the Roman church be grounded only in scripture, as had been done when the early church fought heretics.[39]

## Reforming the Protestant Reformations

Even before Calvin wrote the first version of his *Institutes* in 1536, indeed just a few years after Luther posted his *95 Theses* in 1517, reformers breaking away from the Catholic church began to disagree with one another and, in effect, to reform the Protestant reform. We have already seen Karlstadt pressing Luther's reforms too quickly for Luther's tastes. Although there are many strands or fragments of the Protestant reformations, three in particular illuminate the path the history of reform was traveling at this moment.

The first strand is what has been called the left wing of the Protestant reformations or the Radical Reformation. Groups within this rubric split off at several junctures, but it makes sense to begin with its earliest proponent, Huldrych Zwingli (1484–1531). Less than a year after the 95 Theses appeared, Zwingli began to push the reform of the church in Switzerland. He was less tolerant than Luther of the old Catholic practices and, like Calvin who would follow in Geneva, favored the functional equivalent of a theocracy.

A former Catholic priest, Zwingli preached a reform program that represented a radical *reditus ad fontes* grounded strictly and exclusively in scriptural authority. Zwingli detailed this plan in 1523 as part of a debate with Catholics in Zurich. In the 67 Articles Zwingli prepared for the debate, he removed all images, organs, relics, the intercessory power of the saints, and any Marian devotions. He opposed purgatory, religious orders, the papacy, a celibate priesthood, the sacrament of confession, and rituals like fasting. He sought to restore the archipelago of independent churches that comprised the church of the first few centuries after Jesus.[40]

Luther and Zwingli attempted to resolve their differences, especially the theological issues, at a meeting at Marburg in 1529. They agreed on several major points, but they could not reach accord on the nature of the Lord's Supper. Because they failed to resolve the break between them, these men and their followers split: Lutherans were then known as Evangelicals and Zwinglians as Reformed Protestants, some of whom radicalized further while others were subsumed into Calvinism.

The second strand of the radical Protestant reformations is found among the Anabaptists, who demonstrated a fundamental and ironic challenge to Luther and Zwingli's path. Anabaptists contended that once Luther opened scripture to everyone's interpretation and preached liberty of faith, he could not logically censure anyone who opposed him by interpreting scripture and freely exercising his or her faith in the way Luther himself had sanctioned. The

Anabaptist position might be stated thus: Not only did Luther fail to reform the church, but so did Zwingli, who set out to reform Luther's reform. For this reason, they often complained not only of "popish" practices, but "anti-popish" ones, too.[41]

The Anabaptists rigorously followed scriptural precedents and broke from Zwingli, although they were unorganized in leadership, creed, and organization. Their ideas varied widely, depending on individual interpretations of scripture, but in general they were separatists and pacifists who did not pay taxes, serve in the army, or take oaths. They chose their pastors by lot and owned property communally because that, they explained, was how things were done in the early church according to the Acts of the Apostles. These pastors were religious laymen, not "new priests" who replaced a Catholic clergy with a Lutheran or Zwinglian clergy.

One principle on which all Anabaptist groups agreed was "believer's baptism." Rejecting the Catholic practice of infant baptism, they did not hold baptism to be valid unless taken consciously, usually by an adult. Consequently, they called infant baptism "a senseless, blasphemous abomination, contrary to all scripture, contrary even to the papacy." If their stance meant there would be only a small number of faithful, so be it: "It is much better that a few be rightly taught through the word of God, believing and walking aright in virtues and practices, than that many believe falsely and deceitfully through adulterated doctrine."

The Anabaptists' reform position was summed up in a *Letter to Thomas Müntzer,* sent in September 1524 to a reformer who had withdrawn from Luther. Here they demonstrated their devotion to a reform grounded in scripture. Their ideas touched every aspect of belief and worship, in the process breaking not only with Catholicism, but with other Protestant reform movements, too.

> Just as our forebears fell away from the true God and from the one true, common, divine word, from the divine institutions, from Christian love and life, and lived without God's law and gospel in human, useless, un-Christian customs and ceremonies,...so today too every man wants to be saved by superficial faith, without fruits of faith, without baptism of

trial and probation, without love and hope, without right
Christian practices, and wants to persist in all the old manner
of personal vices, and in the common ritualistic and anti-
Christian customs of baptism and of the Lord's Supper, in dis-
respect for the divine word and in respect for the word of the
pope and of the anti-papal preachers, which yet is not equal
to the divine word nor in harmony with it.... But after we
took scripture in hand, too, and consulted it on many points,
we have been instructed somewhat and have discovered the
great and harmful error of the shepherds, of ours, too....

Two concrete examples of using scripture as the exclusive
model of reform for doctrine and worship are singing and the
mass. Anabaptists took singing to be foreign to the gospels:

We understand and have seen that you have translated the
mass into German and have introduced new German hymns.
That cannot be for the good, since we find nothing taught in
the New Testament about singing, no example of it.

So, too, with the Lord's Supper:

The words found in Matthew 26, Mark 14, Luke 22, and 1
Corinthians 11 alone are to be used, no more, no less.... They
are the words of the instituted meal of fellowship, not words
of consecration.... [T]he Supper is an expression of fellowship, not a mass and sacrament. Therefore none is to receive
it alone, neither on his deathbed nor otherwise. Neither is the
bread to be locked away....[42]

The third strand of the breakaway Protestant reformations
occurred not on the continent but in England, which, as we have
said, was itself a reform apart. After the Catholic-Anglican seesaw
settled down during Elizabeth I's reign, a branch of English
reformers with roots in the decades before her reign contended
that even her actions did not sufficiently reform the church. Like
the Anabaptists who claimed Luther and Zwingli's reforms
needed reform, these Puritans believed their reform of the English
church corrected the Church of England's reform of Roman
Catholicism.

Puritans took their name from their claim to purity in church matters and were essentially the English version of Calvinism. They charged the "popish" Elizabethan settlement was nothing more than Roman Catholicism under a new guise—not unlike the Anabaptists' claim that the Lutherans had simply replaced the Roman clergy with new Lutheran priests. They declaimed Elizabeth's centralized religious authority as nonscriptural, especially in terms of the local election of ministers, and said it only recreated the Roman papal monarchy. These Puritans also singled out for reform simony, pluralism, bad preaching that replaced the good word of God, a lack of education on the part of priests and bishops, and pompous rituals that should be radically simplified in accordance with early church models.

The Puritan ideas of reform are revealed in *An Admonition to Parliament,* written in 1572, which claimed that the English church, though free from "popery," remained far from truly reformed. The authors painted a picture of an Anglican church as bad as the Roman church it had reformed by comparing the *ecclesia primitiva* ("then") and current Elizabethan practices ("now").

> Then the ministers were preachers, now bare readers.... Then, as God gave utterance, they preached the word only: now they read homilies, articles, injunctions, etc..... They ministered the sacrament plainly. We pompously, with singing, piping, surplice and cope wearing.

In fact, these Puritans complained boldly, "We borrow from papists."[43] For these and other reasons, the Puritans took themselves across the Atlantic where, in the "new world," they aimed to start again with a shining city on a hill.

## Catholic Reformations

Catholic reform during this era is plagued by its very name. Was it a Catholic Reformation (or were there Catholic reformations) independent of Luther that pre- and/or postdated him? Is it better to describe the age as a Counter Reformation that only reacted to Luther and without him would not have taken place? Is some combination of these ideas closer to reality? This question is not an historian's parlor game: Naming a reform is a key to understanding it—as the plural allows us to see the Protestant reformations as the complex and multiple efforts they were.[44]

The term "Catholic Reformation" when taken narrowly to refer to the mid–sixteenth century conveniently overlooks the reaction to Luther, while the term "Counter Reformation" ignores Catholic reform efforts before the 95 Theses. In a major review of the state of the question through an exploration of classic and current scholarship, historian William V. Hudon suggested "Tridentine Reformation" may represent the best substitute because the other two common terms are simplifications and generalizations that miss the subtlety, ambivalence, ambiguity, and multiplicity of Catholic reform in these crucial centuries. Another historian noted that "Tridentine Reformation" portrayed sixteenth-century Catholic reform as a proactive, positive, even innovative catalyst that did more than simply respond to the Protestants.

"Tridentine Reformation," however, could focus the reader exclusively on Trent or those ideas flowing into and out of that long, interrupted council. Other authors have suggested dropping the key word *reformation* altogether and referring to "early modern Catholicism," which would include where Trent's reforms came from in terms of prior centuries, how they were discussed at the council itself, and the extent to which they were ignored or implemented in the following century.[45] For our purposes, especially the desire to explore the continuities of Catholic reform, "Catholic reformations" (note the lower case *r* and the plural) here refers to attempts to improve the church just before, during, and after Luther.

## Erasmus

Erasmus (ca. 1467–1536) was a reformer caught between Catholic and Protestant attempts at church reform. Like his friend Sadoleto who corresponded with Calvin, Erasmus admitted the

Catholic church needed major reforms but did not think a break with Rome was the way to achieve them. In the heated atmosphere of the early sixteenth century, neither Catholics nor Protestants trusted Erasmus: both sides considered him a troublemaker and compromiser.

Some Catholics believed Erasmus had encouraged Luther—essentially "aiding and abetting the enemy"—by offering attacks similar to Luther's on Catholic hypocrisy and empty piety while calling for simplicity and reform. As a common phrase used during his lifetime complained, "Either Erasmus lutherizes or Luther erasmianizes." A group of Catholics would have liked to burn him at the stake as a heretic, even as some members of the college of cardinals wanted to reward him with the red hat of their membership.[46] Protestants, meanwhile, resisted Erasmus because he remained Catholic despite all of his complaints about the Roman church and papacy. As Erasmus himself put it, "I am a heretic to both sides."

Erasmus is a bridge between late medieval popular reform and Catholic attempts to respond to Protestant criticisms later in the sixteenth century. Like his contemporary Luther, Erasmus received his early education in a *devotio moderna* school. As a humanist infused with *devotio moderna* spirituality, Erasmus rejected religious formalism and the letter of the law. In his *Enchiridion militis Christiani (Handbook of the Christian Soldier,* 1503), he offered an extended homily to the laity, urging them to practice Christian virtues that sprang from their hearts: they should pursue an active spiritual life of inward piety and outward service. His *Praise of Folly* (1511) used biting satire as a reform technique to criticize ambition, greed, and power in the church's hierarchy. In several works, Erasmus repeatedly singled out Pope Julius II (1503–13), the famous warrior pope, as the worst example of clerical power that neglected pastoral service and humility. Erasmus also criticized empty monastic vows, clerical ignorance, arithmetical piety, spiritual superstition, and scholastic theology that was more sophistic than pastoral.

With Luther, Erasmus returned to the sources of the Christian tradition through close examination of texts, language, and manuscripts. Erasmus published a Greek New Testament in 1516, a year before Luther posted his *95 Theses*, and then editions of the fathers' writings in their original Latin and Greek. All were attempts to restore and make available the classic sources of Christianity so that, as he put it, the housewife at the stove and the plowboy in the fields would sing the psalms as they worked.

Erasmus focused on inner reform and education in order to help the Christian live what he called the philosophy of Christ. Erasmus believed the church must clarify her doctrine and recover her original scriptural and patristic foundations. Then, she must convey them to the minds and hearts of Christians who would act in accordance with Christian principles, thereby fixing Christian society from the inside out. These reform ideas were fundamentally patristic: humanistic, personal, and therefore in touch with the first few centuries of reform history, as well as the resurgence of these ideas in the Twelfth-Century Renaissance and subsequent evangelical awakening. He believed that practicing the faith was the goal of learning the faith; without action, religious knowledge was dead. More than anything else, learning about the faith must lead the Christian to personal reform by embracing the original image and likeness of God: "For what is the philosophy of Christ, which he calls a rebirth, but the renewal of a human nature that was created good?" Erasmus asked in 1516.[47]

One of his lesser-known works, the essay *Sileni Alcibiadis* (1515), summarizes his criticisms and ideas of reform. By contrasting the way things are with the way things should be in the church, Erasmus indicated that the hierarchy must be divested of its worldliness and all Christians must work continuously on their individual goodness.

> They say that the church is being honored and adorned, not when piety is growing among the people, when vices are diminishing and good behavior increasing, when sacred learning is in full bloom, but when the altars glitter with jewels and gold; nay, even when the altars themselves are neglected, and the accumulation of property, troops of servants, luxury, mules and horses, expensive erection of houses or rather

palaces, and all the rest of the racket of life, make the priests no better than satraps.... There are those—I have no wish to mention them—who spend the wealth of the church on wicked purposes, to the great offense of the people. When they have made a gain, we congratulate them and say the church of Christ has been added to; whereas the church has one kind of true wealth and one only—the advance of the Christian life....

I wish the popes to be fully armed, but with the arms of the apostle: that is, with the shield of faith, the breastplate of righteousness, the sword of salvation, which is the word of God. I wish them to be fierce warriors, but against the real enemies of the church: simony, pride, lust, ambition, anger, irreligion.... I want the priests to be acknowledged among the first of the land, but not for their noisy domineering, rather for the excellence of their holy learning, for their outstanding virtues. I want them to be revered, but for their upright and ascetic lives, not only for their titles or dramatic garb. I want them to be feared, but as fathers, not as tyrants.[48]

It is no wonder Catholics in the first half of the sixteenth century often grumbled: "Erasmus laid the egg and Luther hatched it."

## Four Abandoned Catholic Reforms

Catholic reformers clearly saw the need to address problems in the church. Any reform impetus from above, however, had largely failed during the fourteenth and fifteenth centuries as popes resisted conciliar attempts to undermine their authority. But some members of the curia were not afraid to criticize their colleagues. One cardinal drafting a reform plan for Pope Alexander VI said frankly in 1497, "The first thing is that our hearts be cleansed within us." This statement of the need for personal reform, however, was excluded from the subsequent papal bull, which was never promulgated anyway. Despite the fact that many ideas for reform were discussed, the fourteenth- and early-fifteenth-century papacy wasted its opportunity to lead reform by setting an example and reforming itself first. But there were four specific calls for reform in a twenty-five-year period around Luther, which, while stillborn, paved the way to the Council of Trent.

First, even before Luther posted his *95 Theses,* the Catholic church had called a council in 1512 where Giles of Viterbo, head of the Augustinian order, lambasted the papacy and curia in his opening address. He called for the long-awaited renewal to begin. He demanded action, not words, that would return the church to her roots and "finally…call religion back to its old purity, its ancient brilliance, its original splendor, and its own sources." In a famous sentence, he declared "men must be changed by religion, not religion by men"—an eerie foreshadowing of what was to come just a few years later under one of his own Augustinian monks, Martin Luther.

Giles of Viterbo went on to encourage this Fifth Lateran Council to renew the church from its winter with changes that would be like the spring sun and blossoms, just as some previous councils had done.

> For what else is a holy council if not an object of fear for the evil, a hope for the upright, a rejection of errors, a seed-bed and revival of virtues, whereby the deceit of the devil is conquered, the allurements of the senses removed, reason restored to its lost citadel, and justice returned from heaven to earth? Indeed God returns to men.

He bravely pushed the formidable Pope Julius II, who had called the council, to attack the church's problems

> so that God himself by the most evident miracle might restore life to a pope that had expired and the pope by a holy council might restore life to the church that had expired, and so that the church, together with a reviving pope, might restore morals to life…. [God] commands you to tear down, root up, and destroy errors, luxury, and vice, and to build, establish, and plant moderation, virtue, and holiness.[49]

The second call for reform came the next year in the form of a *Libellus* written to Julius II's successor, Leo X (1513–21), who was too busy enjoying the papacy to reform the church. This long memorandum complained that 98 percent of the clergy could not read Latin liturgical rites; most of the Christian faithful knew almost nothing about the faith; and superstitious piety reigned. The authors, a pair of monks, laid the blame squarely at the popes' feet. The papacy should lead the way to reform via inner spiritual progress and oversee reform through the church's hierarchy. Popes should call general councils every five years; bishops should hold synods in their dioceses and provinces to police compliance. They must also carefully examine candidates for ordination, especially inquiring whether they knew scripture and specifically requiring that they had read the entire Bible. The two monks even recommended translating the Bible into the vernacular so the laity could read it for themselves. Anticipating some of the major centralizing reforms of the Council of Trent by half a century, the *Libellus* called for a new missal, breviary, and church calendar so all of Catholicism would quite literally be on the same page.[50] But the Fifth Lateran Council, despite Giles of Viterbo's opening address and the *Libellus*'s plan, failed to institute any lasting reforms. The way was open for Luther.

The third abandoned call for reform was a set of guidelines written by Leo's successor, Adrian VI (1522–23), a pope much more open to self-reflection than Julius II and Leo X. Adrian VI wrote instructions for Francesco Chieregati, his legate to the Diet of Nuremberg. He wanted Chieregati to persuade the German princes meeting there to remain Catholic and oppose Luther. Adrian VI believed admitting papal failures was both honest and a good way to demonstrate good faith. He assigned blame in the highest levels of the church and called for a *reformatio in capite,* which would trickle down *in membris.* As he told Chieregati,

> You will also say that we frankly confess that God permits this persecution to afflict his church because of the sins of men, especially of the priests and prelates of the church.... We know that for many years many abominable things have occurred in this holy see, abuses in spiritual matters, transgressions of the commandments, and finally in everything a change for the worse. No wonder that the illness has spread from the head to

the members, from the supreme pontiffs to the prelates below them. All of us (that is, prelates and clergy), each one of us, have strayed from our paths; nor for a long time has anyone done good; no, not even one.... [Y]ou will promise that we will expend every effort to reform first this curia, whence perhaps all this evil has come, so that, as corruption spread from that place to every lower place, the good health and reformation of all may also issue forth. We consider ourselves all the more bound to attend to this, the more we perceive the entire world longing for such a reformation.

Adrian said he had accepted the papacy "out of obedience to the divine will, in order to reform his deformed bride, the Catholic church." But, just like Luther in the *Invocavit* sermons he had preached only months earlier, the pope called for slow and not sudden reforms, "lest in a desire to reform everything at the same time we throw everything into confusion.... He who scrubs too much draws blood."[51]

Adrian VI could not pursue his reforms, as his pontificate lasted just twenty months. A fourth attempt at Catholic reform did not occur until fifteen years later, when Pope Paul III (1534–49) called a number of leading reformers to Rome. It is under Paul that the papacy finally began to direct a substantial Catholic response to Protestant (and Catholic) complaints.[52]

Interested in calling a general council, Paul III first convoked a committee of reformers and charged them with drawing up a program. None of the members were curialists, which allowed them to speak more frankly and strike at the heart of the problems in the church's head. They included three very influential men: Reginald Pole from England, Erasmus's friend Jacopo Sadoleto, who would write to Geneva two years later, and Gasparo Contarini. In March 1537, they submitted their report, the *Consilium de emendanda ecclesia* or *Counsel on Reforming the Church*, which was "a compilation of those diseases and their remedies" that represented a first step toward "the renewal of the church of Christ."

The *Consilium* directed its reform attacks at the church *in capite*, starting with simony in the papacy that had run rampant since before Avignon and often resulted in poor pastoral care *in membris.*

> From this source as from a Trojan horse so many abuses and such grave diseases have rushed in upon the church of God that we now see her afflicted almost to the despair of salvation and the news of these things spread even to the infidels...who for this reason especially deride the Christian religion so that through us—through us, we say—the name of Christ is blasphemed among the heathens.

To right these wrongs, the *Consilium,* like the *Libellus,* made recommendations that would find their way into Trent's canons. The committee advised, among other measures, reforms in the training and examination of candidates for the priesthood. Pastors should be appointed who desire and know how to care for their flocks. Bishops and parish priests should never be absent from their posts unless for serious reasons. Even the most basic education must be addressed, especially in religious and philosophical matters, and books should be inspected for their suitability. The *Consilium* expressly forbade schoolboys to read Erasmus's *Colloquies,* presumably because, like his *Praise of Folly,* it criticized arithmetical piety and religious orders.

Some of the committee's criticisms mirrored Luther's. These Catholic reformers criticized pardoners, who sold absolution and indulgences and "deceive the peasants and simple people and ensnare them with innumerable superstitions." They warned against allowing too many priests the dispensation to marry, "especially in these times when the Lutherans lay such great stress on this matter." As for Rome, the committee scorned "the hatreds and animosities of private citizens" and the "harlots [who] walk about like matrons or ride on mules, attended in broad daylight by noble members of the cardinals' households and by clerics" in the city that housed "the mother and teacher of the other churches."[53]

Luther was probably pleased to see these Catholic reformers seemed to agree with him. Even though the *Consilium* was supposed to be a secret document, a copy was leaked and Luther published it in a German translation with his own comments in the margins the following year.[54] In his preface, Luther declared, "They cannot let themselves be reformed, and do not want to be," adding later, "[I]f all this filth were to be shaken up in a free council, can you imagine what a stink would rise?"

Right next to the document's first paragraph, where the committee expressed its gratitude to God for selecting Paul III as pope, Luther judged their statements unbelievable.

> Dear me, how seriously the holy see takes this matter! It is too bad that no one believes these scoundrels and liars any longer (providing that anyone could feel sorry about that).

Where the *Consilium* recommended the pope should refrain from profiting through the exercise of his authority and that pastors should live in their parishes and draw reasonable salaries from them, Luther commented:

> Let that one be kept and then see what becomes of the pope, cardinals, bishops, priests, monks, and all their splendor. But they have to talk like that, to make people think that their reformation is in earnest…. Shall the cardinals and prelates give back the parishes they have stolen? That would be dreadful! But what harm does it do to say it, so long as one does not mean it?

When the *Consilium* attacked indulgences, declaring they should not be offered more than once a year in big cities, Luther observed: "That has already been reformed by Luther."

In part because the *Consilium* was leaked and Luther caustically commented on it, yet another Catholic reform effort was abandoned. The papacy, which until now had resisted leading reform, had taken a first step. But Paul III could not move forward with speed and without hindrance, for a few of his own cardinals were identifying problems in the papal office itself. To admit that his office was deformed and required reform might give the Protestants just the evidence they needed to claim that even Rome was questioning the very institution the Protestants had done away with: the papacy. Luther himself noted as much in the preface to the *Consilium* in German: "If [the pope] should now be charged with error in one little point, then all his articles would become suspect." Having largely abdicated leadership in reforming the church for nearly two centuries, the papacy had finally taken some action. Then Luther's publication of the *Consilium* stemmed the rising tide for reform within the Catholic church. The long-awaited council to reform Catholicism would have to wait nearly a decade longer.

## The Council of Trent

After several decades of halting progress, the church made a definite step toward reform by calling the Council of Trent. Historians have debated whether a council would have been called had Luther not posted his *95 Theses*. Even had this been the case and a council had met, it surely would not have acted as Trent did in light of the Protestant challenges.

The Catholic church knew it needed to be reformed. In his keynote address at Trent, Cardinal Pole, one of the authors of the *Consilium de emendanda ecclesia,* sounded the same note of self-reflection and blame Adrian VI had in his instructions to Chieregati a quarter century earlier.

> We ourselves are largely responsible for the misfortune that has occurred—for the rise of heresy, the collapse of Christian morality—because we have failed to cultivate the field that was entrusted to us. We are like salt that has lost its flavor. Unless we do penance, God will not speak to us....[55]

Trent met in three stages: December 1545 to March 1547, May 1551 to April 1552, and January 1562 to December 1563. Each of the three parts addressed different topics with varying levels of debate and agreement. All of the sessions directed themselves to the restatement and conservation of Catholic principles and practices that had come under attack. This agenda has generally given Trent a reputation as a backward-looking, defensive council that sought only to preserve Catholicism. Some would say sixteenth-century Catholic reformers retrenched the Roman church without updating her as Vatican II would.[56] But the Council of Trent's program of reform did take an honest look at core problems, addressing them with reforms and even creating new solutions in one important case: seminaries.

During the first stage (1545–47), Trent's major concern was systematizing doctrinal statements of the Roman Catholic faith—a logical task. The delegates explained the equal and indispensable roles of scripture and tradition, stressing that the proper interpretation of scripture should be in trained hands. They explained the doctrine of original sin, justification, and the fact that both baptism and confirmation were sacraments. Trent in this first stage addressed reform only in a limited way. Brief reforms were legislated: seeking better-formed and better-examined candidates for service, requiring bishops to reside in their dioceses and to make sure pastors were meeting their parishioners' spiritual needs, and restricting pluralism because it detracted from the care of souls.

During its second stage (1551–52), Trent focused on asserting the real presence of Jesus in the eucharist by explaining transubstantiation. The delegates also defended, explained, and asserted penance and final anointing as sacraments. Again, there was limited reform legislation: episcopal residence was mandated once again and some regulations were made for clerical conduct.[57]

For the history of reform, the long third stage of the Council of Trent (1562–63) is the most important, but the documents treated other major matters, too. They asserted ordination and marriage were indeed sacraments, regulated religious orders, and continued the church's use of purgatory, relics, images, and indulgences, all of which Luther had attacked specifically.

As for reform, the Council of Trent in this final stage took several major steps, legislating substantial reform decrees in each of its last three sessions.[58] Bishops and priests, once more, were directed to be present in their dioceses and parishes. Although they could be absent for up to three months with approval, they had to be present for Advent and Christmas, Lent and Easter, Pentecost and Corpus Christi, "for then their flocks need most of all to be renewed and to rejoice in the Lord at the presence of their pastor." Thorough examinations were required for ordination, which should be done by the candidate's own bishop only. Trent's goal was to prevent just the sort of deformation that had occurred and now required reformation.

The 1562–1563 sessions of Trent also focused on how to reform priests, especially their studies, personal suitability, and examination of worthiness for ordination. The major innovation was the creation of a seminary system. The hope was that men who were properly reformed personally would then be able to help their parishioners reform themselves. This was meant to produce an inside-out reform on two levels: The soul of the priest-candidate, once inflamed by the Holy Spirit through his studies, would be able to warm the souls of those to whom he ministered by leading them into a relationship with God. With considerable detail, Trent laid down the form of the seminaries, how they should be funded, what should be taught, and how the students should be examined for promotion and ordination. We have, once again, returned to personal reform as the heart of the matter.

Trent also discussed top-down reform because, as another decree on reform put it, the entire family of the church would be in trouble "if what is required from the body is not found in the head." The delegates therefore devoted a long section to the bishop as the key agent of reform, directing the bishop to root out vices (especially simony, nepotism, and concubinage), implement change, and correct abuses in regular meetings of provincial and diocesan synods. The bishop was essentially to reach back to some of the Gregorian Revolution's goals for clerical behavior, but at Trent he was also charged with making sure the body of the church was healthy, too. It was the bishop's job particularly to make sure his people knew their faith.

> So that the faithful people may approach the reception of the sacraments with greater reverence and spiritual devotion, the holy council charges bishops not only to explain their power and benefit in a way that those receiving can grasp, before they themselves administer them to the people; but to ensure

that the same is done by all parish priests with devotion and wisdom, even in the vernacular tongue, where there is need and it can reasonably be done; and this is to be done according to the form laid down by the holy council for each sacrament, which bishops should take steps to have accurately translated into the vernacular and explained to the people by all parish priests. Similarly, during mass or the celebration of office on every feast or solemnity they should explain the divine commandments and precepts of salvation in the vernacular, and should be zealous to implant them in the hearts of all (leaving aside useless questions) and educate them in the law of the Lord.

Trent's expression of the bishop's role as reformer reminds us that episcopal reform operates not simply as top-down or bottom-up reform. Bishops work through the middle of the church. Because so many bishops were present at Trent and took part in the deliberations, they had a large stake in implementing reform. The bishop's role as defined by Trent is a good example of *reformatio in capite* meeting *reformatio in membris*.

Some judge Trent to have been reactive and unimaginative. This assessment ignores several ways in which this council, while defensive and backward-looking at times, was also innovative and progressive. The stress on preaching in the vernacular provides one example, especially since Luther and other Protestant reformers had made a big issue of reading the Bible and celebrating the liturgy in the people's own language. Trent kept indulgences, but abolished the title of alms collector (*questor,* which was Tetzel's designation). When Trent discussed the importance of tradition in addition to scripture, it also allowed translations of the Bible, provided they were authorized. There was even some discussion that mass should be celebrated in the vernacular, an idea that was judged favorably. The delegates agreed, however, that it would be too abrupt a change and, given the Protestant switch to vernacular liturgies, it might confuse Catholics already baffled by a heady half-century of reform.

# Perspectives

There are several lessons the history of reform teaches from Avignon through Trent. First, at least some members of the Catholic church realized the necessity of reform. Catholics, particularly in the body of the church, were not blind to her faults, but they often lacked the institutional support to make systemic changes. Second, we have discovered change is a process that predated Luther and, as we will see in the next chapter, took centuries to be put into place. Third, both Catholics and Protestants had many ideas of reform that could disagree not only along the Catholic-Protestant divide, but within each group. For instance, the Anabaptists believed if the Bible did not specifically *commend* doctrine or worship, it was *forbidden;* for Luther, if the Bible did not specifically *condemn* doctrine or worship, it was *permitted.* Fourth, self-reflection is necessary for growth, but climate and timing are also important. The *devotio moderna* was generally tolerated, but Erasmus was distrusted by both sides. The ideas of the *Consilium* were helpful, but once Luther printed a German translation with his comments, the reformers' calls were left unheeded.

This long view of reform has also illustrated that popes during the fifteenth century were busy recovering from the conciliarist challenge and, in the early sixteenth century, fighting off the Protestant denial of the papal office itself. Popes and councils, which had worked together during the High Middle Ages but were often at odds after 1300, made a recovery at Trent. Popes took very different approaches to the Protestant challenges: offensive and defensive, proactive and reactive, reaching out and closing down. Paul III (1534–49) and Paul IV (1555–59) stand in sharp contrast to each other. Paul III took a proactive, optimistic approach; he was not afraid to engage cutting-edge religious orders, such as the Jesuits, and take on new tasks, like "New World" missions. Paul IV was a reactive, intransigent, and repressive pope who considered creativity "dangerous innovation" and placed every one of Erasmus's works on his list of forbidden books. Paul IV tried to restore papal monarchy and may be seen as the champion of a reformation that was genuinely "counter." A recent history of the papacy identified these two popes as embodying "a dialectic of reform—creativity versus conservation."[59]

The mixed success and approaches of papal leadership in reform certainly did not stop attempts at reform in the church's body. What occurred while the popes failed to direct reform from the top was a revival *in membris* of reform's patristic foundations: self-reform that was personal, active, gradual, constant, and purgative. Hubert Jedin, who offered the first honest appraisal of Catholic reform from the long perspective of the late Middle Ages, saw the Protestant challenges as the result of rising, not lowered, expectations among Christians *in membris*. Certainly the *devotio moderna* provides a good example of this personal reform, influencing as it did a variety of humanist reformers, among them both Erasmus and Luther. The *devotio moderna* movement also supported interiority among the laity who were particularly attracted to a spirituality based on the imitation of Christ. The same may be said for diocesan priests and bishops who, with mixed success, held local synods during the fifteenth century to treat reform, especially of pastoral care. These bishops foreshadowed Trent's renewal of the episcopal office and its pastoral oversight.

Still, the history of reform explored so far also indicates head and members must reform together. Since they did not, their successes were neither complete nor lasting. Because there was no comprehensive reform coordinated in the church's body by her head, a reformer such as Luther became an inevitability. It was a matter of when, not if.

Finally, this chapter's review of reform (ca. 1300–1600) points to an important continuity in Catholic reform: Tridentine-like personal reform rose from the church's body up to her head before Luther.[60] There were honest self-critiques, but these attempts at reform, at least *in capite,* were generally stunted. While a fair amount of work has been done to find forerunners of the Protestant reformations, it may be time to explore more fully the idea of forerunners (however failed) of the Catholic reformations.

Not every Catholic reformer before the Protestants presented a program that looked to the Protestant solutions, although the writings of a good number of fourteenth- and fifteenth-century Catholic reformers were placed on the *Index of Forbidden Books* after Trent simply because they discussed reform. Many were considered proto-Lutherans, though the programs they advocated had more in common with the Council of Trent than the monk from Wittenberg. Historians have increasingly been tracing the continuities, rather than the discontinuities, among Catholic reformers of the late Middle Ages and sixteenth century. These we may call proto-Catholic reformers, proto-counter reformers, or proto-Tridentine reformers, depending on which phrase eventually dominates the conversation.[61]

Admittedly it may seem odd to talk about late medieval "counter" reformers before they had a Protestant movement against which to react, but there are already precedents. Clarissa W. Atkinson discovered that Margery Kempe's modern editor Hope Emily Allen in private correspondence frequently identified Kempe (ca. 1373–1440) as a "fifteenth-century counter reformer" against Lollardy. *Devotio moderna* scholar John Van Engen similarly noted of his subject, "If they were 'forerunners' of any later developments at all, the closest links may well be to certain aspects of the Counter-Reformation."[62]

Personal reform was an important theme among some high-level church officials before Luther, too. The German humanist Nicholas of Cusa (1401–64) turned from the failure of his reform mission as a papal legate (1451–52) to a *reformatio in membris* during his time as diocesan bishop of Brixen (1452–60). His *Reformatio generalis,* written about the end of this period (1459) outlines a reform of the curia *in capite* and his *De concordantia catholica* (1432–33) mentions a top-down reform. But Cusa also indicated in the *Reformatio generalis* and several sermons that the pope as a faithful, individual Christian must undergo a personal reform even while he serves the church as Christ's vicar. In the *Reformatio generalis,* Cusa described the pope as "most high and holy in dignity," but he added he is at the same time "like other men, sinful and infirm." Gasparo Contarini, one of the authors of the *Consilium,* as early as 1517 advocated personal reform as the starting point for wider reform efforts when discussing bishops' duties.[63]

A fruitful line of inquiry may be to pay more attention to how Trent's focus on personal reform within structural reform was prefigured by Catholic writers before Luther. At least some of these late medieval Catholic reformers, in the end, may have been more in line with Trent's evolutionary idea of reform than some of the Protestants' more radical and revolutionary proposals.

## NOTES

1. Among Protestant scholars looking at forerunners to Luther, Heiko Oberman has led the way in finding continuities before and after the *95 Theses:* see principally Oberman, *The Harvest of Medieval Theology: Gabriel Biel and Late Medieval Nominalism* (Cambridge Mass.: Harvard University Press, 1963) and *Forerunners of the Reformation: The Shape of Late Medieval Thought* (New York: Holt, Rinehart, and Winston, 1966). Oberman declared the idea of discontinuity to be "a tool for apologetics": *Forerunners,* p. 34. Erika Rummel traces several of these issues in "Voices of Reform from Hus to Erasmus," in *Handbook of European History 1400–1600: Late Middle Ages, Renaissance and Reformation,* vol. 2, *Visions, Programs and Outcomes,* eds. Thomas A. Brady, Jr., Heiko A. Oberman, and James D. Tracy (Leiden: E. J. Brill, 1995), pp. 61–91.

2. Quoted in *Readings in Western Civilization,* vol. 4, *Medieval Europe,* eds. Julius Kirshner and Karl F. Morrison (Chicago: University of Chicago Press, 1986), pp. 427–28.

3. The clearest statement of this principle is found in a sermon from the Council of Constance and the council's most famous decree, *Haec sancta,* based on it: C. M. D. Crowder, ed., *Unity, Heresy and Reform, 1378–1460: The Conciliar Response to the Great Schism* (New York: St. Martin's Press, 1977), pp. 76–83. Pope Pius II (1458–64), ironically a former conciliarist, explicitly condemned the principle of conciliarism in his bull *Execrabilis:* Crowder, *Unity, Heresy and Reform,* pp. 179–81.

4. John "XXIII" is correct. He was deposed at the Council of Constance in 1415, which effectively wiped him off the papal lists as an official pope. This papal name was considered dead. When Cardinal Angelo Roncalli famously said, "I will be called John" at the conclave to elect Pius XII's successor in 1958, his choice of name was taken as the first sign of his unexpected independence.

5. These three major agenda items are discussed in Crowder, *Unity, Heresy and Reform,* pp. 11–24, with translated texts at pp. 65–138. Faith and heresy were largely directed toward the trial, condemnation, and execution of Jan Hus, whose complaints about the church contained elements of a reform program. Hus may have been the victim of a council eager to decide on matters of faith in the pope's absence, thereby employing the principles of conciliarism to prove that a general council and not the pope was the church's ultimate authority. For Hus's

trial and execution, see Matthew Spinka, trans., *Jan Hus at the Council of Constance* (New York: Columbia University Press, 1965).

6. Phillip H. Stump, *The Reforms of the Council of Constance (1414–1418)* (Leiden: E. J. Brill, 1994), p. 138. Many of the reform ideas that competed at Constance provided a rich heritage from which later reformers, especially at Trent, drew.

7. Stump, *The Reforms of the Council of Constance,* pp. 16–48, 56–145, 149–52, 168–69, and 188–93 with the text of the proposals at pp. 345–49, 358–59, 363–67, and 370. See also Phillip H. Stump, "The Reform of Papal Taxation at the Council of Constance (1414–1418)," *Speculum* 64 (1989): pp. 69–105.

8. Jürgen Miethke, "Kirchenreform auf den Konzilien des 15. Jahrhunderts: Motive—Methoden—Wirkungen," in *Studien zum 15. Jahrhundert,* eds. Johannes Helmarth and Heribert Müller, 2 vols. (Munich: Oldenbourg, 1994), vol. 2, pp. 16–22, 39–42; Johannes Helmrath, "Reform als Thema der Konzilien des Spätmittelalters," in *Christian Unity: The Council of Ferrara-Florence 1438/39–1989,* ed. Giuseppe Alberigo (Leuven: Leuven University Press, 1991), pp. 75–152; Gerald Christianson, "Annates and Reform at the Council of Basel," in *Reform and Renewal in the Middle Ages and the Renaissance,* eds. Thomas M. Izbicki and Christopher M. Bellitto (Leiden: E. J. Brill, 2000), pp. 198–202; Stump, *The Reforms of the Council of Constance,* pp. 239–45; Francis Oakley, *The Western Church in the Later Middle Ages* (Ithaca: Cornell University Press, 1979), pp. 219–31.

9. Gerald Strauss, "Ideas of *Reformatio* and *Renovatio* from the Middle Ages to the Reformation," in Brady, Oberman, and Tracy, *Handbook of European History 1400–1600,* vol. 2, pp. 3–4, 12–13.

10. Giles Constable, "Twelfth-Century Spirituality and the Late Middle Ages," *Medieval and Renaissance Studies* 5 (1971): pp. 27–60, and "The Popularity of Twelfth-Century Spiritual Writers in the Late Middle Ages," in *Renaissance Studies in Honor of Hans Baron,* eds. Anthony Molho and John A. Tedeschi (Dekalb Ill.: Northern Illinois University Press, 1971), pp. 5–28.

11. For a summary of late medieval spirituality, see the following syntheses in Jill Raitt, ed., *Christian Spirituality: High Middle Ages and Reformation* (New York: Crossroad, 1987): Richard Kieckhefer, "Major Currents in Late Medieval Devotion," pp. 75–108; Alois Maria Haas, "Schools of Late Medieval Mysticism," pp. 140–75; Ewert Cousins,

"The Humanity and the Passion of Christ," pp. 375–91. See also Oakley, *The Western Church in the Later Middle Ages,* pp. 82–100.

12. On these *imitatio Christi* texts as used by preachers and spiritual directors to guide personal reform, see Lawrence F. Hundersmarck, "Preaching the Passion: Late Medieval 'Lives of Christ' as Sermon Vehicles," in *De Ore Domini: Preacher and Word in the Middle Ages,* eds. Thomas L. Amos, Eugene A. Green, and Beverly Mayne Kienzle (Kalamazoo Mich.: Medieval Institute Publications, 1989), pp. 147–67, and "Reforming Life by Conforming It to the Life of Christ: Pseudo-Bonaventure's *Meditaciones Vitae Christi,*" in Izbicki and Bellitto, *Reform and Renewal in the Middle Ages and the Renaissance,* pp. 93–112.

13. John F. D'Amico, "Humanism and Pre-Reformation Theology," in *Renaissance Humanism: Foundations, Forms, and Legacy,* 3 vols., ed. Albert Rabil, Jr. (Philadelphia: University of Pennsylvania Press, 1988), vol. 3, pp. 349–79, especially p. 366: "In general, humanist reform thought emphasized personal amelioration rather than institutional change." See also Oakley, *The Western Church in the Later Middle Ages,* pp. 252–59.

14. For the history, spirituality, and documents of the *devotio moderna,* see John Van Engen, trans., *Devotio Moderna: Basic Writings* (New York: Paulist Press, 1988), on which this section relies for examples and quotations. See also Otto Gründler, *"Devotio Moderna,"* in Raitt, *Christian Spirituality: High Middle Ages and Reformation,* pp. 176–93.

15. Nikolaus Staubach details the movement's libraries, translations, themes, and reading programs in *"Memores pristinae perfectionis.* The Importance of the Church Fathers for *Devotio Moderna,"* in *The Reception of the Church Fathers in the West,* 2 vols., ed. Irena Backus (Leiden: E. J. Brill, 1997), vol. 1, pp. 405–69. On the importance of Carthusian spirituality for Grote, see Otto Gründler, *"Devotio Moderna Atque Antiqua:* The Modern Devotion and Carthusian Spirituality," in *The Spirituality of Western Christendom,* vol. 2, *The Roots of the Modern Christian Tradition,* ed. E. Rozanne Elder (Kalamazoo Mich.: Cistercian Publications, 1984), pp. 27–45.

16. Gründler believes it is this move from complete isolation to involvement in works of charity and mercy that made the movement "modern": *"Devotio Moderna,"* p. 190. However, this move may be modern only if the similar Franciscan efforts that arose nearly two centuries earlier are also considered modern.

17. On Thomas à Kempis (1380–1471) as the alleged author, see Van Engen, *Devotio Moderna: Basic Writings*, pp. 8–10, especially n. 5. Giles Constable offers a comprehensive portrait of *imitatio Christi* piety in *Three Studies in Medieval Religious and Social Thought* (Cambridge: Cambridge University Press, 1995), pp. 145–248.

18. Edward Peters, ed., *Heresy and Authority in Medieval Europe* (Philadelphia: University of Pennsylvania Press, 1980), pp. 265–307; Matthew Spinka, ed., *Advocates of Reform: From Wyclif to Hus* (Philadelphia: Westminster Press, 1953), pp. 21–88 and 187–278.

19. John Van Engen, "Late Medieval Anticlericalism: The Case of the New Devout," in *Anticlericalism in Late Medieval and Early Modern Europe*, eds. Peter A. Dykema and Heiko A. Oberman (Leiden: E. J. Brill, 1993), pp. 19–30, with quotation on p. 29.

20. Carter Lindberg, *The European Reformations* (Oxford: Basil Blackwell, 1996), p. 61.

21. Oakley, *The Western Church in the Later Middle Ages*, pp. 113–30; Lawrence G. Duggan, "The Unresponsiveness of the Late Medieval Church: A Reconsideration," *SCJ* 9 (1978): pp. 3–26.

22. Quoted in Strauss, "Ideas of *Reformatio and Renovatio*," p. 18. A judicious evaluation of Luther as an individual man and not a cultural icon is provided by Heiko A. Oberman, *Luther: Man Between God and the Devil*, trans. Eileen Walliser-Schwarzbart (New Haven: Yale University Press, 1989).

23. *LW*, vol. 31, pp. 25–33. It is not widely known that Luther the next year expounded at great length on his very brief propositions to answer charges of heresy: *Explanations of the Ninety-Five Theses or Explanations of the Disputation Concerning the Value of Indulgences: LW*, vol. 31, pp. 83–252.

24. *LW*, vol. 44, pp. 123–217.

25. *LW*, vol. 44, p. 154.

26. *LW*, vol. 36, pp. 11–126.

27. Jaroslav Pelikan, an historian of dogma, critiques the approach and principles Luther took in this pamphlet: "Renewal of Structure Versus Renewal by the Spirit," in *Theology of Renewal*, vol. 2, *Renewal of Religious Structures*, ed. L. K. Shook (New York: Herder and Herder, 1968), pp. 21–41. Susan C. Karant-Nunn explores how Protestant reformers attempted to correct Catholic practices that had devolved into superstitions by replacing or refreshing them with rituals from the early church. This process, she concludes, restored a bareness of

ritual, liturgy, and devotions that produced discipline within Protestant communities, but also a more remote experience of God: *The Reformation of Ritual: An Interpretation of Early Modern Germany* (London: Routledge, 1997), especially pp. 190–201.

28. *LW,* vol. 44, pp. 175–79.

29. *LW,* vol. 44, pp. 141–43, 169–72, 180–83.

30. *LW,* vol. 31, pp. 333–77.

31. *LW,* vol. 31, pp. 372–74.

32. *LW,* vol. 51, pp. 70–100; Lindberg, *The European Reformations,* pp. 91–110.

33. *LW,* vol. 51, pp. 72, 75–76, 77. It is ironic that the criticism Luther leveled at the earliest Protestants in terms of the rapidity and extremity of their reforms was also applied to the initial wave of Vatican II changes, especially in the liturgy.

34. William Bouwsma, *John Calvin: A Sixteenth-Century Portrait* (New York: Oxford University Press, 1988). The *Institutes* has been called the "Protestant *Summa Theologica*": E. G. Rupp, "The Reformation in Zurich, Strassburg and Geneva," in *The New Cambridge Modern History,* vol. 2, *The Reformation: 1520–1559,* 2d ed., ed. G. R. Elton (Cambridge: Cambridge University Press, 1990), p. 116. For the final edition of the *Institutes,* see John T. McNeill, ed., and Ford Lewis Battles, trans., *Calvin: Institutes of the Christian Religion,* 2 vols. (Philadelphia: Westminster Press, 1960).

35. J. K. S. Reid, trans., *Calvin: Theological Treatises* (Philadelphia: Westminster Press, 1954), pp. 26, 29–31.

36. These two texts are conveniently published one after the other in John C. Olin, ed., *A Reformation Debate: Sadoleto's Letter to the Genevans and Calvin's Reply* (Grand Rapids Mich.: Baker Book House, 1976).

37. For the details of this portrait of Geneva, see Robert M. Kingdon, "International Calvinism," in Brady, Oberman, and Tracy, *Handbook of European History,* vol. 2., pp. 229–47. The *Ecclesiastical Ordinances* are found in Reid, *Calvin: Theological Treatises,* pp. 58–71.

38. Eamon Duffy, *The Stripping of the Altars: Traditional Religion in England, c. 1400–c. 1580* (New Haven: Yale University Press, 1992) generally rebuts A. G. Dickens, *The English Reformation,* 2d ed. (University Park: University of Pennsylvania Press, 1991), who argues that the English wanted change before Henry acted, and considered Mary a throwback who needed to be thrown back.

39. Hans Hillerbrand, ed., *The Protestant Reformation* (New York: Harper Torchbooks, 1968), pp. 248–57.

40. Zwingli's opening remarks and the 67 *Articles* are in Lewis W. Spitz, ed., *The Protestant Reformation,* 3d rev. ed. (Needham Heights Mass.: Ginn Press, 1990), pp. 77–88.

41. Lindberg provides a thought-provoking discussion of the Anabaptists in *The European Reformations,* pp. 199–228.

42. This *Letter* is included in Hillerbrand, *The Protestant Reformation,* pp. 122–28. The Anabaptists also summarized their tenets in another document several years later, the *Brotherly Understanding of Some Children of God about Seven Articles,* sometimes known simply as the 7 *Articles* or the *Schleitheim Confession of Faith:* Hillerbrand, *The Protestant Reformation,* pp. 129–36.

43. For selections from the *Admonition,* see Hillerbrand, *The Protestant Reformation,* pp. 257–66.

44. The author of a recent book stated he deliberately avoided the debate in his title: R. Po-Chia Hsia, *The World of Catholic Renewal: 1540–1770* (Cambridge: Cambridge University Press, 1998). Robert Bireley placed one of the controversial terms in his subtitle: *The Refashioning of Catholicism, 1450–1770: A Reassessment of the Counter Reformation* (Washington D.C.: Catholic University of America Press, 1999).

45. William V. Hudon, "Religion and Society in Early Modern Italy: Old Questions, New Insights," *American Historical Review* 101 (1996): pp. 783–804. Eric W. Cochrane championed "Tridentine Reformation" or "Age of Consolidation" (which has not caught on): "Counter Reformation or Tridentine Reformation? Italy in the Age of Carlo Borromeo," in *San Carlo Borromeo: Catholic Reform and Ecclesiastical Politics in the Second Half of the Sixteenth Century,* eds. John M. Headley and John B. Tomaro (Washington D.C.: The Folger Shakespeare Library, 1988), pp. 31–46. See also Elisabeth G. Gleason, "Catholic Reformation, Counterreformation and Papal Reform in the Sixteenth Century," in Brady, Oberman, and Tracy, *Handbook of European History 1400–1600,* vol. 2, p. 333; and John W. O'Malley, "Catholic Reform," in *Reformation Europe: A Guide to Research,* ed. Steven Ozment (St. Louis: Center for Reformation Research, 1982), pp. 297–319, particularly its bibliography. Elsewhere, O'Malley suggested the phrase "early modern Catholicism": "Was Ignatius Loyola a Church Reformer? How to Look at Early Modern Catholicism," *CHR* 77 (1991): 177–93. He recounted the historiography of the nomenclature

debate and expanded his *apologia* for "early modern Catholicism" in *Trent and All That: Renaming Catholicism in the Early Modern Era* (Cambridge, Mass.: Harvard University Press, 2000).

46. Duggan, "The Unresponsiveness of the Late Medieval Church," p. 13.

47. James D. Tracy, *Erasmus of the Low Countries* (Berkeley: University of California Press, 1996), p. 111. Tracy studied Erasmus's reform ideas, focusing especially on their nuances (which he called "slippery" and "circumspect") and how they were used and misused by both Catholics and Protestants who claimed Erasmus foreshadowed Luther. Tracy also recounted how Erasmus tried to defend himself, while maintaining what he believed to be valid criticisms of the Roman church.

48. John C. Olin, ed., *The Catholic Reformation: Savonarola to Ignatius Loyola* (New York: Fordham University Press, 1992), pp. 79, 83.

49. John C. Olin, ed., *Catholic Reform from Cardinal Ximenes to the Council of Trent: 1495–1563* (New York: Fordham University Press, 1990), pp. 47–60. See also John W. O'Malley, *Giles of Viterbo on Church and Reform* (Leiden: E. J. Brill, 1968).

50. The *Libellus* remains untranslated but may be found in *Annales Camaldulenses* (Venice, 1773), vol. 9, cols. 612–719, with reform addressed at cols. 668–714. Jedin describes its contents in *History of the Council of Trent*, vol. 1, pp. 128–30.

51. Olin, ed., *The Catholic Reformation: Savonarola to Ignatius Loyola*, pp. 122–27.

52. Because of this, Elisabeth G. Gleason identified Paul III as the first "Counter-Reformation" pope: "Who was the First Counter-Reformation Pope?" *CHR* 81 (1995): pp. 173–84.

53. Olin, ed., *Catholic Reform from Cardinal Ximenes to the Council of Trent: 1495–1563*, pp. 65–87. Elisabeth G. Gleason judged the *Consilium* to be "backward-looking, at times downright timid," offering standard complaints, albeit in striking terms, but failing to put forward innovative solutions: "Catholic Reformation, Counterreformation and Papal Reform in the Sixteenth Century," pp. 322–24. For a different assessment, see William V. Hudon, "The *Consilium de emendanda ecclesia* and the 1555 Reform Bull of Pope Julius III: Dead Letters or Building Blocks?" in Izbicki and Bellitto, *Reform and Renewal in the Middle Ages and the Renaissance*, pp. 240–58.

54. *LW*, vol.34, pp. 235–67.

55. Jedin, *History of the Council of Trent*, vol. 2, p. 26.

56. John W. O'Malley believes the concept of aggiornamento would have been foreign to Trent: "As a matter of fact, it is hard to imagine an intellectual atmosphere in which reform through a program of bringing things up to date would have received a more startled and uncomprehending hearing": "Historical Thought and the Reform Crisis of the Early Sixteenth Century," *TS* 28 (1967): p. 537.

57. Tanner, *Decrees,* vol. 2, pp. 686–89, 714–18.

58. Tanner *Decrees,* vol. 2, pp. 744–53, 759–73, 784–96.

59. Eamon Duffy, *Saints and Sinners: A History of the Popes* (New Haven: Yale University Press, 1997), p. 169; Gleason, "Who was the First Counter-Reformation Pope?"

60. These paragraphs rely on Jedin, *History of the Council of Trent,* vol. 1, pp. 139–65.

61. Jean Gerson, a leader and conciliarist at Constance, is an example of a fifteenth-century Catholic reformer who advocated reform by using the *ecclesia primitiva* as a model, as would Protestants a century later, without necessarily foreshadowing Luther or Calvin: Louis B. Pascoe, "Jean Gerson: The *Ecclesia Primitiva* and Reform," *Traditio* 30 (1974): pp. 379–409.

62. Clarissa W. Atkinson, *Mystic and Pilgrim: The Book and World of Margery Kempe* (Ithaca: Cornell University Press, 1983), p. 105, especially n.7, and p. 151; Atkinson added the Carthusians as part of this "counter" effort. Van Engen, *Devotio Moderna: Basic Writings,* pp. 10–11.

63. For Cusa's *Reformatio generalis,* see Morimichi Watanabe and Thomas M. Izbicki, "Nicholas of Cusa: *A General Reform of the Church,*" in *Nicholas of Cusa on Christ and the Church,* eds. Gerald Christianson and Thomas M. Izbicki (Leiden: E. J. Brill, 1996), pp. 175–202 with quotation at p. 197. Elisabeth G. Gleason, *Gasparo Contarini: Venice, Rome, and Reform* (Berkeley: University of California Press, 1993), pp. 97–98, 105–7; see three related letters of Contarini in Gleason's *Reform Thought in Sixteenth-Century Italy* (Chico Calif.: Scholars Press, 1981), pp. 24–33. Scott H. Hendrix raised the issue of the extent to which personal reform is clerical reform, linking reform *in capite* with reform *in membris:* "Nicholas of Cusa's Ecclesiology Between Reform and Reformation," in Christianson and Izbicki, *Nicholas of Cusa on Christ and the Church,* pp. 122–26.

# Chapter 4
# Catholic Reform in Changing Times

The next phase in the history of reform entailed putting Trent's program of personal and pastoral reform into practice. This process took initial steps in the decades immediately following Trent's conclusion, but ultimately occurred over a long period of time and within a changing context. The church tried to achieve her reform goals in an age of unique transition as the world faced many versions of Christianity for the first time.

Factors other than religion also affected church reform in these centuries. The enlightenment and scientific revolution of early modern history (ca. 1600–1800) and the industrialization of modernity that followed (ca. 1800–1900) influenced society as a whole and religion in particular. The intellectual, social, economic, and political changes brought on by these movements significantly altered the church's reform program. New questions emerged: How should the church respond to changes that replaced the dominant Christian culture with a secular mentality? To reform herself, should the church resist those developments or embrace them?

It is important to note the Tridentine church did not at first meet these changes with her infamous (and clichéd) "siege mentality." The church was not a monolith; Trent did not build up the church's walls and raise the drawbridge.[1] The century after Trent was in fact somewhat imaginative and progressive: full of charismatic figures and new religious orders with innovative solutions. Over time, however, some in the church did fail to reform, or even consider reform necessary, by embracing new ideas and developments. In 1832, Pope Gregory XVI dismissed the very idea that the church could require reform since, he contended, she could never be deformed. But the nineteenth century also witnessed the hesitant birth pangs of certain movements, among them social Catholicism and modernism, which would become full-blown reforms only in the context of Vatican II.

Far from being a period of complete stagnation, the four centuries between Trent and Vatican II need to be revisited as a time of vibrant, bubbling, and controversial reform efforts. Especially during the nineteenth century and at the turn of the twentieth, these reform innovations, especially *in membris,* encountered some opposition *in capite* but lived to fight another day.

## The Age of Trent

### Popes and Bishops

In the immediate aftermath of the Council of Trent, the papacy reasserted its authority by taking the lead in reforming the church—another example of a top-down idea of reform. Rome wanted to institutionalize reforms *in capite* and then export them *in membris,* much as the papal monarchists had done during the High Middle Ages beginning with Pope Gregory VII in the late eleventh century. These centralized reforms were designed to trickle down to the church's body through certain institutions, such as Roman congregations led by cardinals, and materials, including catechisms, ritual books, and Bibles.

The popes after Trent directed their efforts to asserting papal authority, which had recently come under assault from Protestant, and even some Catholic reformers. Fifteenth-century popes, in particular, focused on this recovery after the conciliarist challenge at the councils of Constance and Basel-Ferrara-Florence-Rome. They largely ignored what needed correction because the papacy itself had become the object of criticism. But in the late sixteenth century, the papacy acted as the agent of reform. Of the twenty-nine popes between 1540 and 1770, nineteen were lawyers but only three were theologians, a reminder of the canon lawyers who dominated the high medieval papacy and located reform within the goal of building a papal bureaucracy. They focused on administration and married the recovery of their authority with the act of reform.[2]

Pope Pius IV (1559–65) led the implementation of Trent's reforms by approving the council's decrees. His next step had critical implications: Before doing anything else, the pope reserved the exclusive right to decide how Trent's reforms were to be implemented and understood. In practice, he appointed in 1564 a small but powerful council of cardinals, later called the Congregation on the Council. They reviewed questions about Trent's documents or new circumstances that arose that required those documents to be reinterpreted. Because of this committee, the popes effectively held reform's reins, telling most of the rest of the church how to read and apply Trent's statements.

The papacy also directed Tridentine reform by controlling the council's documents: While bishops were permitted to proclaim Trent's decrees aloud in their dioceses, they were not allowed to read Trent's working committee reports (which were not even published until the late nineteenth century). This rule prevented clergy and laity from hearing the debates, disagreements, and proposals that worked out the final forms of those decrees. The restriction succeeded to a degree in controlling Trent's interpretation and reform implementation. But it could be argued that the centralized Roman council's decisions (and the prohibition against merely reading earlier alternatives) stifled some progressive steps that would have emerged if clergy and laity had been allowed to experiment more.

In quick succession, the Tridentine popes issued reform documents so all Catholic dioceses would be, quite literally, on the same page: a profession of faith (1564), a catechism (1566), a breviary (1568), a missal (1570), and a revised Vulgate Bible (1593). Historian Elisabeth G. Gleason observed: "That almost all these works contained the word 'Roman' in their titles underlined that Rome was the nerve center of the Catholic church."[3] Pope Sixtus V (1585–90) reorganized the curia into fifteen congregations to oversee temporal and spiritual matters. Among these were congregations to examine doctrine, oversee rites, produce the *Index of Forbidden Books,* control printing, and supervise prelates, clergy, and religious orders.

Tridentine popes acted as more than administrators in implementing Trent's reforms: They worked to stress the papacy's link with Christianity's roots. They may have done this to counter Protestant charges that the papacy, curia, and college of cardinals were innovations that were not found in the early church. Tridentine popes wanted to demonstrate the continuity of sixteenth-century Catholicism with first-century Christianity out of which, Rome asserted, it had developed authentically.

Under Sixtus V, for example, the pope celebrated Lenten liturgies in Rome's oldest churches, places where those liturgies had first been observed. In his Ash Wednesday address in 1587 before the pope, a Franciscan preacher praised the ties between early and sixteenth-century Christianity in Rome:

> We see the venerable beauty renewed, that form of the stations reinstated; in this we see restored the most illustrious discipline of the primitive church.... O blessed are we, we who behold today living and breathing that ancient form of the church![4]

Popes also used the early church to strengthen their authority and respond to Protestant challenges to the papacy itself. Sixtus V continued the rebuilding of St. Peter's Basilica, whose very name proclaimed papal authority, on a massive scale. Paul V (1605–21) added a longer nave to the basilica, which Urban VIII (1623–44) finally consecrated in 1626. Bernini aided the effort by centering the eye on Peter's tomb—the iconographic foundation of papal authority—with his towering altar balcony and by providing a physical "chair of St. Peter" in the apse behind the main altar.[5]

While the popes directed reform from Rome, it fell to the bishops to implement reform on the local level. Trent identified diocesan bishops as the key agents of reform, serving as the connective tissue between the church *in capite* and *in membris*. Carlo Borromeo (1538–84), the archbishop of Milan, is often cited as the model bishop for putting Trent into practice in his home diocese.

Borromeo was nephew to Pius IV, but even though his uncle made him a cardinal in his early twenties, Borromeo was not a useless creature of nepotism. Energetic and well trained, Borromeo backed Pius IV's Tridentine program. He worked behind the scenes at Trent, especially concerning the creation of seminaries and the discussions that led to reforming the missal, breviary, liturgy, music, and the catechism. As archbishop of Milan, the twenty-seven-year-old Borromeo was perfectly placed to implement the Tridentine decrees he had helped formulate.

Borromeo went to Milan as its first resident bishop in eighty years and personally moved from luxury to poverty. Though a cardinal, he dressed and signed his name as a bishop. Borromeo selected several issues on which to focus. First, he created a seminary to train the clergy in mind and spirit, as Trent directed, and made sure pastors lived in their parishes and held only one office charged with the care of souls. Second, he took his role as chief shepherd of his diocesan flock seriously and visited many parishes himself. Third, he reorganized the diocesan administration, mirroring on the local level the centralization above him in the papal curia. He especially relied on local synods to gather together clergy with common problems. Fourth, he devoted great energy to teaching the laity, especially children, by leading religious education classes each Sunday.

Borromeo became known as such a model shepherd that many fellow bishops wrote him for advice on specific matters in their own dioceses. The demand for precedents proved so strong that Borromeo had to print six thousand copies of the decrees from his first provincial synod at Milan. Because of this voluminous correspondence and careful record keeping, Borromeo left a very practical paper trail, and this in accessible Italian, for bishops to use as a guide.[6]

Beyond the well-documented example of Borromeo, scholars have researched how and to what degree Trent took root on the local level after the council ended and Rome published its core documents. One such study examined the diocese of Perugia (ca. 1560–1630), where bishops took a leading role in printing materials to teach the faith and support reform. They tried to train good preachers and teachers; they wanted priests to support one another; they facilitated an active piety among the laity by repairing and building hospitals, schools, and churches.[7] All of these reform attempts met with mixed success, but even the failures bear testimony to explicit, overt, and intentional efforts to reform the church under episcopal leadership.

But the major initiative of Trent, building seminaries, took only hesitant steps. Schools were established in Rome, but this is not surprising. Gregory XIII (1572–85) established the English College and heavily supported the Roman College (renamed the Gregorian University for his patronage) and the German College. On the diocesan level, Perugia's seminary, which began functioning in 1564, less than a year after Trent concluded, became a standard, especially in terms of its academic reputation and library. In other dioceses, however, seminaries emerged slowly and with considerably mixed success. It took more than a century before Trent's decrees had a tangible, lasting impact, and this after very slow progress and some failed attempts due to lack of funding, enthusiasm, and other factors. In Italy, for instance, not even half of the dioceses set up seminaries in the sixteenth century, and the seventeenth century did not see many more. Trent's crucial reform goal—providing priests trained carefully in faith and reason so they could lead their parishioners to their own personal conversions—met short-term failure and only slow, long-term success.[8]

## Spanish Reformers

While the Tridentine church reformed *in capite,* individuals were already reforming themselves *in membris.* Three Spanish mystics illustrate how attempts at personal reform led to revitalizing existing religious orders and inventing new ones.

Spain had long been a vibrant area of spirituality, given the long occupation of the Iberian peninsula by the Moslems and the sometimes contentious mix of Islam, Judaism, and Christianity that distinguished Spanish territories. After Trent, the Spanish royal families took a leading role in implementing its reform plans by continuing the core Christian mission of reinvigorating souls. Philip II (1556–98) militantly put Trent into practice in his territories. He saw the monarchy taking a leading role, even over the episcopacy, in combating heresy. In 1565, Philip ordered the Spanish bishops to call councils and begin applying Trent's reforms. He named every bishop, prelate, and head of religious orders in his territories. Over the objections of the Council of Trent itself, Philip refused to release the Dominican archbishop of Toledo Bartolomé Carranza, who had been arrested by the Inquisition in 1559, even though the prelate had participated at Trent, worked with Cardinal Pole, and composed a Spanish catechism.

While Philip directed Tridentine reform from the top of the Spanish political and religious hierarchy, Teresa of Avila (1515–82), John of the Cross (1542–91), and Ignatius Loyola (1491–1556)—three mystics whose lives spanned the initial Tridentine period—influenced reform on the local level.

Teresa of Avila led a comfortable life as a Carmelite nun for twenty years in an important, nearly luxurious convent before undergoing a personal conversion experience. She recorded her insights about the spiritual journey in the famous *Interior Castle* (1577), which noted that personal conversion comes in stages: an unsteady process full of both consolation and desolation. The Spanish tradition of a mystical spirituality based on purgation, interiority, and a return to original sources influenced Teresa's concept of personal conversion.[9] Her personal *metanoia* led her to apply her inner reform to her order. This attempt to reinvigorate the Carmelites consumed the next twenty years of her life. Teresa laid this reform out in 1560; two years later, she formed with some companions a reformed branch, the Discalced Carmelites, based on an austere return to her order's basics. Within five years, the reform began to spread to other houses.

John of the Cross met Teresa in 1567 and joined her in reforming the Carmelites, even though he had contemplated entering the rigorous Carthusian order. He agreed that spiritual conversion entailed ecstasy and great pain, describing the latter as his dark night of the soul. Their ideas, however, met with opposition and intervention from bishops and even kings, especially concerning jurisdiction and oversight. By 1575, the Carmelites decided to halt the Discalced reforms. Two years later, John of the Cross was physically taken to Toledo blindfolded and ordered to renounce the reform. He refused and was jailed in a Carmelite monastery's six-by-ten-foot cell with barely any sunlight from its two-inch-wide window and only bread and water for sustenance. He escaped after nine months.

Teresa and John came under suspicion of heresy and innovation, in part, because of the reform climate in Spain. John's mysticism especially raised questions: Was he a Lutheran who emphasized the inner path of conscience over the outer form of authority? With a history of inquisition and heresy, Spanish religious and political authorities were quick to suspect any movement that seemed to deviate from orthodoxy. Though Tridentine reformers understood spiritual renewal of orders would aid larger reform agendas, it eventually took a papal decree from Gregory XIII in 1580 to allow the Discalced Carmelites to exist legally and govern themselves.[10]

As Teresa of Avila and John of the Cross reformed an existing religious order, Ignatius Loyola created a new one for the changing times. His *Spiritual Exercises* embody a program of personal reform and decision making. By contemplating certain scenes from Christ's life and particular religious themes for about thirty days (or four unequal "weeks"), the retreatant comes to an understanding of God's unique plan for him and then makes a conscious choice—or "election"—to follow that plan. Ignatius described the choice as one that tied personal reform with service.

> In every good election insofar as it depends on us, the eye of our intention ought to be single. I ought to focus only on the purpose for which I was created, to praise God our Lord and to save my soul....

Therefore nothing whatever ought to move me to choose such means or deprive myself of them, except one alone, the service and praise of God our Lord and the eternal salvation of my soul.

This election he applied not only to major changes of life, such as the decision to marry or enter a religious order, but also to the daily practice of personal conversion and Christian service that brings one closer to God: "For everyone ought to reflect that in all spiritual matters, the more one divests oneself of self-love, self-will, and self-interests, the more progress one will make."[11]

The form and content of Ignatius's *Exercises* mirror many reform ideas that had their roots in the patristic period and that recurred throughout the Middle Ages and the period surrounding Trent. Ignatius's emphasis on personal conversion recalls the *metanoia* at the core of the monastic experience. His concept of good and evil spirits being at war with each other echoed elements of personal reform common to numerous writers. Ignatius implicitly drew on the positive, optimistic humanism of the Twelfth-Century Renaissance and its late medieval resurgence to champion what human beings could do to participate in God's reforming work of salvation for them. These facts mark the *Exercises* as a critical moment in the history of reform where core traditions were rejuvenated to push Catholicism's renewal forward.[12]

Ignatius did not establish his Society of Jesus to fight Luther and Calvin, although Jesuits ended up doing just that, among other tasks. At least initially, Jesuits did not see themselves as systematic reformers so much as a band of priests devoted to helping souls. Ignatius's apostolate of personal conversion ran parallel to much sixteenth-century reform, but at a vital juncture turned perpendicular. His inside-out reform met top-down efforts once he and his companions placed themselves, through their famous fourth vow, at the disposal of the pope. Especially at Trent, the Jesuit idea of personal reform intersected with the institutional church's program. Ignatius wanted his order to serve the needs of the time; during his life, that need happened to be implementing Trent's reforms and countering Protestantism.[13]

At a fortuitous moment for the council, the order, and the church, Ignatius's concern with personal conversion came together with Trent's reform schema. The Jesuits had a specific impact on the reform of priests, but this did not exclude others. When Ignatius said his goal was to help souls, he did not specify that they must be clergy. However, although laypeople were attracted to the *Exercises* in its full thirty-day as well as shorter adapted forms, priests and members of religious orders made the Jesuit retreat more than any other group. After Jesuits participated in drafting Trent's legislation on seminaries, Jesuits built and staffed the first seminaries and colleges to train priests. Their contemporaries regarded Jesuits as "reformed priests" who offered personal models for the laity, and especially the clergy, to follow.[14]

## Priests, Nuns, and Laity

In addition to the reformed branch of Discalced Carmelites and the new Society of Jesus, innovators created other religious orders in the age of Trent to meet reform challenges creatively and bring them to laypeople. So important were original orders that half of all the saints named between 1540 and 1770 were founders and members of these new orders—a sign that the church wanted to recognize and literally canonize their directions.

This movement *in membris* began with reformed priests who, like the Jesuits, placed their own spiritual houses in order so they could help parishioners do the same. Other new orders, especially female congregations like the Ursulines, used education as a tool to promote personal reform. Their efforts were more systematic and organized than any other the institutional church had attempted. Finally, the laity often formed themselves into groups called confraternities to support their own inner conversion and outer service.

Even before the popes called the Council of Trent, priests knew they needed to band together and make improvements. Many believed that renewing the church did not require a break from Catholicism and chose to reform from within. Principal among them was a group of priests known as the Theatines. Formed in

Rome in 1524, they dedicated themselves to a level of austere spirituality traditionally reserved for cloistered or mendicant religious orders, but lived their vocations as parish priests. Like others before them, they turned to the *ecclesia primitiva* for examples to re-create. These "clerks regular" found their reform model in a collection of priests who lived something of a common life in Augustine's diocese of Hippo in North Africa in the early fifth century.

Theatine spirituality echoes some of the earliest elements of personal reform: humility, obedience, self-denial. The Theatines lived these virtues in the context of the *imitatio Christi,* the hallmark of late medieval spirituality that reminded Christians, cleric and lay, they were made in the *imago Dei.* Their influence as model reformed priests grew in the seventeenth century: A good number of Theatines were made bishops and missionaries who spread the group's reform goals among priests and laity.[15]

While the Theatines and others had a great impact on priestly formation, orders of religious women represented a key link between the institutional church's reform goals and their implementation among the laity. Many new female orders were created as part of the innovative reform climate of sixteenth century Catholicism, perhaps none so exemplary as the Ursulines. Angela Merici (1470–1540) established the order in 1532 and repeatedly fought attempts to enclose her group in the traditional cloister. The Ursulines, like other innovative groups of women trying to adapt to changing times, were especially challenged by Trent's order to seal off all religious communities of women, all third orders, and all convents with prior exemptions. Enclosure promoted interiority and mysticism for those who accepted the cloister, but other groups felt called to apostolic service and resisted the requirement. Influenced by the Jesuit model, the Ursulines wanted to live a very active spiritual life. The order embraced regular members and lay affiliates, some of whom lived outside a community with families. The Ursulines cared for widows, orphans, the ill, prostitutes, and the poor.

Many religious orders selected education as their key arena for reforming the church *in membris*. The Jesuits, for example, believed that if they educated an elite corps of young men who would then become leaders in society, this cluster of laity would bring their vocation and values to their work and those they oversaw. This goal underlies the motto: *puerilis institutio renovatio mundi*—the education of young men [leads to] the renewal of the world. For their part, Ursulines and other orders ensured that young women also received an education. The Ursulines believed young girls would be the primary teachers of religious knowledge in their homes as mothers. Nuns dedicated themselves to academic, vocational, and religious education, using vernacular catechisms for the latter. In fact, the reform bishop Carlo Borromeo specifically brought the Ursulines into Milan to teach because of their excellent reputation in education.

These educational efforts, especially by nuns dedicated to teaching girls, proved a major force for reform *in membris*. One historian has identified a direct correlation: Where Christians, especially laywomen, were educated in the faith, reform flourished. Educated nuns and priests taught personal reform, offering their own lives as examples. They produced an educated laity, which, in turn, was often an active laity. The earliest confraternities of Christian doctrine not only taught lay men and women, but also enlisted them as teachers once they had been trained.[16]

The laity, on its part, embraced education and practiced a lively faith. Preached missions drew huge crowds to penance, eucharistic adoration, and other traditional devotions, which the Catholic laity championed despite, or perhaps because of, the Protestant challenge to them. Catholics increasingly received communion (in some places even monthly), were confirmed, and celebrated their marriages sacramentally. Devotions emphasized personal conversion, sin, and repentance. Sodalities devoted to Mary celebrated an aspect of Roman piety Protestants had criticized. The Society for the Veneration of the Holy Sacrament was established in 1554 at a Jesuit college in Naples with Ignatius's specific approval. Members regularly confessed their sins, received the eucharist once every two weeks, and served the poor. One of the Society's rules explicitly invokes reform: the members had to promise to "reform oneself each day, giving a good example and edification to others." The hope was like the Ursulines': Young people would imbibe these devotions and then pass them on in their own homes when they became parents.[17]

Laypeople in the age of Trent also turned to parishes and confraternities to organize their personal reform and direct it toward pastoral service. The confraternity sometimes competed with the parish for a layperson's money, energy, and allegiance. They could be organized around a particular devotion (the Sacred Heart of Jesus), social-economic activity (helping prostitutes), or education (teaching religion to poor children or adults). There were all types: open and closed, clerical and lay, male and female, aristocratic and artisan.[18]

The laity appears to have responded well to the invitation and opportunity to become more involved in their own reform, as they had done in the years before Luther when the institutional church stumbled *in capite* during the Avignon Papacy, Great Schism, and conciliar period. The Spanish pumped money into publishing spiritual materials for these eager masses. Between 1500 and 1670, one out of every two books published in Spain concerned religion. Were they read and assimilated? One investigation revealed that in 1590, 68 percent of the Christians questioned knew the *Pater Noster, Ave Maria, Salve Regina,* Creed, and Ten Commandments. By the early decades of the seventeenth century, that percentage climbed to 82 percent including, remarkably, nearly three out of every four peasants asked to recite these prayers and statements.[19] Tridentine reform was bubbling up and trickling down.

## Encountering Modernity: 1700–1900

Catholicism's reform program was daunting enough in the best circumstances, but the centuries after Trent saw massive paradigm shifts in the way people thought about government, science, religion, economics, and social classes. Europe exploded and imploded several times during the early modern period, the "New

World" came into its own, and African and Asian cultures struggled to maintain their identities while being colonized. Christianity had to adapt to all of these outward changes while dealing with Trent's impact and the reformations' multiple legacies.

These innovative movements, which had a dramatic impact on the history of religious reform, can be gathered under the rubric "liberalism"—but not in the sense of "liberal" or "conservative" politicians today. Early modern liberalism was the general idea that human beings should be free (from the Latin adjective *liber* and noun *libertas*) from any control. This concept led to *laissez-faire* economics, which limited government intervention in the economy and, in politics, to self-determination that resulted in constitutional republics. Liberalism also opened the world of science and mathematics to human ingenuity. No longer would people be content to attribute the movement of the heavens or the workings of the human body merely to God. Building on medieval advances in anatomy and astronomy, early modern scientists opened the universe to scientific study.

In terms of religion, this tended to split into two directions: toward atheism, a new option almost entirely unheard of before the reformations, or toward an affective, emotional practice of the faith as a reaction against science and even sometimes theology. Some of the faithful tried to marry the social, economic, and political activism that liberalism created with religion, producing an important movement known as social Catholicism. The career and writings of John Henry Newman allow us to see where Catholicism stood in its embrace and rejection of early modern developments and their impact on religion. Finally, the disparate intellectual ideas grouped under the term *modernism* permit insights into how the church at first rejected reforms she would later embrace.

Most would not view these four items—romanticism, social Catholicism, Newman's ideas, and modernism—as reform movements. But when seen from the long view of the past from which they emerged and the future they helped form, they reveal themselves as important steps toward the spirituality, activism, theology, ecclesiology, and intellectual ideas that ultimately shaped Vatican II.

## Romanticism

Romanticism was a reaction against the scientific revolution and enlightenment. It was an attempt to rehabilitate religion, to prove it worthy of intellectuals' interest. During the seventeenth and eighteenth centuries, religion had increasingly been seen as superfluous, out of step with contemporary developments, antiquated, something for the simple-minded and uncultured, and no longer useful, applicable, or even necessary.

However, many Europeans rejected enlightened liberalism. They objected to the excesses of the French Revolution, seen by some as liberalism's highest moment or logical conclusion, because it had departed from its original calls for liberty, equality, and fraternity. Robespierre and his Committee of Public Safety had produced a reign of terror. The reaction against the Terror's bloody exercise of authority caused many in politics and religion to circle their proverbial wagons and close themselves off from some of liberalism's results. Disillusioned with the idea that government and natural science could be "figured out," they reformed by returning to an emotive understanding of religious matters.

Significantly, Catholics and Protestants both responded this way. Among Protestant churches, reactions against arithmetical piety, scholastic sophistry, and strict religious organization resulted in Pietism, which emphasized a return to scripture, active piety, religious emotion, and sometimes overly strict moral rigorism. The austere Quakers represent Pietism in Europe and North America. The Puritan preacher Jonathan Edwards (1703–58) started a "Great Awakening" of the faith in New England using fiery, apocalyptic language to return congregations to his vision of religion's true path. The Wesley brothers John (1703–91) and Charles (1707–88) split from the Anglican church with their renewed Methodist practices. In the nineteenth century, Newman's Oxford Movement would try to return Anglicanism to its basics.

The German theologian Friedrich Schleiermacher (1768–1834) also felt the influence of Pietism. He was one of the most eloquent spokesmen for a return to religious emotion as a way of renewing the very idea of faith in an age of enlightenment. In 1799, he published

*On Religion: Speeches to Its Cultured Despisers.* In these essays, Schleiermacher argued that the contemporary intelligentsia missed the point of religion as they tried to use a purely intellectual vocabulary to explain God. Condemning a certain arrogance and sterility in their writings, he focused on piety as the true expression of a Christian's inner identification with the *imago Dei.* He also offered piety as an alternative to more traditional, systematic, scholastic modes of theology, but noted that devotions could themselves become superstitious and devoid of meaning if they ran unchecked.

Schleiermacher specifically wished to bring religious discussion back from the terms used by the secular sciences: Deism, natural religion, rationalism. While some of this theological inquiry may expand one's knowledge of God, it did not necessarily increase a devotional, felt, faithful experience of religion that bridged the gap between what could be known about God and what remained unknowable. Feeling and intuition, which were both emotional and cognitive, comprised the essence of religious faith. Intuition reminded the Christian of his dependence on God, but this dependence did not denigrate the human condition. Recalling the medieval humanists' idea of human and divine partnership, Schleiermacher argued that dependence on God raised humans and placed them once more in their proper relationship with God.

Schleiermacher's ideas recall important aspects of religious reform, notably the idea of a constant effort to renew oneself and the need for an active spiritual life. He argued Christians know God within their inner, natural religious consciousness and activities in a world that contains God. The dynamic element of this religious knowledge was based on the concept of becoming, not being: A Christian will never be with God totally in this world, but if he lives his life rightly, he will come close enough and be with God fully in eternity. History, he declared, acted as an important teacher because her lessons illustrated humanity's "becoming" in action.[20]

Catholic romanticism centered around the scholars at Tübingen where, from 1817 on, a seminary was linked with the city's university. These scholars laid the foundations for modern methods in scripture study as well as historical, moral, and sacramental theology that would follow in the modernism of the late nineteenth century. They rejected many of liberalism's most extreme positions, such as the strict separation of faith from reason, but embraced the free inquiry of ideas by which liberalism pursued questions in secular and religious matters.

Johann Sebastian Drey (1777–1853) established the Catholic seminary at Tübingen and later moved it within the university there. He renewed the study of theology by updating the curriculum. Drey added courses on ancient and foreign languages, epistemology, comparative religion, psychology, history, and art. He focused not on a static faith but a living tradition, which under the guidance of the Holy Spirit developed in the context of world events. The church, he argued, consisted more of an inner essence than an exterior form.

Drey described church and society as a joined, living organism and romanticized the Middle Ages because he believed it contained a fully Christianized context. He appreciated medieval mysticism specifically because mystics recognized the divine spark in the material world. Simultaneously, he rejected scholasticism as sophistry because the method tried to reduce that divine spark to empirical terms. As he put it in 1812, theologians must appreciate the mystics' insight: Christian faith is dynamic, always developing, and cannot be reduced to purely intellectual terms.

> This empirical...spirit pushed aside mysticism, which is, after all, the very soul of Christianity. With the disappearance of mysticism there vanished also the exalted conception of Christianity as a great divine decree encompassing the whole history of mankind. Also lost was the concept of the church as the infinitely progressive realization of this decree, and there necessarily sprang up a view of Christianity that treated it as a contingent occurrence in human history, undertaking to explain it from similarly contingent causes.[21]

Romanticism was not just a reform movement among Catholic elites: the laity at large, educated or not, continued to adopt a lively, emotive faith. Among the various spiritual activities of the eighteenth-and nineteenth-century laity, we find increased liturgical participation, more frequent reception of the eucharist, a greater attendance at sermons, and more pilgrimages. This period also witnessed, however, a return to the arithmetical piety of the late Middle Ages that Protestant and Catholic reformers had criticized. These devotions were typically individual, demonstrative, and focused on the suffering Christ.

Although Trent had emphasized individual piety, some devotions, taken to an extreme, prejudiced the communal nature of liturgy. This is another reminder that reforms sometimes go so far that they must at a certain point be reformed again. Romanticism as a reform was itself subject to correction. An early leader against overly romanticized individual and superstitious practices was the Italian priest and historian Lodovico Antonio Muratori (1672–1750), who sought to balance criticism with encouragement. One historian called his work *On a Well-Ordered Devotion* (1747) the "most important reform book in the eighteenth century." In it, Muratori criticized false miracles, masses with little congregational participation, idolatry or indifference to the eucharist, legends and superstitions concerning saints and their relics, private revelations, and empty rituals. Echoing the *devotio moderna* and Trent, Muratori called for inward devotions that produced outward service. His attacks on popular religion and its abuses drew criticism, but they were translated from Italian into German, French, Spanish, Hungarian, Czech, and English.

There was also in Italy an increasing focus on the importance of the parish liturgy on Sunday, pulling people away from their loyalties to competing chapels and shrines. To promote liturgical participation, in some parishes the gospel was read out first in Latin and then in the vernacular; certain reformers even then were calling for the entire mass to be celebrated in the people's language. The priest recited the canon aloud instead of privately to himself and encouraged all in attendance to receive the eucharist if they could. To remove distractions, one mass was celebrated at a central altar without other masses at side altars to distract the congregation.

The people in the pews did not always embrace these reforms, especially those concerning their traditional practice of favorite devotions. Reformers removed legends, cults, and indulgence tables, while literally taking off the layers of clothing parishioners used to decorate saints' statues. Crowds often fought the changes. Faith in relics ran so deep that, when a rumor spread in Prato in May 1787 that the local bishop planned to destroy an altar dedicated to Mary's girdle, the people rioted, occupied the cathedral, tore out and burned the bishop's throne, and ransacked his home. It took an army to restore order.

Trent's centralized reform program slowed down in the eighteenth and nineteenth centuries. During this period, the papacy was distracted from the Tridentine task of supervising internal reform. In response to the excesses of the French Revolution, popes cooperated with Europe's old order to restore and protect monarchical systems—even as the papacy's fellow monarchs tried to make Rome their puppet. With the papacy fighting for its life, reform moved slowly in the institutional church.

Only in the mid-nineteenth century did the pace of reform quicken once again. The scene of vibrant action moved from Europe to the American and Asian missions, where questions of evangelization and inculturation made spreading the faith a lively and challenging endeavor. Among religious orders, increased membership indicated a revived spiritual yearning. Worldwide, there were only 1600 Benedictines and 1284 Trappists in 1850, but just 50 years later there were 6000 Benedictines and the Trappists had nearly tripled their numbers to 3700. The Jesuits grew even more exponentially: 4652 existed in 1852, a number multiplied more than three and one-half times to 16,894 by World War I.

Missionary and female groups especially flourished, with the Oblates of Mary Immaculate growing from 270 members in 1850 to 3,110 in 1914. There were 900 Salesians in 1888, but over 3,500 in 1914 working in 31 countries, including 16 Latin American nations. As had occurred right around the time of Trent, innovative opportunities for women grew in the mid-nineteenth century. Between 1850 and 1860, 48 new congregations for women were established; in only three years, between 1862 and 1865, 74 more were created.

The question arises: Why the upsurge in spirituality? The answer seems to lead back to romanticism, which continued to attract adherents. The Industrial Revolution contributed to romanticism's draw. When business owners treated their workers like cattle and drew the population into grimy urban conditions, religion offered individuality and a sense of personal worth. In the face of the cold rationalism of the enlightenment and the harsh realities of the factory, Europeans and Americans found refuge in romantic, often idealized, notions of the Christian Middle Ages. Just as intellectual reformers like Drey in Tübingen had romanticized the Middle Ages as a model to be recreated so, too, did the largely unlettered masses.

These ideas were popularized in pamphlet stories available in the penny press and in various pious practices that tended toward sentimentality and hagiography. The popular portrait of medieval society highlighted the close integration of work and faith, the "secular" and the "sacred." This integration stood in sharp contrast, some reformers thought, to the enlightenment denigration of faith and modernity's separation of church and state. As England's Cardinal Manning lamented succinctly in 1877: "Modern civilization is civilization without Christianity."[22] In response, Catholics worked to reform the church by restoring what they romantically identified as her golden age.

## Social Catholicism

Liberalism had generally been seen as an enemy of the church. As with the Tübingen reformers, however, liberalism could have a positive impact on theology, history, liturgy, and sacraments. Pope Leo XIII (1878–1903) also adopted one aspect of liberalism more than his predecessors: social Catholicism. Leo XIII was no ideological liberal, but he was an experienced diplomat who tried to place the church into dialogue with the many changes characterizing modern society. As chief shepherd, Leo XIII was especially concerned with the castoffs created by the Industrial Revolution and the mass political movements capitalism had engendered. He championed parts of social Catholicism while defending the church from some of its more radical socialist aims. Leo juggled several conflicting goals in his efforts to bring the church and world in closer contact—with the hope of rejuvenating both.

As factory workers unionized, they often employed a Marxist-socialist vocabulary to call for participatory political and economic power. Some Catholics linked socialist principles with the gospel message of sharing gifts in a community where all worked for one another and each individual had a stake in an entire assembly's well-being. Catholics were often in the leadership of workers' organizations. England's Cardinal Manning championed child labor laws to fight the kinds of conditions familiar through Dickens's novels. In 1874, he wrote *The Rights and Dignity of Labor,* in which he stated that workers had a right to organize themselves into unions, should work regular hours, and should not be subject to abuses. Manning also helped mediate the London dock strike in 1889. When he died three years later, workers showed up in huge numbers to honor him at his funeral. Other priests, prelates, and even lay factory owners in Europe and the United States fought for fair wages, workers' councils, adequate and affordable housing, and insurance for illness, unemployment, and job-related accidents.

Leo XIII put the church behind social Catholicism and the call for social justice in his 1891 encyclical *Rerum Novarum,* often referred to as the movement's Magna Carta. This encyclical anticipated Vatican II's paradigm shift by placing the church squarely in the middle of the social and political events of the day. Surprisingly to many who read the encyclical for the first time, Leo carefully avoided complete support or condemnation of either capitalism or socialism: He defended and criticized aspects of each.

As if to exemplify the balance necessary for reform, Leo had harsh things to say to both socialists and capitalists. He declared private property to be a natural right, not an evil. The family, not the state, was the key unit of any society. He saved his sharpest rebuke for a seminal Marxist principle: According to Leo, class warfare was neither inevitable nor necessary. The pope also pushed against capitalist claims. Although he preferred decentralization to centralization, some state intervention in the economy was required, particularly to protect the interests of workers; Leo thereby rejected the liberal economic idea of complete laissez-faire. That principle often produced a brutal invisible hand that did not guarantee fair treatment for the workers who, Leo declared, could organize themselves to protect their interests.

Leo XIII believed religion should foster justice and charity between employer and employee, giving an example of how Christianity was relevant to modern society.

> It is the church that insists, on the authority of the gospel, upon those teachings whereby the conflict can be brought to an end, or rendered, at least, far less bitter; the church uses her efforts not only to enlighten the mind, but to direct by her precepts the life and conduct of each and all; the church improves and betters the condition of the working man by means of numerous organizations; [and] does her best to enlist the services of all classes in discussing and endeavoring to further in the most practical way, the interests of the working classes....
>
> ...[T]here is no intermediary more powerful than religion (whereof the church is the interpreter and guardian) in drawing the rich and the working class together, by reminding each of its duties to the other, and especially of the obligations of justice.

Anticipating Vatican II's mandate for Catholics to bring Christianity to their workplaces, in 1891 Leo challenged Christians to renew themselves and the world by getting involved in social justice activities. This he did by using explicit renewal language to call Christians back to an individual reform, which would then move outward to societal renewal. To move forward at this particular moment, the church must first look back to her origins and her history. Leo explained that by doing so Christians would discover that only the church's remedies and teachings

> can reach the innermost heart and conscience, and bring men to act from a motive of duty, to control their passions and appetites, to love God and their fellow men with a love that is

outstanding and of the highest degree and to break down courageously every barrier which blocks the way to virtue....
...[C]ivil society was renovated in every part by Christian institutions;...in the strength of that renewal the human race was lifted up to better things—nay, that it was brought back from death to life, and to so excellent a life that nothing more perfect had been known before.... [I]f human society is to be healed now, in no other way can it be healed save by a return to Christian life and Christian institutions. When a society is perishing, the wholesome advice to give to those who would restore it is to call it to the principles from which it sprang; for the purpose and perfection of an association is to aim at and to attain that for which it is formed, and its efforts should be put in motion and inspired by the end and object which originally gave it being. Hence, to fall away from its primal constitution implies disease; to go back to it, recovery.[23]

The pope's calls gave life to Christian trade unions, some of which had organized before the encyclical, while others appeared in response to it. The German Workers' Welfare Association, established in 1879, and the Belgian Democratic League, established in 1891, flourished. In 1920, many groups on both sides of the Atlantic forged ties through the International Federation of Christian Trade Unions. In the United States, Dorothy Day led the Catholic Worker movement, which spread to other countries.[24]

Reform from above supported reform below, renewing both the church and the wider societies in which she lived. Viewed from this perspective, the social Catholicism movement of the late nineteenth century was an important step toward a central Vatican II reform: the détente between the church and the world at the heart of *Gaudium et Spes*.

## John Henry Newman

Newman (1801–90) embodies many of the nineteenth-century reform activities, though he is not always labeled a reformer. Newman saw his own life as a constant reform of self as he encountered, in turn, childlike faith, a Bible-based religion of stories and images, enlightenment challenges like liberalism, Calvinists' notions of a pietistic and individual sense of God's presence, Anglicanism, and then Roman Catholicism. The constant process of reassessment took time and entailed what we might identify as a religious version of the Hegelian dialectic: A thesis meets its antithesis and then works out a synthesis.

Before his conversion to Roman Catholicism and subsequent ordination as a Catholic priest, Newman and a group of like-minded Anglicans tried to reform the Church of England, which, they believed, had strayed from her origins. This Oxford Movement, as it was called, saw the Anglican church as a reforming *via media* between Roman excesses and the minimalism of certain Protestant groups. But Newman feared the Church of England had become stuck in this middle way and lost her vitality. He fought secularism, liberalism, and what he saw as the state's interference in church affairs. Newman led the way in calling for a revival of the liturgy and spirituality of the original Church of England. In his sermons and pamphlets, Newman called especially for a return to a vital inner prayer life. Ironically, while many criticized the Oxford Movement for opposing the papacy and the Roman church, many of its followers ended up converting from Anglicanism to Catholicism.

Another aspect of Newman's reform was his idea of the development of doctrine. Newman did not claim dogma itself developed. For example, Jesus was fully divine and fully human long before the fourth-century councils said so, not because they issued creeds defining his humanity and divinity; such a truth is transhistorical and everlasting. Human language and intelligence, however, do develop, allowing for increasingly clearer expressions of dogma.

Newman's idea of the development of doctrine entailed a crucial reform idea: Eternal truths grounded in immutable first principles can be expressed in new ways, proving theology to be a living tradition subject to organic growth. In fact, growth was evidence of life, according to Newman. This growth entailed the conservation of unchangeable truths expressed in innovative ways that respected both faith and reason, past and present, tradition and progress. Orthodoxy, for Newman, was always undergoing reform because it is alive and dynamic. This notion of a vibrant tradition, or dynamic orthodoxy, would finally emerge as a hallmark of Vatican II's paradigm shift.

Finally, Newman's position on the role of the laity also contributed to church reform in the nineteenth and twentieth centuries. He offered a rationale for the laity's increased participation in the church's attempts to revitalize herself. About a hundred years before Vatican II met, Newman called for laypeople to learn about their faith (though he framed his call in nineteenth-century terms which seem to exclude laywomen).

> I want a laity, not arrogant, not rash in speech, not disputatious, but men [sic] who know their religion, who enter into it, who know just where they stand, who know what they hold, and what they do not, who know their creed so well that they can give an account of it, who know so much of history that they can defend it. I want an intelligent, well-instructed laity; I am not denying you are such already: but I mean to be severe, and, as some would say, exorbitant in my demands. I wish you to enlarge your knowledge, to cultivate your reason, to get an insight into the relation of truth to truth, to learn to view things as they are, to understand how faith and reason stand to each other, what are the bases and principles of Catholicism.... I have no apprehension you will be the worse Catholics for familiarity with these subjects, provided you cherish a vivid sense of God above, and keep in mind that you have souls to be judged and to be saved. In all times the laity have been the measure of the Catholic spirit....

In his enthusiastic call for an honest perspective on the church's developing history and dynamic traditions, Newman anticipated many of the reforms that would mark the path toward Vatican II.[25]

## Modernism

The modernists were never an organized group of scholars so much as a number of French, Italian, English, and German priests and laypeople working in different fields. One of them called modernism a "tendency" that sought a renewal of religious life through historical and critical methodology, which they believed they should be free to exercise. Their opponents saw modern scholarly methods as skeptical, destructive, and disrespectful rationalism. The modernists' methods and the church's response recall earlier tense moments in the history of reform when innovators applied new methods of reason to matters of faith. Just as the partisans of tradition and progress battled each other in the Middle Ages, so too modernists and their opponents argued about the proper way to reform the church in the late nineteenth and early twentieth centuries.

Some church leaders considered modernity too secular, rational, and dangerous. They opposed intellectuals who, embracing certain parts of liberalism and romanticism, were optimistic with respect to Catholicism's ability to stand up to modernity's freedom of thought. Modernists wanted to meet the world with the world's methods by using historicism, archaeology, and textual criticism to address theology and scripture. At an 1863 conference in Munich, the German theologian and historian Johann von Döllinger presented a keynote speech entitled "The Past and Future of Theology" in which he called for intellectual freedom, not censorship, for Catholic scholars based on the principle that by examining errors, they could come to a greater understanding of religious truth.

In response, Pope Pius IX (1846–78) issued a *Syllabus of Errors* in 1864 in which he denounced rationalism, naturalism, socialism, liberal capitalism, freedom of religion, and the very idea of progress. Among the "errors" he condemned, two stand out:

> It is no longer expedient that the Catholic religion should be treated as the only religion of the state, all other worships whatsoever being excluded. (Error #77)

> The Roman Pontiff can and ought to reconcile and harmonize himself with progress, with liberalism, and with modern civilization. (Error #80)

Modernism continued despite this condemnation. One development occurred in biblical studies when exegetes suggested scriptural interpretation should be more open and flexible. Leo XIII (the champion of social Catholicism but, again, not an ideological radical liberal) responded in his encyclical *Providentissimus Deus* (1893) that error in the Bible was impossible. The French biblical scholar Alfred Loisy (1857–1940) studied Jesus as an historical figure, claiming he was a prophet who did not know he was the messiah and did not intend the church to be a hierarchical institution. The church, Loisy said, was a human institution in which dogma developed and where scripture should be subject to the same rigid textual analysis as any historical document. Historians fought against ecclesiastical legends and hagiography taken as fact. Other modernists wanted a democratic church without papal authoritarianism and infallibility.

The institutional church struck back. In 1906, the Biblical Commission required all Catholics to believe Moses wrote the Pentateuch. Pope Pius X (1903–14) identified sixy five "errors" in his July 1907 decree *Lamentabili Sane* and strengthened his condemnation two months later with the biting encyclical *Pascendi Dominici Gregis,* which characterized modernism as a monolith. According to Pius X's chronicle of their errors, modernists said the Jesus of history was inferior to the Christ of faith; Jesus' knowledge was limited and he did not know he was the messiah; Jesus could have erred and he did not institute the church or the sacraments; and papal primacy was not of divine origin. The last "error" summed up the rest: "Modern Catholicism can be reconciled with true science only if it is transformed into a non-dogmatic Christianity; that is to say, into a broad and liberal Protestantism."

The papal reaction against the modernist reforms led to investigatory commissions and censors in dioceses and seminaries. These vigilance committees often operated in secret and through self-appointed informers who could destroy a career with a mere accusation: Parish priests and seminary professors were denounced with no knowledge of their accusers.[26] *Pascendi* struck a forceful blow against modernism, but reforming scholarship suffered only a delay, not death. The papal reaction put reformers and the institutional church into an adversarial relationship. It would be left for later scholars in the twentieth century to foster dialogue that aided, instead of hindered, the inevitable march toward reform.

## Perspectives

The period from 1600 to 1900 did not begin with a siege mentality. It was first an age of innovation peopled by charismatic reformers like Borromeo, Teresa of Avila, and Ignatius who energetically worked to reform the church from the top down and the bottom up. Women especially stepped forward as reformers during these centuries, taking their place as the educators who helped implement personal reform to the broadest degree possible. Only gradually did larger forces—enlightenment liberalism, scientific revolution, and industrialization—challenge the intimate *metanoia* at the heart of Trent's program. These major societal movements caused some in the church to insulate her from the world and slow down reform's momentum.

Reform did not die during this period, but it did not exist in a vacuum either. Secularization and rationalism competed with the very idea of faith for loyalty, making reform harder to accomplish. This context explains why reform slowed a bit during the early modern period, at least institutionally. But enthusiasm did not fail to flourish, especially among religious orders who renewed Catholicism by exporting it to the missions. There, nuns, priests, and brothers reinvented their presentations of Catholicism in light of the diverse cultures they encountered.

Reform in the period between 1600 and 1900 was marked by ambivalence. The Leo XIII who made Newman a cardinal and championed social Catholicism was the same Leo XIII who declared error in the Bible an impossibility, criticized certain aspects of socialism, and was no friend of the modernists. Romanticism, social Catholicism, Newman's ideas of development, and modernism generated reforms *in membris,* but also caused tension with the institutional church *in capite.*

Reform also had its share of opponents. Newman was distrusted and at times denounced by some Catholics. Social Catholicism could produce as much opposition as support. Popes seriously hindered the modernists' methods and agendas. Nevertheless, these movements paved the way for Vatican II. The swiftly changing times between 1600 and 1900 are perhaps the least studied chapter in the history of reform, but they also may be the most formative and crucial for our own times, for this period fertilized the soil in which Vatican II was born.

## NOTES

1. Giuseppe Alberigo reappraises Trent by rebutting the image of the monolithic siege mentality during the council itself, but he recognizes that Roman intransigence and centralization eventually triumphed in the centuries following: "The Council of Trent," in *Catholicism in Early Modern History: A Guide to Research*, ed. John W. O'Malley (St. Louis: Center for Reformation Research, 1988), vol. 2, pp. 211–13, 217–23.

2. Elisabeth G. Gleason summarizes the papal reform initiatives after Trent in "Catholic Reformation, Counterreformation, and Papal Reform in the Sixteenth Century," in *Handbook of European History 1400–1600: Late Middle Ages, Renaissance and Reformation*, vol. 2, *Visions, Programs and Outcomes*, eds. Thomas A. Brady, Jr., Heiko A. Oberman, and James D. Tracy (Leiden: E. J. Brill, 1995), pp. 334–39. For other details, see R. Po-Chia Hsia, *The World of Catholic Renewal: 1540–1770* (Cambridge: Cambridge University Press, 1998), pp. 92–105.

3. Gleason, "Catholic Reformation," p. 339.

4. Frederick J. McGinness, *Right Thinking and Sacred Oratory in Counter-Reformation Rome* (Princeton: Princeton University Press, 1995), pp. 183–85.

5. Hsia, *The World of Catholic Renewal*, pp. 155–56; Robert Bireley, *The Refashioning of Catholicism, 1450–1700: A Reassessment of the Counter Reformation* (Washington D.C.: Catholic University of America Press, 1999), pp. 65–66; Eamon Duffy, *Saints and Sinners: A History of the Popes* (New Haven: Yale University Press, 1997), pp. 172, 183, 186.

6. John B. Tomaro, "San Carlo Borromeo and the Implementation of the Council of Trent," in *San Carlo Borromeo: Catholic Reform and Ecclesiastical Politics in the Second Half of the Sixteenth Century*, eds. John M. Headley and John B. Tomaro (Washington D.C.: The Folger Shakespeare Library, 1988), pp. 67–84.

7. Christopher Black, "Perugia and Post-Tridentine Church Reform," *JEH* 35 (1984): pp. 429–40, 451.

8. Kathleen M. Comerford, "Italian Tridentine Diocesan Seminaries: A Historiographical Study," *Sixteenth Century Journal* 29 (1998): pp. 999–1022; Black, "Perugia and Post-Tridentine Church Reform," pp. 441–43.

9. For insights into the Spanish background of reform, as well as the social, economic, and political issues at stake, see Jodi Bilinkoff, *The Avila of Saint Teresa* (Ithaca: Cornell University Press, 1989), pp. 78–151; Kieran Kavanaugh and Otilio Rodriguez, trans., *The Collected Works of St. Teresa*

*of Avila,* 3 vols. (Washington D.C.: Institute of Carmelite Studies, 1976–85), vol. 3, pp. 20–23, 58–61.

10. For the story of her reforms and the struggle, challenges, and distrust they encountered, see Teresa's account in her autobiography: Kavanaugh and Rodriguez, *The Collected Works of St. Teresa of Avila,* vol. 1, pp. 213–51. John's reform perspective, opposition, and imprisonment are discussed in Kieran Kavanaugh, *John of the Cross: Selected Writings* (New York: Paulist Press, 1987), pp. 9–20. Lawrence S. Cunningham notes the sixteenth-century culture of suspicion at work against Teresa and John in *The Catholic Heritage* (New York: Crossroad, 1983), pp. 94–100.

11. George E. Ganss, ed., *Ignatius of Loyola: The Spiritual Exercises and Selected Works* (New York: Paulist Press, 1991), pp. 161, 166.

12. Robert E. McNally, "The Council of Trent, the *Spiritual Exercises,* and the Catholic Reform," *CH* 34 (1965): pp. 36–49.

13. John W. O'Malley, "Was Ignatius Loyola a Church Reformer? How to Look at Early Modern Catholicism," *CHR* 77 (1991): pp. 180–83, 188–89; *The First Jesuits* (Cambridge Mass.: Harvard University Press, 1993), pp. 16–19.

14. Mark Lewis, "The First Jesuits as 'Reformed Priests',"" *Archivum Historicum Societatis Iesu* 65 (1996): pp. 111–27 discusses the context of other sixteenth-century reformed priests, demonstrating how they affected the Jesuits and were in turn influenced by them.

15. William V. Hudon presents the Theatines' spiritual goals in *Theatine Spirituality: Selected Writings* (New York: Paulist Press, 1996); for the order's history, see pp. 16–29.

16. Bireley, *The Refashioning of Catholicism,* pp. 25–44, 121–46.

17. Louis Châtellier, *The Europe of the Devout: The Catholic Reformation and the Formation of a New Society,* trans. Jean Birrell (Cambridge: Cambridge University Press, 1989), pp. 3–6; Bireley, *The Refashioning of Catholicism,* pp. 96–120.

18. Black, "Perugia and Post-Tridentine Church Reform," pp. 444–47.

19. Hsia, *The World of Catholic Renewal,* p. 51.

20. Friedrich Schleiermacher, *On Religion: Speeches to Its Cultured Despisers,* trans. Richard Crouter (Cambridge: Cambridge University Press, 1988).

21. Johann Sebastian Drey, "Toward the Revision of the Present State of Theology," in *Romance and the Rock: Nineteenth-Century*

*Catholics on Faith and Reason,* ed. Joseph Fitzer (Minneapolis: Fortress Press, 1989), p. 69.

22. Owen Chadwick, *The Popes and European Revolution* (Oxford: Clarendon Press, 1981), pp. 391–444; Roger Aubert, *The Church in a Secularised Society* (London: Darton, Longman and Todd, 1978), pp. 110–28; Philip Gleason, "American Catholics and the Mythic Middle Ages," in *Keeping the Faith: American Catholicism Past and Present* (Notre Dame: University of Notre Dame Press, 1987), pp. 14–25; Joseph A. Komonchak, "Modernity and the Construction of Roman Catholicism," *Cristianesimo nella storia* 18 (1997): pp. 353–85.

23. Leo XIII, *Rerum Novarum,* nos. 16, 19, 26, 27, in *The Papal Encyclicals 1878–1903,* ed. Claudia Carlen (Raleigh N.C.: McGrath, 1981), pp. 245, 248. This translation of no. 27 complies with the language of renewal, restoration, and recalling in the original Latin as found in *Acta Sanctae Sedis* 23 (1890–91): pp. 653–54.

24. Aubert, *The Church in a Secularized Society,* pp. 144–64. Some twentieth-century American Catholics reached to the Middle Ages for models, as the romantics had done in the nineteenth century, this time for examples of medieval social justice activities: Eugene McCarraher, "American Gothic: Sacramental Radicalism and the Neo-Medievalist Cultural Gospel, 1928–1948," *Records of the American Catholic Historical Society of Philadelphia* 105 (1995): pp. 3–23.

25. Vincent Ferrer Blehl, ed., *The Essential Newman* (New York: New American Library, 1963), p. 274. For excerpts of Newman's most important writings, many of which entail reform, consult Ian Ker, ed., *Newman the Theologian: A Reader* (Notre Dame: University of Notre Dame Press, 1990). Avery Dulles explored the connections between Newman and Vatican II in his keynote address at a conference in Morristown N.J., 24 June 1996. My thanks to Cardinal Dulles for supplying a copy of this unpublished paper, "Newman and Vatican II," in which he concludes that Vatican II was only partially "Newman's council."

26. This account relies on Aubert, *The Church in a Secularised Society,* pp. 186–203. For modernist writings themselves, see the selections in Bernard M. G. Reardon, ed., *Roman Catholic Modernism* (Stanford: Stanford University Press, 1970). Thomas J. Shelley provides a case study of how vital scholarship in a seminary was cut off by the reaction against modernism in *Dunwoodie: The History of St. Joseph's Seminary* (Westminster Md.: Christian Classics, Inc., 1993), pp. 148–70.

# Chapter 5
# Vatican II

Since the church is still living through Vatican II's growing pains, it is a risky enterprise to interpret the council's ultimate meaning. Historians and historical theologians need time to assess developments. Any observations of Vatican II at this moment must be seen like journalism—the first draft of history. Nevertheless, it is not impossible to place Vatican II, which some have equated with Pentecost as the most influential event in Christianity's life, into the history of reform, at least in a preliminary manner for future generations to judge.

This chapter does not discuss all of the many paradigm shifts Vatican II initiated. Like the other chapters in this history of reform, this one primarily examines this council's ideas of reform in the long view: where they came from, how they developed, and to what degree they are being implemented or turned back. An effective way to approach Vatican II is to look first at what came before, especially pre-Vatican II scholarship, spirituality, and liturgical renewal. Next, we will look briefly at the council itself as an event in the early 1960s, a focus that is often lost in its implementation over the next several decades. Then, we must attempt at least an initial assessment of the council's fallout. This approach reveals Vatican II as one more case study of reform as a process.

# The Gear-Up

Vatican II, like the Twelfth-Century Renaissance and Luther, did not appear out of nowhere. Today's reform movements grew from nineteenth-century developments. Some of these reforms moved from the church's body to her head in Rome; others were directed from the Vatican outward to the world's dioceses and parishes.[1]

## Scholarship and Popular Devotions

Despite curial opposition to modernism, Rome did promote reform and active spirituality in the first half of the twentieth century. Pope Pius XI (1922–39) encouraged social Catholicism's energy on the diocesan level. Groups like Catholic Action invited Christians to bring their faith to the workplace decades before Vatican II made that effort one of its hallmark missions. Pius XII (1939–58) especially applied his hand to the renewal of religious orders, which experienced greater fervor. Orders directed their attention increasingly to their founders' unique charisms and initial apostolates, but they also tried to adapt them to changing conditions. This dynamic came to characterize the revitalization of many orders in the wake of Vatican II's calls for updating throughout the church. Pius XII sent out about twenty documents each year on this topic and even used the word *aggiornamento,* which would become Vatican II's buzzword.

Other reforms bubbled *in membris,* especially among the laity who stepped up their participation in church matters long before Vatican II asked them to live a lay life as a special mission. Groups like the Christian Family Movement and the Legion of Mary promoted individual devotions; a series of secular institutes gave order and direction to laypeople who wanted to live the gospel in their vocations as spouses and parents. Teachers used new educational theories and materials to improve the quality and quantity of catechetical instruction, particularly for children. Popular literature reached a wider audience, promoting the life of

Christ, the models of the saints, and Marian piety. Private devotions proved a two-edged sword: they had to be corrected and redirected like the arithmetical piety of the late Middle Ages. In response, reformers emphasized communal feasts instead of private devotions and encouraged laypeople to read primarily about Christ's suffering, rather than the triumphalist saints' lives that dominated popular literature after Trent.

Although modernism had seriously damaged the reputations of leading scholars, others bravely continued to apply new scholarly concepts and methods to theology, scripture, church history, and liturgy. Leo XIII's 1893 encyclical *Providentissimus Deus* stated that the Bible cannot be in dialogue with natural science nor be dissected in the language of scientific truth. But this same pope also established the Biblical Commission, planned the Pontifical Biblical Institute, opened the Vatican Archives in 1883 to scholars of all faiths, and promoted the use of modern methods in astronomy, the hard sciences, archeology, theology, and scriptural exegesis. On the more popular level, Leo encouraged laypeople to read the Bible in the vernacular and lifted the restriction that banned them from reading parts of the mass in their native languages. Pius XII's 1943 encyclical *Divino Afflante Spiritu* recognized several literary genres in the Bible, cautioned against fundamentalism, and accepted modern methodologies to interpret scripture.

Scholarship promoted reform by marrying academic study with faith without the burden of confessional apologetics and biases. Scholars in many fields returned *ad fontes,* to the sources, and established institutes, journals, and publication series to recover and disseminate original texts. This effort provided a sound historical and theological basis for spiritual, sacramental, and liturgical renewal. The Jesuits focused on spirituality by establishing the *Revue d'ascétique et de mystique* in 1920 and the *Dictionnaire de spiritualité* in 1932. Other French and Italian histories of devotions and religious practices followed. The fathers were translated into English and appeared in several affordable series that became standard reading in Catholic seminaries and colleges. Historians and historical theologians looked back at key moments of reform, especially the period from 1300 to 1600, to find models and lessons for the twentieth-century renewal that was taking place with mounting urgency.

Marian devotions illustrate the synthesis between rejuvenated popular piety and scholarship. With interest in Mary rising because of Fatima and Lourdes, pilgrimages and congresses proliferated. Marian institutes were founded in France, Rome, Spain, Canada, and Germany. The proclamation of the Assumption in 1950 and the centennial anniversary of the proclamation of the Immaculate Conception in 1954 revitalized and promoted further study of Mary's place in history, theology, spirituality, liturgy, and art.

## Liturgical Renewal

Many of these reforms in scholarship and religious practice came together in the liturgical renewal, which foreshadowed the great changes Vatican II would introduce. The liturgical renewal deserves close attention because the liturgy is the most visible and controversial manifestation of Vatican II. For many, the vernacular mass *is* Vatican II.

Scholars have identified two periods of liturgical renewal in the modern era: The first followed the Council of Trent for about fifty years; the second occurred during the twentieth century, with roots a bit earlier. But in between stood a long period of dry, arithmetical worship one historian called "three centuries of a stability rendered immobile by rubricism." Glorious solemn high masses were celebrated in some monasteries, convents, cathedrals, and seminaries. But many parish priests walked through a stale recitation of rites, adhering rigidly to the letter of the "rubrics" (directions) written in red in their ritual books. "Read masses" rarely inspired a congregation.

Some reformers began to water this liturgical desert in the nineteenth century, led in France by Dom Prosper Guéranger, a Benedictine abbot influenced by romanticism. He oversaw the publication of a nine-volume work designed to help pastors enliven their liturgical rites; Guéranger's enthusiasm quickly spread to Germany and Belgium. His particular desire to revive Gregorian chant caught the attention of Giuseppe Sarto, the cardinal archbishop of Venice who immediately promoted liturgical reform when he assumed the papal throne in 1903.

Pius X (1903–14) published in the first year of his pontificate *Tra le sollecitudini,* which encouraged Gregorian chant, congregational singing, and the active participation of the faithful in the liturgy. Sixty years later, active participation of the faithful would be the key idea of *Sacrosanctum concilium,* Vatican II's document on the liturgy. He also favored frequent, even daily reception of the eucharist—a revolutionary suggestion, as prior to the twentieth century most Catholics received communion only two or three times a year. Pius X cut down the restrictions for reception, saying in a 1905 decree that the communicant only had to desire to do God's will and could not be in a state of mortal sin. This removed the requirement that the communicant might approach the altar rail only if confession had been made almost immediately beforehand. The pope also extended frequent reception to children: The age of first communion was moved back to about the age of seven. Pius X's other reforms touched catechesis, the missal, the breviary, the curia, and canon law. It must be remembered, however, that this was the same pope who fiercely condemned and rooted out modernism: Pius X, like Leo XIII before him, reminds us reformers are not always reformers in everything.

If Catholics were to participate so intimately in liturgy, they had to know what was going on. Permitting the laity to follow the Latin mass by reading missal translations in their own languages and encouraging them to sing fostered lay participation. Priests used vernacular prayers for burials and certain sacraments. Toning down the liturgy's pomp made it more intimate, although some complained that the mass consequently lost its majesty and reverence. Pius XII's *Mediator Dei* (1947) gave these reform developments a tremendous boost by providing papal support for increased lay participation at mass, just as *Tra le sollecitudini* had legitimated certain aspects of liturgical reform before it. According to the theologian Johannes H. Emminghaus, *"Mediator Dei* became the Magna Carta of liturgical reform" by promoting the atmosphere for vernacular rites and a new translation of the psalms; it also further restricted the burdens of the eucharist fast, making it easier to receive more frequently, much as Pius X had done several decades earlier.

Liturgical renewal *in membris* and *in capite* enjoyed a dialectical growth. Dom Lambert Beauduin (1873–1960) picked up on the phrase "active participation of the faithful" from *Tra le sollecitudini* and spent years pursuing this goal. Beauduin sponsored yearly conferences on liturgical renewal in Louvain and addressed emerging questions in a journal. In the 1920s, Virgil Michel brought the enthusiasm he caught in Europe to the United States, where he spread the gospel of liturgical renewal in the journal *Orate Fratres* (now *Worship*), through the publisher Liturgical Press, and at annual meetings. So strong was the call to revitalize the liturgy that in Paris in 1943, right in the middle of the Nazi domination of Europe, Beauduin and others established a center for pastoral liturgical study.

Reforms spread on the lay level through "dialogue" masses in which the congregants said the *Gloria, Credo, Sanctus, Pater Noster,* and *Agnus Dei* along with the celebrant. As early as the 1920s, the archbishop of Cologne celebrated dialogue masses in his cathedral while facing the congregation. Such masses enjoyed only slow progress, however. In 1922, Belgian priests sought approval for their dialogue masses: While they were not banned, they were not encouraged, either. In 1935, the archbishop of Genoa requested Roman approval; it came, but with the admonition that a diocesan bishop must oversee this type of liturgy.

Right after World War II, Pius XII gathered together the key players of liturgical renewal, who began a major overhaul of liturgical practices. In 1955, for instance, Holy Week liturgies were dramatically revitalized and brought more in line with original traditions. To further increase lay participation and understanding, after the epistle and gospel were read out in Latin at mass, a vernacular translation followed. By 1958, a layman was permitted to act as lector at mass using vernacular translations. Even bigger changes were just around the corner.

## *The Council*

Angelo Roncalli may have been elected as a caretaker pope, but as John XXIII (1958–63) he had other things in mind. Despite the fact he was seventy-six and his pontificate lasted less than five years, we can hardly overstate John XXIII's impact on the history of reform. From the start, his pastoral and reform concerns were pre-eminent: he chose the feast of Carlo Borromeo, the reforming bishop of Trent's program and the subject of Roncalli's own five-volume study, for his coronation. Less than three months after his election, John XXIII informed the world he had received a sudden insight while praying: The church required an ecumenical council to keep up with a new era in the world's history. In his December 25, 1961, address formally convoking the council, John declared this was a moment for courage and change for the church and her children.

> [T]hough the world may appear profoundly changed, the Christian community is also in great part transformed and renewed. It has therefore strengthened itself socially in unity; it has been reinvigorated intellectually; it has been interiorly purified and is thus ready for trial.[2]

He envisioned this council as a new Pentecost, a chance to open the church's windows to let the dusty old air out and the refreshing breeze in.

Although John XXIII wanted a reforming council, Vatican curialists tried to stem the pope's call for change. A central planning commission drew up an agenda and organization for the council, including ten preparatory committees, but these were generally stocked with conservative curialists. It seems the Roman curia was trying to stall for time and impede John's call for aggiornamento. This central commission produced agenda items from a Roman perspective and sent materials to bishops in the summer of 1962, only three months before the first session of the council met that October. A rear-guard action was firmly in place. It appeared John's Pentecost might be stillborn.

Nevertheless, three innovations would lead to reform: a commission for the laity was created, though no Roman congregation for laypeople then existed; a secretariat to promote Christian unity was established; and noncurial diocesan bishops and theologians were appointed to the commissions. These experts (*periti,* to use the familiar Latin word) included some theologians whose work had been suspected and even censured in earlier decades. Their ideas soon overcame the curialists' program and their talks during the four autumn sessions of Vatican II (1962–65) drew overflow crowds of bishops eager to update their own theological training. Each fall during the early 1960s, Rome turned into one big seminar.

About 2,500 bishops, theologians, and other representatives met in October 1962 to hear John XXIII, in his opening address, call them to face new challenges, to renew the church's ancient tasks, and to focus themselves on pastoral implications. Already, this council differed radically from earlier councils, for it was a global meeting, full of young churches. While Europeans made up 33 percent of those in attendance, 35 percent came from North and South America, and another 10 percent each from Africa and Asia. Eventually, nearly one hundred non-Catholic observers from twenty-eight churches and denominations attended and were consulted by the commissions.

Almost from the start of the council, a spirit of independence upset the curialists' stalling maneuvers. The bishops asked to postpone the election of committee members: Rather than draw members from lists prepared by the curia, the bishops wanted to elect whomever they wanted from among themselves. By the end of the first session in the fall of 1962, the bishops had redrawn the Roman bureaucracy's narrow agenda to reflect their own diocesan, international, and pastoral concerns. The bishops declared they wanted to discuss matters, not rubber-stamp Roman motions. The council elected a new central commission with noncurial bishops making up the majority and placed in control of revisions.

After John XXIII's death, some curialists hoped the council would not continue, but Paul VI (1963–78) made it clear very quickly that the council would proceed as John and the world's bishops wanted. Paul added almost thirty laymen to the second session in 1963 and seven laywomen to the third in 1964. They were particularly helpful in the formulation of *Gaudium et Spes,* which declared that the church should be in dialogue with the wider world, as the modernists had said. Lay participation at Vatican II helped promote the important idea that all Catholics (and all Christians) had a vocation and a duty to bring the gospel to their workplaces, as lay reformers *in membris* had been doing since the Middle Ages.

Especially for the laity, Vatican II (like Trent) spoke the language of continual, humanistic, and inner renewal, as in *Gaudium et Spes* (1965, nos. 13, 58):

> Thus the human being is divided interiorly, and the whole of human life, whether singly or shared, is shown to be a dramatic struggle between good and evil, light and darkness. People find themselves incapable of overcoming the onslaughts of evil by themselves, and individuals feel bound and helpless. But the Lord has come to liberate them and strengthen them, renewing them interiorly *(interius renovans)* and expelling the prince of this world, who kept them in the slavery of sin. For sin diminished them and prevented them from attaining their fulfillment.
>
> ...The good news of Christ continually renews *(continenter renovat)* the life and behavior of fallen humanity and attacks and dispels the errors and evils which flow from the ever-threatening seduction of sin. It ceaselessly purifies and enhances the ways of peoples. As if from the inside, it enriches with heavenly resources, strengthens, completes and restores in Christ the spiritual endowments and talents of every people and age.[3]

Vatican II promoted several shifts in the history of reform, but these often reached back to earlier precedents that had never fully broken into the mainstream or lasted for long. The active role of the laity, as we have just noted, was one such shift, as was the spirit of détente Paul VI established between the church and the modern world. The very idea of the church moved from a strictly institutional, hierarchical concept to one of the church as the people of God, to use Paul's favorite phrase. In this, Paul VI picked up on the original idea of the Hebrews as God's chosen race as well as Pius XII, who in his encyclical *Mystici Corporis* (1943) described Christ as the head of the church who lives simultaneously within the hearts of his people.

Other Vatican II reforms included intra- and interreligious dialogue, the idea of civil tolerance for all faiths, episcopal collegiality and reform synods on the local level, the recognition that there were diverse ways to celebrate the sacraments and liturgies within Catholic unity, and a renewed call for all Christians to study the Bible according to modern methods within the church's traditional teaching authority.[4]

Perhaps the most important aspect of Vatican II was its very vocabulary of reform. The church recognized herself as a pilgrim, both perfect and imperfect at the same time. Therefore, since tomorrow, "today" will be "yesterday," the task of aggiornamento ("today-ing") never ends. The council asked the church to read the signs of the times during a period of drastic global change in politics and social values. The historian John W. O'Malley believes Vatican II embraced change by contradicting a basic principle illustrated at the Fifth Lateran Council in 1512. Giles of Viterbo, delivering its opening address, said then: "Men must be changed by religion, not religion by men." According to O'Malley's long view,

> What Vatican II's *aggiornamento* called for was precisely the opposite. It determined that religion should be changed by men, in order to meet the needs of men.... In the breadth of its applications and in the depth of its implications, *aggiornamento* was a revolution in the history of the idea of reform.

This change in the very idea of reform may be why, for the first time in twenty-one general councils, the church overwhelmingly chose "renewal" language over "reform" language in its documents.

Moreover, Vatican II, unlike other councils, did not lay down canons of what the church held and what it did not, the latter known by the litany of *anathema sit* ("let him be anathema") that for centuries rang ominously down on the heads of heretics and dissenters. Instead, Vatican II's documents were more open-ended than prescriptive. Renewal, the council seemed to say, was not a list of items to be imposed, but a process. The council—in its theoretical, not precisely directive documents—acted only as an impetus, motivator, and clearinghouse of ideas. The way was open to reach back to the models and sources of the early church, but to update, not simply to restore them. Vatican II spoke the language of progress, innovation, development, and trial-and-error. For Vatican II, renewal would always be an experiment and never a complete achievement.[5]

## The Fallout

Councils need decades to work their implications out, which was certainly the case with Trent. So, too, Vatican II is still being interpreted, implemented, and fought over. To this degree, it is impossible to gauge the council's final legacy, but it appears Vatican II remains up for grabs.

At the moment, it seems clear opinions are split about what Vatican II produced. Soon after the council ended in 1965, Catholics lined up on opposing sides. One side wanted the council's decrees and natural progressions to be implemented as quickly as possible with no hindrances to aggiornamento or creativity. From this angle, Vatican II still has not gone far enough. The other side tried to stem the council's tide and push its more provocative changes back, especially when it came to liturgies. For them, Vatican II went too far; they believe the church needs to restore the pre-Vatican II ways, especially the Latin mass and traditional devotions. Restoration has become a model of reform that competes with—indeed, literally opposes—the concept of aggiornamento.[6]

Both sides can interpret the same developments quite differently: by 1970, one side feared the initial impetus and enthusiasm of reform was dying out, while at the very same time the other side lamented the rapidity and extent of change. Conflicting interpretations frequently produced factionalism, extremism, and rigidity on both ends of the spectrum. While many degrees of moderate perspectives exist between these two ends, zealous positions often attract the most media attention because of their radical rhetoric.[7]

Part of the confusion stems from what precisely Vatican II was and is. How were clergy and laity to interpret and implement documents that did not lay down doctrines or programs as earlier councils had done? Unlike Pope Pius IV after Trent, Paul VI after Vatican II did not establish a congregation of cardinals to oversee the interpretation and implementation of the council's documents. Some critics of Vatican II see the failure to create an instrument of oversight as a major error. Their opponents say such an instrument would itself go against "the spirit of the council," a phrase often invoked by those who wish to allow Vatican II to play itself out in a process of unhindered experimentation and development.

Some prelates wasted no time in trying to work against the council. Little more than six months after the council adjourned, Cardinal Alfredo Ottaviani, head of the Congregation for the Doctrine of the Faith, sent a confidential letter to bishops' conferences. Ottaviani had largely opposed and tried to forestall John XXIII's Vatican II initiative, but the council progressed under the bishops' independence. In the letter released so soon after the council ended, Ottaviani reminded these same bishops of their task to oversee the renewal the council had inaugurated. Ottaviani said he wrote the letter because

> alarming news has come from various quarters on the subject of growing abuses in the interpretation of the council's doctrine and with strange and audacious opinions greatly upsetting the minds of many faithful.

Ottaviani then listed ten areas in which errors and dangers had appeared, a list reminiscent of the syllabi of errors the church had published in the nineteenth and early twentieth centuries.[8] Innovation was under attack.

Once again, the liturgy provides a good case study because of its high visibility. Liturgical renewal took time to play out. Between 1964 and 1966, the physical rearrangement of sanctuaries turned the altar around so the celebrant faced the congregation; then reception of communion under both species was encouraged. During 1967, music, the missal, the lectionary, and eucharistic prayers were all revised. In 1969, the changes truly hit home with the renewal of sacraments and rites that touched people at the most important moments of their lives: baptism, marriage, and funerals. The vernacular was permitted for mass in 1971, a formal statement that played catch-up with reality. Vatican II did not specify switching from Latin and in fact said Latin should be preserved. However, local bishops could permit the vernacular in liturgies and the administration of sacraments for the good of their people. Confirmation and the RCIA process were introduced in the early 1970s; a new code of canon law followed in 1983, and a new catechism appeared about a decade later.[9]

The liturgical movement since Vatican II has become a battlefield, perhaps because it is the most visual representation of a paradigm shift that has gone too far for some and not far enough for others. Annibale Bugnini, one of the architects of liturgical reform in Rome since the 1940s, noted that change, especially after Vatican II, has been a bumpy ride: "…a continual alteration of green, yellow, and red lights…. I mean the expectations, oppositions, second thoughts, forward thrusts, and setbacks." His memoirs are part remembrance and part chronicle of the hesitant and controversial liturgical reforms of the late twentieth century.

As passionately as Bugnini promoted liturgical renewal, others like Klaus Gamber contended that change went too far too fast. His own reflections, published about the same time as Bugnini's, admit liturgy had become stale because of rubricism. He does not argue with the need for reform, but rather with the form it took in the spirit of Vatican II. Gamber's work reads like an apologia for restoration of former rites and an indictment of wholesale change: "[T]oo much emphasis is being given to the congregation actively participating in the liturgy…. Also, we are now experiencing—and this applies especially to worship in larger group settings—a diminishing sense of solemnity." The church, according to Gamber, has broken with her liturgical tradition, not renewed it, and should have moved with greater caution and on an experimental basis only. The result of rapid, innovative change has been "a liturgical destruction of startling proportions—a debacle worsening with each passing year."[10] The battle continues.

## Perspectives

Vatican II is an ongoing development, a continuing debate, and in some cases an open wound. But it is also simply the latest in a long series of events in the history of reform. Where does Vatican II fit into that history?

The council forced the church to reexamine how she can best move forward. Should she retrench and restore the past? Would it be better to cut herself off from the past and give herself over to modernity? Perhaps a combination of these options is more in order: a combination of backward-looking reform and forward-looking renewal. If this is the case, then the Roman god Janus surveying past and future simultaneously reemerges as the symbol of aggiornamento seeking to strike a careful, delicate, and often contentious balance of old and new, conservation and innovation, restoration and progress. These pairs of goals are in a constant dialectic, as we have seen often. Creative tension is a standard theme that continues to characterize Vatican II's growing pains. In that sense, the church is right where it should be as she thinks aloud and tries to play out this latest reform council.

In addition, discussing aggiornamento in the context of the word *tradition* is a helpful way to understand contemporary renewal. The Twelfth-Century Renaissance witnessed both a fixed and fluid notion of tradition. Trent pronounced the unalterable doctrines of the Catholic faith, but that council also pushed a progressive agenda and to some degree created a climate in which innovative religious orders could meet new challenges with new models. For John Henry Newman and other theologians of the nineteenth and twentieth centuries, tradition is not a closed book, but a living organism requiring constant updating.

Vatican II did not deny tradition: On the contrary, at and since the council, the church has taken a more serious look at the early church than in a very long time. But Vatican II asked the church to look at tradition with new glasses to renew its life. Tradition builds or develops and is not as rigidly fixed as we might think—or like to think—although there are, of course, nonnegotiable elements of dogma. The history of reform demonstrates tradition is not the kind of traditionalism onto which some restorationists tenaciously grab. The notion that the church does not and cannot change is fundamentally ahistorical and goes against the oldest events in the church's development of dogma, especially at the first councils. Whenever the church has tried to fix herself in time, she ended up gasping for air.

And yet, few would argue that the church can move too quickly in implementing change. There is a consensus that some of Vatican II's updates, especially of the liturgy, were good ideas, but were not always presented clearly to parishioners. Ironically, the Catholic church could have learned from Luther when he opposed Karlstadt's rapid and bold attempts to offend Catholic sensibilities. In his *Invocavit* sermons of 1522, as we have seen, Luther cautioned that reforms must be introduced gradually and explained carefully, or else people will hold onto their old ways and reject new ways with great vehemence, even if they might otherwise agree with the new.

The problem is that the church seems to be polarizing since Vatican II. Hans Küng, the German theologian silenced in 1979, identified factionalism as a deplorable by-product of the council as early as 1973. He regretted that less than a decade after the council ended, the pace of reform had slowed down.[11] The church's inner division may have even touched Paul VI, who appeared remarkably ambivalent about the council. Each side of the debate has claimed him as its own, decried his alleged loyalty to the other side, or criticized his attempts to walk a tightrope between them.

Despite his personal mixed feelings, Paul VI did not fail to remind Catholics that, like Trent, Vatican II ultimately had personal and not structural reform in mind. Trent created the seminary as an institution, but to train the hearts and minds of priests who would then guide their parishioners' spiritual journeys. Likewise, all of the changes, especially liturgical, of Vatican II may seem primarily structural, but those changes were only the visible means to a more personal end.

Paul VI tried to explain in 1969 that structural change had an important purpose. At the same time, he tried to limit calls for more revolutionary innovations in the church's hierarchical system:

> ...[T]here has been, and still is, a good deal of talk about church "structures," with intentions that are not always aware of the reasons justifying these structures and of the dangers that would arise if they were changed or destroyed. It should be noted that interest in renewal has in many cases taken the form of insistence on the exterior and impersonal transformation of the ecclesiastical edifice, and of acceptance of the forms and spirit of the Protestant Reformation, rather than the essential and principal renewal desired by the council: moral, personal, and inner renewal.... We would like to invite all of you to meditate on this fundamental intention of the council: to bring about our inner and moral reformation.[12]

Vatican II comes into focus when we place it side by side with Trent, with which it is more typically placed in opposition. The French theologian Yves Congar, for example, believed Vatican II marked the end of the "Counter Reform" (defined in intransigent, conservative terms) and a step closer to renewing theology by integrating a juridical mentality with pastoral concerns.[13] But Congar seemed to draw too strict a line between Trent and Vatican II, placing them in contradiction to one another, as many people often do. Might we not see Vatican II as completing what Trent could not because of sixteenth-century circumstances? Once we separate the caricature of Trent from the reality, the siege mentality falls away. The Tridentine fathers' inventive ideas begin to emerge, if only from the ideas that did not make it to the council's final decrees but were discussed seriously in working committees, like the call for a vernacular liturgy. In the end, if we link a true picture of Trent with Vatican II, we may uncover some overlooked intersections, places of fundamental agreement. In that case, we may yet find more instructive continuities in the history of reform.

## NOTES

1. Roger Aubert summarizes late-nineteenth-and early-twentieth-century reforms in *The Church in a Secularised Society* (London: Darton, Longman and Todd, 1978), pp. 165–85, 574–623.

2. John XXIII, *Humanae salutis,* in Walter M. Abbott, *The Documents of Vatican II* (New York: Herder and Herder, 1966), p. 705.

3. Tanner, *Decrees,* vol. 2, pp. 1076, 1109; nos. 1–22 and 40–45 especially treated these topics.

4. Avery Dulles summarized the council's paradigm shifts in "Vatican II Reform: The Basic Principles," *Church* 1 (1985): pp. 3–10, reprinted in his *The Reshaping of Catholicism* (San Francisco: Harper and Row, 1988), pp. 19–33.

5. John W. O'Malley, "Reform, Historical Consciousness, and Vatican II's *Aggiornamento,*" *TS* 32 (1971): pp. 575–76; "Developments, Reforms, and Two Great Reformations: Towards a Historical Assessment of Vatican II," *TS* 44 (1983): pp. 391–402. See the discussion of conciliar vocabulary in this study's introduction.

6. For summaries of the several sides of the debate over Vatican II, see Joseph A. Komonchak, "Interpreting the Council: Catholic Attitudes toward Vatican II," in *Being Right: Conservative Catholics in America,* eds. Mary Jo Weaver and R. Scott Appleby (Bloomington: Indiana University Press, 1995), pp. 17–36; Avery Dulles, "Vatican II and the American Experience of Church," in *Vatican II: Open Questions and New Horizons,* ed. Gerald M. Fagin (Wilmington, Del.: Michael Glazier, 1984), pp. 38–57, reprinted as "American Impressions of the Council," in Dulles, *Reshaping of Catholicism,* pp. 1–18. For closer attention to traditionalists, restorationists, and Vatican II's opponents, see Daniele Menozzi, "Opposition to the Council (1966–84)," in *The Reception of Vatican II,* eds. Giuseppe Alberigo et al. (Washington, D.C.: Catholic University of America Press, 1987), pp. 325–48; William D. Dinges, "'We Are What You Were': Roman Catholic Traditionalism in America," in Weaver and Appleby, *Being Right,* pp. 241–69.

7. One observer noted that by the early 1970s, "The demand for absolute purity of teaching (orthodoxy) or of practice (orthopraxy) betrays a fanatical purism from whichever side it comes ('conservative' or 'progressive'), and leads it in its turn to inhuman and un-Christian behavior": Karl-Heinz Ohlig, "The Theological Objectives of Church Reform," *Concilium* 73 (1972): p. 51.

8. Samuel J. Thomas, "After Vatican Council II: The American Catholic Bishops and the 'Syllabus' from Rome, 1966–1968," *CHR* 83 (1997): pp. 254–57.

9. These and earlier details of liturgical renewal are drawn from P. Jounel, "From the Council of Trent to Vatican Council II," in *The Church at Prayer*, ed. A. G. Martimort, trans. Matthew J. O'Connell, vol. 1, *Principles of the Liturgy* (Collegeville, Minn.: Liturgical Press, 1987), pp. 63–84; Owen Chadwick, *A History of the Popes: 1830–1914* (Oxford: Clarendon Press, 1998), pp. 359–65; Johannes H. Emminghaus, *The Eucharist: Essence, Form, Celebration,* trans. Linda M. Maloney (Collegeville, Minn.: Liturgical Press, 1997), pp. 88–94; Clifford Howell, "From Trent to Vatican II," in *The Study of Liturgy,* rev. ed., eds. Cheslyn Jones et al. (London: SPCK, 1992), pp. 285–94.

10. Annibale Bugnini, *The Reform of the Liturgy: 1948–1975,* trans. Matthew J. O'Connell (Collegeville, Minn.: Liturgical Press, 1990), p. xxvi; Klaus Gamber, *The Reform of the Roman Liturgy: Its Problems and Background,* trans. Klaus D. Grimm (San Juan Capistrano, Calif.: Una Voce Press/Harrison N.Y.: The Foundation for Catholic Reform, 1993), pp. 3–9. Gamber's book is discussed in a review symposium in *Antiphon* 3:3 (1998): Cassian Folsom, "Defending Continuity and Organic Development," pp. 33–38, and Kevin W. Irwin, "Glorifying the Old: Caricaturing the New," pp. 38–42. Two other articles declare the present to be a natural time to evaluate the first generation of liturgical changes after the council: M. Francis Mannion, "Agendas for Liturgical Reform," *America,* 30 November 1996, pp. 9–16, and Rembert G. Weakland, "Liturgy and Common Ground," *America,* 20 February 1999, pp. 7–11.

11. Hans Küng, *Reforming the Church Today: Keeping Hope Alive* (New York: Crossroad, 1990) gathers together essays he published between 1969 and 1989 as Vatican II played itself out against a backdrop of increasing division among a spectrum of Catholic opinions of the council.

12. Menozzi traces Paul VI's ambivalence in "Opposition to the Council," pp. 332–35, 339–41; for Paul's quotation, see p. 333 n. 33.

13. Noëlle Hausman, "Le Père Yves Congar au Concile Vatican II," *Nouvelle revue théologie* 120 (1998): pp. 275–78.

# Conclusions

In some ways, the history of Christianity is the history of reform. If one theme resonates throughout that history, it is the need for personal reform. Beginning with John the Baptist and Jesus, we hear a repeated call for *metanoia* regardless of what is occurring more formally within religious groups or the institutional church. The fathers were among the first to recognize personal reform as the sine qua non of the Christian life; their voices frequently acted as a north star keeping diverse reform movements on course. As a leading patristics scholar, Boniface Ramsey, observed, "needed renewal has come to the church only when it has reappropriated for itself the legacy of the fathers."[1]

We have seen this call for personal reform in different parts of the church during various periods. The Carolingian capitularies and the Gregorian Revolution attempted to initiate personal reform and establish norms for behavior within which people could pursue their own paths to God. This leaves open the question: How far does religious feeling penetrate when imposed from above? The Twelfth-Century Renaissance coupled Gregorian, top-down, political concerns with a vibrant, humanistic spirituality from the bottom up. Institutional synods and councils give evidence of concern for pastoral and personal reform. A canon of Lateran II warned against formalism, directing bishops and priests to instruct their flocks that outward penitential actions must be accompanied by true inner repentance.[2] Grassroots reform movements also complemented the institutional church's shortcomings. Once the papacy became the object and not the agent of reform in the fifteenth century because of the Avignon papacy and schism, which ground reform *in capite* to a halt, Christians *in membris* kept reform's fires burning. Reform, in short, never disappears, but it does locate itself in different places at different times through different ideas, people, and methods.

During Vatican II, the papacy tried to spread personal reform throughout the church's body by offering encouragement from her head. In *Ecclesiam Suam* (1964), Paul VI asked rhetorically:

> ...[D]id not Jesus Christ himself call upon men to receive God's kingdom interiorly? Was not his whole teaching technique concerned with inculcating and fostering the soul's interior life?...
>
> ...[L]et us repeat once again for our common admonition and profit: the church will rediscover its youthful vitality not so much by changing its external legislation, as by submitting to the obedience of Christ and observing the laws which the church lays upon itself with the intention of following in Christ's footsteps. Herein lies the secret of the church's renewal, its *metanoia,* to use the Greek term, its practice of perfection.[3]

Personal reform continues to be critically important in today's church. Contemporary culture is used to looking within, sometimes to a fault. Self-help books, talk shows, and videos create in some cases self-involved, self-absorbed, and indeed selfish people. But introspection in religious terms may represent an area where Protestants and Catholics can unite. Protestants in the sixteenth century focused urgently on each individual's intimate, unique relationship with Christ—a focus mirrored by evangelical calls to accept Christ as a personal savior in the late twentieth century. Since Vatican II, Catholics have caught a similar spirit as they search for an individual bond with their God.

Personal reform can represent a common yearning, a shared heritage, and an area of contemporary agreement between Catholics and Protestants. Personal reform therefore can have ecumenical implications if it leads to an honest reappraisal of the ways in which Christian denominations have not acted in brotherhood.

In turn, this reappraisal can lead to a recognition of what all Christian denominations share liturgically, biblically, and spiritually, making reform an important aspect of intra-Christian dialogue. Vatican II recognized this very point in its document on ecumenism, *Unitatis redintegratio* (1964, no. 6):

> Such renewal has therefore notable ecumenical importance. In various spheres of the church's life, this renewal is already taking place. The biblical and liturgical movements, the preaching of the word of God and catechetics, the apostolate of the laity, new forms of religious life, the spirituality of married life and the church's social teaching and activity—all these should be considered as promises and guarantees for the future progress of ecumenism.

The council made a similar link between reform and ecumenism in *Lumen Gentium* (1964, no. 15):

> ...[T]he spirit arouses in all of Christ's disciples desire and action so that all may be peacefully united, in the way established by Christ, in one flock under one shepherd. To obtain this the church does not cease to pray, to hope and to work, and it exhorts its children to purification and renewal so that the sign of Christ may shine more clearly over the face of the church.[4]

In order to accomplish these goals, the church must grow more comfortable with another enduring theme in the history of reform: the tension between tradition and progress that is best illustrated by the Roman god Janus with his two faces simultaneously looking past and forward. Jesus himself directed his followers to be like the master of a household who draws from his storehouse treasures that are both old and new (Matt 13:52). This review of the history of reform offers several precedents of cooperation and struggle between old and new treasures.

In the twelfth century, conservation and innovation, along with tradition and progress, both competed with and complemented each other. From the perspective of fourteenth-century spirituality, an historian of the *devotio moderna* concluded: "One could say that tradition, in order to stay alive, demands innovation while the latter depends upon tradition for its authenticity and legitimacy."[5] After the multiple Protestant reformations attempted to reform the church by recovering her original sources and ways in the sixteenth century, the Catholic Church tried to marry conservation of the past with innovative methods to spread the faith. This uneasy dance gives historical perspective to a similar struggle taking place in today's church as Vatican II's aggiornamento is played out. As one side complains that the council's excitement has fizzled out and even been reversed (which also occurred in the seventeenth century), another side claims "the spirit of Vatican II" has been allowed to run amok.

One of the goals of reform, especially in the wake of Vatican II, must be to explore these precedents to find a middle way between tradition and progress, conservation and innovation, rigidity and flexibility. Reform councils have sometimes tried to build a bridge between these seemingly contradictory pairs. For all of its many and precise canons, for example, the great medieval reform council Lateran IV was not entirely a machine of papal monarchy and ecclesiastical administration. In discussing restrictions prohibiting marriage, Lateran IV urged a lighter touch.

> It should not be judged reprehensible if human decrees are sometimes changed according to changing circumstances, especially when urgent necessity or evident advantage demands it, since God himself changed in the New Testament some of the things which he had commanded in the Old Testament.[6]

In his analysis of true and false reform in the church published just before Vatican II and then again afterward, the French theologian Yves Congar similarly reminded reformers to find a middle way of balancing ancient custom with new circumstances. He warned against two extremes or temptations that could beset reformers or their opponents. Congar identified the first temptation as a pharisee-like adherence to religious formalism and obligation. In the sixteenth century, Erasmus had objected to just this type of religious activity, which he called dry and stuffy, producing actions devoid of meaning. Such "reformers" (more frequently those fighting reform) do not want to see changes to standard religious forms, although they may agree that abuses, especially arithmetical piety, should be curtailed. This perspective tends to hold onto tradition as fixed inflexibly in time and place.

Congar identified the opposite reform extreme as the wholesale rejection of what is termed "old." This temptation was toward revolutionary reform cut off from the traditions that give Christianity her heritage and roots. The church should adapt, but she should not lose touch with her core and her past, he warned. The exercise of reform was characterized by the act of distinguishing between what is necessary and permanent, on the one hand, and what is relative and temporary, on the other. One must be open to both the letter of the law and natural developments in the spirit of tradition. Finding the middle way between these two extremes produces a reform mentality, spirit, or mindset. This exercise has always been, and remains, the challenge of reforming.[7]

But should reform progress slowly or quickly? Is revolution or evolution the way to proceed? Can revolution move too fast or evolution too slowly? Another lesson from the history of reform surely relates to the rate of change.

Timing and pace, many heretics learned, could mean everything. Many reformers whom the medieval church condemned as heretics said at least some things in line with the Gregorian Revolution's goals. This was the case with the earliest Waldensians; however, the institutional church and these critics parted company on the issue of obedience. The *devotio moderna* reformed *in membris* just when the church *in capite* was imploding in the late Middle Ages. This movement trained both Erasmus and Luther; by laying the egg Luther hatched, Erasmus knew he was a villain to some Catholics and a hero to others. Luther's own hopes for change snowballed rapidly to the point where he had to chastise radical reformers like Karlstadt who were taking axes to organs. Proceed slowly, Luther reminded them in his *Invocavit* sermons, or else you may turn away those who are on your own side—a lesson sometimes lost in the late 1960s and early 1970s. The modernists were condemned in their own day, but their ideas helped fuel Vatican II's surge of renewal.

Finally, this study has taken for granted an essential element of church history: in this life, the church will never get the gospel completely right. Why should the church reform at all, then, if she knows she cannot fully succeed? Vatican II answered that question in *Lumen Gentium:* The church must reform because she has been given the skills and mandate to do so.

> ...[The holy spirit] apportions his gifts "to each individually as he wills" (1 Cor 12:11), and among the faithful of every rank he distributes special graces by which he renders them fit and ready to undertake the various tasks and offices which help the renewal and the building up of the church, according to that word: "To each is given the manifestation of the spirit for the common good" (1 Cor 12:7).[8]

The church must move from inner reform to spreading the gospel, a point made explicitly in Vatican II's document on missionary activity, *Ad gentes divinitus* (1965, no. 35):

> Since the entire church is missionary and the spreading of the gospel is a fundamental duty of the people of God, this synod invites everyone to a profound interior renewal, so that having a lively awareness of their personal responsibility for the spreading of the gospel, they may play their part in missionary work among the nations.[9]

Certainly there is no question the church will only be reformed fully at the end of time. Vatican II understood this hard fact when it asserted: "The church...will reach its completion only in the glory of heaven, when the time for the restoration of all things will come...."[10] Until then, the church cannot fail to try to renew herself. To stop renewing means she will stop growing; to stop growing means dying. As John Henry Newman put it, "to live is to change, and to be perfect is to have changed often."[11] The church must realize she can never be truly perfect in this life, but she must never stop trying to improve the human imperfection that is her earthly lot. To live, she must reform; to try to be perfect, she must reform often.

## NOTES

1. Boniface Ramsey, *Beginning to Read the Fathers* (New York: Paulist Press, 1985), p. 2.

2. Tanner, *Decrees*, vol. 1, p. 202.

3. Paul VI, *Ecclesiam Suam*, nos. 21, 51, in *The Papal Encyclicals 1958–1981*, ed. Claudia Carlen (Raleigh, N.C.: McGrath, 1981), pp. 138, 146.

4. Tanner, *Decrees*, vol. 2, pp. 913, 861.

5. Otto Gründler, "*Devotio Moderna Atque Antiqua*: The Modern Devotion and Carthusian Spirituality," in *The Spirituality of Western Christendom*, vol. 2, *The Roots of the Modern Christian Tradition*, ed. E. Rozanne Elder (Kalamazoo, Mich.: Cistercian Publications, 1984), p. 28.

6. Tanner, *Decrees*, vol. 1, p. 257.

7. Congar, *Vraie et fausse réforme*, pp. 141–78.

8. Tanner, *Decrees*, vol. 2, p. 858.

9. Tanner, *Decrees*, vol. 2, p. 1037.

10. Tanner, *Decrees*, vol. 2, p. 887 (*Lumen Gentium*, no. 48).

11. Quoted in Ian Ker, *John Henry Newman: A Biography* (Oxford: Clarendon Press, 1988), p. 304, from Newman's *An Essay on the Development of Christian Doctrine* (1845; rev. ed. 1878).

# For Further Reading

This section is intended to point the interested reader in the direction of primary sources and secondary studies related to each chapter. I have tried to select those works that represent entry points because of their synthetic treatment of these topics and the resources often contained in their scholarly apparatus. For the most part, I have not repeated here sources already appearing in the notes.

## Chapter 1

The best way to understand the fathers in their cultural world and to be introduced to their writings is to read Boniface Ramsey's *Beginning to Read the Fathers* (New York: Paulist Press, 1985), which includes a bibliography of the fathers' writings in translation along with a helpful chronology. A guide to two millennia of monasticism and the religious orders that grew from the patristic period and early Middle Ages, often reacting against or working to improve one another, is Karl Suso Frank's *With Greater Liberty: A Short History of Christian Monasticism and Religious Orders*, trans. Joseph T. Lienhard (Kalamazoo Mich.: Cistercian Publications, 1993). Three articles in *Christian Spirituality: Origins to the Twelfth Century*, eds. Bernard McGinn, John Meyendorff, and Jean Leclercq (New York: Crossroad, 1985) treat the topics covered in the first sections of this chapter: Charles Kannengiesser, "The Spiritual Message of the Great Fathers," pp. 61–88; Jean Gribomont, "Monasticism and Asceticism I: Eastern Christianity," pp. 89–112; and Jean Leclercq, "Monasticism and

Asceticism II: Western Christianity," pp. 113–31. All include further bibliographies. Irish spirituality was as ascetic as the practices of the earliest desert fathers and played a decisive role in forming the sometimes extreme penitential focus of northern European monasticism: see John T. McNeill and Helena M. Gamer, trans., *Medieval Handbooks of Penance* (New York: Columbia University Press, 1990), especially pp. 75–270.

On the Carolingian Empire and Renaissance, see principally the surveys by Heinrich Fichtenau, *The Carolingian Empire: The Age of Charlemagne*, trans. Peter Munz (New York: Harper and Row, 1964); Rosamond McKitterick, *The Frankish Church and the Carolingian Reforms, 789–895* (London: Royal Historical Society, 1977); and J. M. Wallace-Hadrill, *The Frankish Church* (Oxford: Clarendon Press, 1983).

# Chapter 2

R. N. Swanson has synthesized the current state of scholarship in *The Twelfth-Century Renaissance* (Manchester: Manchester University Press, 1999). On the multiple issues of the investiture controversies in context, see Uta-Renate Blumenthal, *The Investiture Conflict: Church and Monarchy from the Ninth to the Twelfth Century* (Philadelphia: University of Pennsylvania Press, 1988). For more specific cases of how Gregorian reforms played out in diverse circumstances, see among many studies Robert Somerville, *Pope Alexander III and the Council of Tours (1163): A Study of Ecclesiastical Politics and Institutions in the Twelfth Century* (Berkeley: University of California Press, 1977); Kenneth Pennington, *Pope and Bishops: A Study of the Papal Monarchy in the Twelfth and Thirteenth Centuries* (Philadelphia: University of Pennsylvania Press, 1984); and Paul B. Pixton, *The German Episcopacy and the Implementation of the Decrees of the Fourth Lateran Council, 1216–1245: Watchmen on the Tower* (Leiden: E. J. Brill, 1995). On reform in action at synods, consult the bibliography accompanying Robert Somerville's *Dictionary of the Middle Ages* entry (cited in notes);

and Uta-Renate Blumenthal, *The Early Councils of Pope Paschal II, 1100–1110* (Toronto: Pontifical Institute of Mediaeval Studies, 1978). Two books examine how church reform had an expanding impact on social, political, demographic, and economic change, in essence uncovering the culture of reform: John Howe, *Church Reform and Social Change in Eleventh-Century Italy: Dominic of Sora and His Patrons* (Philadelphia: University of Pennsylvania Press, 1997) and Maureen C. Miller, *The Foundation of a Medieval Church: Ecclesiastical Change in Verona, 950–1150* (Ithaca: Cornell University Press, 1993).

On canon law, readers should start with James A. Brundage, *Medieval Canon Law* (London: Longman, 1995) and, for primary sources, Robert Somerville and Bruce C. Brasington, *Prefaces to Canon Law Books in Latin Christianity: Selected Translations, 500–1245* (New Haven: Yale University Press, 1998). A longer view is taken by Manlio Bellomo, *The Common Legal Past of Europe, 1000–1800,* trans. Lydia G. Cochrane (Washington, D.C.: Catholic University of America Press, 1995). More particular analysis is offered in Stanley Chodorow, *Christian Political Theory and Church Politics in the Mid-Twelfth Century: The Ecclesiology of Gratian's Decretum* (Berkeley: University of California Press, 1972). On scholastic theology, especially as it emerged from earlier traditions of monastic theology, see principally Jaroslav Pelikan, *The Christian Tradition,* vol. 3, *The Growth of Medieval Theology (600–1300)* (Chicago: University of Chicago Press, 1978); Marcia L. Colish, *Peter Lombard,* 2 vols. (Leiden: E. J. Brill, 1994) and *Medieval Foundations of the Western Intellectual Tradition, 400–1400* (New Haven: Yale University Press, 1997). Primary sources are offered by Eugene R. Fairweather, ed. and trans., *A Scholastic Miscellany: Anselm to Ockham* (Philadelphia: Westminster Press, 1956).

On monasticism, in addition to Karl Suso Frank's *With Greater Liberty,* see Giles Constable, *Medieval Monasticism: A Select Bibliography* (Toronto: University of Toronto Press, 1976) and, especially, Jean Leclercq, *The Love of Learning and the Desire for God: A Study of Monastic Culture* (New York:

Fordham University Press, 1961). For the female monastic experience, see Penelope D. Johnson, *Equal in Monastic Profession: Religious Women in Medieval France* (Chicago: University of Chicago Press, 1991) and Sally Thompson, *Women Religious: The Founding of English Nunneries after the Norman Conquest* (Oxford: Clarendon Press, 1991). Cistercian spirituality is treated by Louis Bouyer, *The Cistercian Heritage* (London: A. R. Mowbray, 1958) and Louis J. Lekai, *The Cistercians: Ideals and Reality* (Kent, Ohio: Kent State University Press, 1977); for the relationship between contemplation and environment, consult Peter Fergusson, *Architecture of Solitude: Cistercian Abbeys in Twelfth-Century England* (Princeton: Princeton University Press, 1984). For the Franciscans and Dominicans, begin with C. H. Lawrence, *The Friars: The Impact of the Early Mendicant Movement on Western Society* (London: Longman, 1994). Primary sources are found in Regis Armstrong and Ignatius C. Brady, ed. and trans., *Francis and Clare: The Complete Works* (New York: Paulist Press, 1982). Margaret Carney discusses female Franciscans in *The First Franciscan Women: Clare of Assisi and Her Form of Life* (Quincy, Ill.: Franciscan Press, 1993); see also Ingrid J. Peterson, *Clare of Assisi: A Biographical Study* (Quincy, Ill.: Franciscan Press, 1993). On the key Franciscan topic of poverty, see M. D. Lambert, *Franciscan Poverty: The Doctrine of the Absolute Poverty of Christ and the Apostles in the Franciscan Order, 1210–1323* (London: SPCK, 1961). For the Dominicans, see Benedict Ashley, *The Dominicans* (Collegeville Minn.: Liturgical Press, 1990); for primary sources, consult Simon Tugwell, ed., *Early Dominicans: Selected Writings* (New York: Paulist Press, 1982). A comprehensive guide to heresies is Malcolm Lambert, *Medieval Heresy: Popular Movements from the Gregorian Reform to the Reformation,* 2d ed. (Oxford: Basil Blackwell, 1992). For the very interesting path of the Waldensians, see Gabriel Audisio, *The Waldensian Dissent: Persecution and Survival, c.1170–c.1570,* trans. Claire Davison (Cambridge: Cambridge University Press, 1999).

# Chapter 3

The Center for Reformation Research in St. Louis published overviews and bibliographies concerning this period in three volumes: vol. 1, Steven Ozment, ed., *Reformation Europe* (1982); vol. 2, John W. O'Malley, ed., *Catholicism in Early Modern History: A Guide to Research* (1988); vol. 3, William S. Maltby, ed., *Reformation Europe: A Guide to Research* (1992). For theological shifts, the standard study is Jaroslav Pelikan, *The Christian Tradition*, vol. 4, *Reformation of Church and Dogma (1300–1700)* (Chicago: University of Chicago Press, 1984). James D. Tracy views this period of multiple changes from three angles—developments in doctrine, politics, and society and community: *Europe's Reformations, 1450–1650* (Lanham Md.: Rowman and Littlefield, 1999).

The most complete and even-handed appraisal of the Avignon papacy is G. Mollat, *The Popes at Avignon*, 9th ed., trans. Janet Love (New York: Harper and Row, 1965). Walter Ullmann provides a narrative and analysis of the disputed 1378 papal elections in *Origins of the Great Schism* (London: Methuen, 1948). For papal recovery at Basel, consult the very detailed study by Joachim W. Stieber, *Pope Eugenius IV, the Council of Basel, and the Secular and Ecclesiastical Authorities in the Empire: The Conflict over Supreme Authority and Power in the Church* (Leiden: E. J. Brill, 1978).

For reform in terms of popular developments and humanism (within both Catholic and Protestant circles), consult John F. D'Amico, *Roman and German Humanism: 1450–1550*, ed. Paul F. Grendler (Brookfield Vt.: Variorum, 1993); Erika Rummel, *The Humanist-Scholastic Debate in the Renaissance and Reformation* (Cambridge: Harvard University Press, 1995); Reinhard P. Becker, ed. *German Humanism and the Reformation* (New York: Continuum, 1982); and Alister McGrath, *The Intellectual Origins of the European Reformation* (New York: Basil Blackwell, 1987).

For some possible proto-Tridentine reformers, see Louis B. Pascoe, *Jean Gerson: Principles of Church Reform* (Leiden: E. J.

Brill, 1973); Christopher M. Bellitto, *Nicolas de Clamanges: Personal Reform and Pastoral Renewal on the Eve of the Reformations* (Washington, D.C.: Catholic University of America Press, 2001); Donald Sullivan, "Nicholas of Cusa as Reformer: The Papal Legation to the Germanies, 1451–1452," *Medieval Studies* 36 (1974): pp. 382–482; and Anton Weiler, "Nicholas of Cusa on the Reform of the Church," *Concilium* 77 (1962): pp. 94–102. On the continuities of the period, see Steven Ozment, *The Age of Reform 1250–1550: An Intellectual and Religious History of Late Medieval and Reformation Europe* (New Haven: Yale University Press, 1980); Heiko Oberman, "Fourteenth-Century Religious Thought: A Premature Profile," *Speculum* 53 (1978): pp. 80–93, and *Masters of the Reformation: The Emergence of a New Intellectual Climate in Europe* (Cambridge: Cambridge University Press, 1981). John W. O'Malley uncovers Catholic calls for reform before and immediately after Luther in *Praise and Blame in Renaissance Rome: Rhetoric, Doctrine, and Reform in the Sacred Orators of the Papal Court, c. 1450–1521* (Durham, N.C.: Duke University Press, 1979); Frederick J. McGinness continued the story, like O'Malley linking reform with the rapidly emerging field of sermon studies, in *Right Thinking and Sacred Oratory in Counter-Reformation Rome* (Princeton: Princeton University Press, 1995). A convenient collection of classic articles debating the "Catholic" or "Counter" reformations is David M. Luebke, ed., *The Counter-Reformation* (Oxford: Basil Blackwell, 1999).

On Erasmus, see the biography by Roland H. Bainton, *Erasmus of Christendom* (New York: Scribner, 1969) and two volumes edited by John C. Olin: *Christian Humanism and the Reformation: Selected Writings of Erasmus*, 3rd ed. (New York: Fordham University Press, 1987) and *Luther, Erasmus, and the Reformation: A Catholic-Protestant Reappraisal* (New York: Fordham University Press, 1969). Erika Rummel provides selections from sixteenth-century polemics in *Scheming Papists and Lutheran Fools: Five Reformation Satires* (New York: Fordham University Press, 1993).

# Chapter 4

Several studies explore the spirituality and reform of the Spanish mystics as pursued in this chapter: G. T. W. Ahlgren, *Teresa of Avila and the Politics of Sanctity* (New York: Cornell University Press, 1996); Kieran Kavanaugh and Otilio Rodriguez, trans., *The Collected Works of St. John of the Cross* (Washington, D.C.: Institute of Carmelite Studies, 1979); and John E. Dister, *A New Introduction to the Spiritual Exercises of St. Ignatius* (Collegeville, Minn.: Liturgical Press, 1993).

Owen Chadwick treats modernity's intellectual paradigm shift and its impact on religion in *Secularization of the European Mind in the Nineteenth Century* (New York: Cambridge University Press, 1975). On social Catholicism's roots, developments, and paradoxes, see M. P. Fogarty, *Christian Democracy in Western Europe 1820–1953* (Westport Conn.: Greenwood Press, 1974); Etienne Gilson, ed., *The Church Speaks to the Modern World: The Social Teachings of Leo XIII* (Garden City: Doubleday Image Books, 1954); and Richard L. Camp, *The Papal Ideology of Social Reform: A Study of Historical Development, 1878–1967* (Leiden: E. J. Brill, 1969). David Goslee discusses Newman's ambivalent relationship with romanticism and liberalism: *Romanticism and the Anglican Newman* (Athens: Ohio University Press, 1996). Peter Benedict Nockles discusses Newman's *via media* in *The Oxford Movement in Context: Anglican High Churchmanship, 1760–1857* (New York: Cambridge University Press, 1994). Two recent books explore religious reform and the social movements with which they were often associated on the grassroots level: Michael P. Carroll, *Veiled Threats: The Logic of Popular Catholicism in Italy* (Baltimore: Johns Hopkins University Press, 1996) and David K. Adams and Cornelis A. van Minnen, eds., *Religious and Secular Reform in America: Ideas, Beliefs, and Social Change* (New York: New York University Press, 1999).

The literature on modernism is extensive and there are many biographies of key players. For surveys and analyses, see especially Marvin R. O'Connell, *Critics on Trial: An Introduction to the Catholic Modernist Crisis* (Washington, D.C.: Catholic University of America Press, 1994); Gabriel Daly, *Transcendence and Immanence: A Study in Catholic Modernism and Integration* (Oxford: Clarendon Press, 1980); Thomas Michael Loome, *Liberal Catholicism, Reform Catholicism, Modernism* (Mainz: Matthias-Grünewald-Verlag, 1979).

# Chapter 5

For the early stages of the liturgical reform, see J. D. Crichton, *Lights in Darkness: Forerunners of the Liturgical Movement* (Collegeville, Minn.: Liturgical Press, 1996), which deals with the European scene, and an American counterpart, Keith F. Pecklers, *The Unread Vision: The Liturgical Movement in the United States of America, 1926–1955* (Collegeville, Minn.: Liturgical Press, 1998).

A team of international scholars is currently compiling a definitive *History of Vatican II* (Maryknoll, N.Y.: Orbis Books), edited by Giuseppe Alberigo and Joseph Komonchak. The first volume, published in 1995, chronicles the preparation for the council; the second and third, published in 1997 and 2000, look at the first two sessions and intersessions in 1962–1964. Each of the next two volumes will look at the subsequent sessions (1964–1965).

Several collections have tried to chronicle and analyze the council's impact from multiple perspectives: Adrian Hastings, ed., *Modern Catholicism: Vatican II and After* (London: SPCK, 1991); Rene Latourelle, ed., *Vatican II: Assessment and Perspectives, Twenty-Five Years After (1962–1987)*, 3 vols. (New York: Paulist Press, 1988–89); Alberic Stacpoole, ed., *Vatican II Revisited by Those Who Were There* (Minneapolis: Winston Press, 1986). For divergent opinions of the council's program of reform, compare Heinrich Fries, *Suffering from the Church: Renewal or Restoration?*, trans. Arlene Anderson Swidler and Leonard Swidler (Collegeville, Minn.: Liturgical Press, 1995); Hans Küng and Leonard Swidler, eds., *The Church in Anguish: Has the Vatican Betrayed Vatican II?* (New York: Harper and Row, 1987); and Joseph Ratzinger, *The Ratzinger Report: An Exclusive Interview on the State of the Church* (San Francisco: Ignatius Press, 1986).

# Index